M000291052

"Jackson W. provides Western readers, indeed glo[]
mented Eastern perspective on Paul's epistle to the Romans. Arguing that Asian and Middle Eastern cultures share similarities in worldview, he brings us new vistas and nuances to this wonderful epistle. While he does not challenge Western thinking, he does challenge us to see more than that. In doing so, his thoughts will certainly provide for vigorous but necessary and long-overdue discourse. I found it a refreshing and insightful read."

Duane H. Elmer, G. W. Aldeen Professor of International Studies, retired, distinguished professor of educational studies, emeritus

"Jackson W.'s work *Reading Romans with Eastern Eyes* provides a long-overdue contribution to Pauline theology and biblical studies. Blending the first-century cultural dynamics of honor and shame, patronage, and collectivism alongside traditional understandings of the book of Romans, Jackson unpacks the importance of a comprehensive interpretation of this fundamental book of the faith. He brings a sensitivity to the many issues that strikes at the heart of the global majority while highlighting the latest in New Testament studies. This is an indispensable read for any pastor, scholar, or Christian who desires to have a deeper grasp of the apostle Paul's magnum opus."

Benjamin C. Shin, associate professor of Christian ministry and leadership, Talbot School of Theology, Biola University

"Jackson W. has gifted us with a fresh and delightfully insightful reading of Romans. Because his Eastern perspective shares much in common with that of Paul's first-century world, the book offers many aha moments for Western Christians. Over and over, issues such as honor and shame, collective identity, and ancestral authority shed significant light on the text, at times challenging traditional readings. What's more, this highly readable book teems with applications that speak to the church today. I strongly commend it to students, teachers, and pastors."

Dean Flemming, MidAmerica Nazarene University, author of *Contextualization in the New Testament: Patterns for Theology and Mission*

"Brilliantly presented! Jackson W. masterfully retraces Paul's use of the Tanakh, the prevailing worldview of honor and shame, and subverts our settled view of Romans. With crystalline prose and energetic bursts of insight, this scholarly work with modern-day relevancy is highly recommended."

Samuel E. Chiang, president and chief executive officer, The Wycliffe Seed Company

"Honor and shame were at the heart of first-century Roman sociopolitical categories and remain the bedrock of social categories in many parts of East Asian countries today. Yet honor and shame are elusive to most Christians and biblical scholars in the West. As such, they are typically overlooked or, at most, undervalued as important substrata of Paul's letters, especially his letter to the Romans. In this book, *Reading Romans with Eastern Eyes*, Jackson W. has gifted those of us in the West with firsthand insight into this important Pauline motif, in a way that makes the entire letter take on new characteristics. Perhaps most importantly, Jackson challenges scholars to read beyond discussions of apocalyptic, covenantal, participationist, or forensic categories and to see the ways in which filial and divine honor are at the heart of every section of the letter. It is an excellent study and a must-read for every interpreter of Romans in the West today."

Haley Jacob, assistant professor of theology at Whitworth University, author of *Conformed to the Image of His Son*

"How can I follow Jesus without forsaking my parents, my people, and my country? This question concerns everyone from the Californian surfer dude to the Harvard humanities professor. *Reading Romans with Eastern Eyes* is an impressive book that goes a long way in answering these universal questions. Jackson W. uses shame and honor to give us a far richer understanding of the message of Romans."

Sam Chan, City Bible Forum, Australia

"Drawing from his personal experience and combining insight and principles from diverse disciplines (not just biblical theology), Jackson W. has written another practical book that will reorient the way we read the letter to the Romans. There aren't enough resources written that take into consideration the cultural nuances and implications that aren't immediately evident, but this book does exactly that. Hence, this book isn't just another Bible study or hermeneutics resource but a key reference if we are to fully grasp the message of the epistle. While Jackson deals specifically with Romans here, I believe it will help and inspire us to begin reading the rest of Scripture with the same cultural awareness and intelligence. This is a must-read for everyone—not just crosscultural workers!"

I'Ching Thomas, author of *Jesus: The Path to Human Flourishing: The Gospel for the Cultural Chinese*

"In this culturally sensitive and theologically insightful reading of Romans, Jackson W. invites us to consider the East Asian notion of 'face' as a key for unlocking the significance of the themes of honor and shame in Paul's epistle to the Romans. Through this contemporary conceptual analog, the author is able to guide the reader through the relational world that Paul took for granted and to illuminate how social capital affects various dimensions of this most important letter. Well researched and yet accessibly written, *Reading Romans with Eastern Eyes* is a useful and reliable resource for anyone interested in journeying into Romans by way of a culture closer to the apostle's own than that shared by many of us in the West today."

John K. Goodrich, associate professor of Bible, Moody Bible Institute

"The epistle to the Romans stands for Paul's efforts in reaching out to communities in Rome, a city epitomized by the ideology of law and justice. That explains the reason why the epistle appears to be dominated by the theme of law and guilt. However, Paul, a former Pharisee, was indoctrinated and saturated with an Eastern heritage—namely, the Jewish culture. Furthermore, the community that Paul was addressing consisted mainly of diaspora Jews, a group of Easterners sojourning in a Western city. Hence, the epistle to the Romans was like an archeological site loaded with multiple layers of cultures. In this book, Jackson W. digs deeper into the cultural roots of this epistle. The lens through which he reinterprets should be considered legitimate and ought to be taken seriously. As a theologian trained in the West, Jackson—just like Paul—makes all efforts of rendering the gospel relevant to the honor-shame type of Asian cultures. By doing this, he restores the original cultural nuances of both the author and the audiences of this powerful text."

Zhiqiu Xu, associate professor of theology, coordinator of Chinese seminary studies, Columbia International University

JACKSON W.

READING ROMANS

with

EASTERN EYES

HONOR *and* SHAME *in*
PAUL'S MESSAGE
and MISSION

Foreword by E. Randolph Richards

IVP Academic

An imprint of InterVarsity Press
Downers Grove, Illinois

InterVarsity Press
P.O. Box 1400, Downers Grove, IL 60515-1426
ivpress.com
email@ivpress.com

InterVarsity Press® is the book-publishing division of InterVarsity Christian Fellowship/USA®, a movement of students and faculty active on campus at hundreds of universities, colleges, and schools of nursing in the United States of America, and a member movement of the International Fellowship of Evangelical Students. For information about local and regional activities, visit intervarsity.org.

Scripture quotations, unless otherwise noted, are from The Holy Bible, English Standard Version, copyright © 2001 by Crossway Bibles, a division of Good News Publishers. Used by permission. All rights reserved.

Figure 1 used courtesy of Werner Mischke, The Global Gospel: Achieving Missional Impact in Our Multicultural World *(Scottsdale, AZ: Mission One, 2015).*

Cover design and image composite: David Fassett
Interior design: Daniel van Loon
Images: grained paper: © GOLDsquirrel / iStock / Getty Images Plus
Pantheon ceiling in Rome: © Sasaki Makoto / Moment / Getty Images
Flowers of the Four Seasons: © Flowers of the Four Seasons by Shiko Wantanabe at Ashmolean Museum, University of Oxford, UK / Purchased with the aid of the National Art Collections Fund / Bridgeman Images

ISBN 978-0-8308-5223-9 (print)
ISBN 978-0-8308-7361-6 (digital)

Printed in the United States of America ∞

InterVarsity Press is committed to ecological stewardship and to the conservation of natural resources in all our operations. This book was printed using sustainably sourced paper.

Library of Congress Cataloging-in-Publication Data
A catalog record for this book is available from the Library of Congress.

P   25   24   23   22   21   20   19   18   17   16   15   14   13   12   11   10   9   8   7   6   5   4   3   2

Y   38   37   36   35   34   33   32   31   30   29   28   27   26   25   24   23   22   21   20   19

This book is dedicated

to two men whose encouragement and vision

spurred the creation of this book.

To Dr. Scott Hafemann,

my former professor at Gordon-Conwell Theological Seminary,

who never tired of teaching me and others to think rigorously about the Bible

and follow the text wherever it leads.

To Jayson Georges,

a dear friend and collaborator, who exemplifies humility in dialogue,

passion for sound exegesis, and a longing to make everything practical

so that everyone can apply God's word wherever they serve.

CONTENTS

FOREWORD

E. Randolph Richards

I f you are looking for an exegetical book on Romans, you have come to the right
place. Did that comment surprise you? Lots of books on Eastern and Western
readings of Scripture talk from the ten-thousand-foot level, trying to give us a big
picture of how our worldview can color the way we read God's Word. I think those
books can be very helpful; I've written a couple of them myself. Describing in sweeping
terms how an ancient Mediterranean person looked at the world—his worldview—
can be very enlightening. Broad overviews, though, are only so that we can later find
insights to read specific Bible passages better. We aren't supposed to stay at ten
thousand feet. In the end I want to know, So what? I want to know how as a Westerner
I can read Romans better.

I have been looking forward to this book for two reasons. First, Jackson is an expert.
He was born and raised a Westerner but has spent most of his adult life in the East. He
is fluent in an Eastern language, is deeply immersed in an Eastern culture, has been
studying Eastern worldviews for decades, and has a keen interest in how modern
Eastern Christians interpret the Bible. This makes him the ideal person to help me. He
understands the kinds of questions Westerners have, the ways that Westerners misread
Scripture, and importantly, when and how a more Eastern perspective can help me.

Second, before opening the book, I knew *Reading Romans with Eastern Eyes*
would upset my twentieth-century Western method of reading Romans. The "Roman
Road" makes perfectly logical sense to me. All the dots in Romans connected com-
fortably for me. Romans was neat, simple and clean. The problem is that Paul ended
up looking a lot—a whole lot—like me. Instead of me imitating Paul, as I am supposed
to (1 Corinthians 4:16), Paul imitated me. I suspect I had created a Paul in my own
image. No wonder I liked and understood Romans so well!

Rather, Jackson is helping Westerners like me (and perhaps you) see how we might
misread Romans because of our own cultural lenses. I don't intend to read my modern,
Western biases into Romans. It is subconscious, unintentional, but pervasive and serious. For example, we Westerners don't usually sit around talking about the importance of individualism or how guilt is used to motivate us. Yet somehow Romans
seems (to me) to be a book about my individual guilt before God. The fact that the

word *guilt* doesn't occur even once in Romans seems irrelevant. Even though Paul only refers to "guilty" once in all his letters (1 Corinthians 11:27), I am still convinced that individual guilt is the most important theme in Paul. Well, is it vitally important to Paul or to me? Has my Western worldview colored how I read Paul? What really are the major themes in Paul?

Are there other ways in which my Western worldview has colored how I read Romans? Romans talks a lot about grace. We often define grace as undeserved kindness: getting what we don't deserve. Paul would like that definition. He says, "While we were still sinners, Christ died for us" (Romans 5:8). We don't deserve the gift of Christ, but we got it anyway. Great. So, why do Americans struggle with this? Why do we keep trying to earn grace?

As modern Americans, we don't usually talk about how folktales help us organize our world. Yet, how I interpret the teachings of Jesus about giving to the poor is heavily influenced by the children's story of the Little Red Hen. Those we help need to be trying to help themselves; they need to be deserving; they need to be grateful. Otherwise, they are not worthy of help. When someone stops me on the sidewalk asking for a handout, up pops a little Jesus on my right shoulder telling me to give to those in need (Matthew 5:42), but the Little Red Hen pops up on my left shoulder, telling me that I should only help those who are worthy (and grateful). Suddenly I'm conflicted, even though the very definition of grace is helping those who aren't worthy. (If you are a Westerner, you may at this very moment be coming up with reasons to defend the viewpoint of the Little Red Hen!) More importantly, I find myself thinking that God is like the Little Red Hen and really only wants to help those who are worthy. My head knows otherwise. I know I can't earn grace. Christian songs on the radio remind me that I can't earn grace. Yet, my worldview, in a powerful undercurrent, keeps telling me that only the worthy should be helped, and I need to be worthy in order to be given grace.

My American culture is a lens that influences what I notice in the biblical stories I read (and what I *don't* notice). The story of the patriarch Joseph with his coat of many colors is reinterpreted in my mind to look like the American success story of the boy who leaves his home, overcomes adversity, and ends up striking it big. This is why for me the story really ends with Joseph becoming Pharaoh's right-hand man. I dismiss the remainder of the story as epilogue, even though it is *more than half* the story.

Recently, some Eastern friends got to the first scene of Joseph having conflict with his brothers. One stood up, waving his arms and in a raised voice exclaimed, "Where is the father?" I wasn't even thinking about Jacob. "Fathers are supposed to resolve conflict between sons," he insists. "He is neglecting his fatherly duties. Jacob is failing!" When we got to the second half of the Joseph story, the part I found confusing (and boring) about the brothers going back and forth, hidden cups, etc., my Eastern friends perked up. Now we were getting to the good parts. When Jacob is reconciled to Joseph and Joseph to his brothers, they were all smiles—a happy ending. The story, after all, was about family. I never even saw it; I thought it was about an individual named Joseph.

Recently, I was teaching a church Bible study and pointed out some important themes that were in the undercurrent of a biblical story—what went without being said. One person was confused and objected, "I don't see *any* of that in the story." Exactly. When we got to the end, many members of the Bible study said, "Now the story makes sense." It had seemed like the story had some missing pieces. The story did. The writer omitted the parts *everybody knows*. Those parts went without being said. A thousand years later and half a world away, those things can no longer go without being said. This book points out better ways to read Paul in some places in Romans where my Western lenses caused me to overlook what to Paul and his readers seemed obvious.

While this book is not a cultural study, this book is also not a commentary. I love commentaries; I'm writing one myself, but commentaries work on Scripture from the ground level. Commentaries are in the weeds. Good commentaries on Romans talk about each verse and how the Greek syntax impacts how we should be reading that phrase. It will discuss archaeological insights, Latin inscriptions, and many other factors that drill down into the details of a very close reading of Romans. This book doesn't go verse-by-verse through Romans. So the book you have picked up is probably not like any other books you have read. It is not a broad-stroke, cultural study of the East and West, nor is it a commentary. You have found an exegetical study of Romans unlike those you and I are used to. You may find new viewpoints, fresh ways to read, and even expose a few of our Western misreadings of Romans. Enjoy!

EDITOR'S NOTE

The author of this book, here using the pseudonym "Jackson W.," has also published in other contexts under the pen name Jackson Wu. He lives and works in East Asia and must write under a pseudonym for security reasons. For the almost two decades that he's lived there, he has followed a practice common in his context of foreigners taking a Chinese name out of respect for his host culture and with the missiological aim of connecting most effectively with those he's in immediate contact with.

Jackson is not Chinese and does not claim to be. He has not used that pen name from an intent to mislead readers about his ethnicity. We trust that readers will understand the author's need for a pseudonym and the good faith behind his previous choices in international context.

ACKNOWLEDGMENTS

A s Romans 16 makes plain, Paul knew his ministry was the fruit of a community of saints. The same proves true for me. Without the encouragement and patience of my wife, I never could have completed this journey.

While writing, some friends, like Wendel Sun, have been like brothers. Thank you for your willingness to dialogue at any time of day and share your joy for Scripture. Given the context I live in, others cannot be named here. Yet I am especially grateful for GL, GZ, WB, SC, and BR. In life, God ordains that we meet certain people and have key conversations that set us in a new direction. Of course, this book would not exist were it not for the countless hours of conversation with my students.

Thank you, Andy Crouch, for your advice and encouragement to write this book. Finally, I shudder to think what this book would look like without the insights and feedback given by my editors, Dan Reid and Anna Gissing, concerning the content and communication of ideas.

INTRODUCTION

I was still new as the youth pastor of a large, well-off suburban church. The job offered a stable salary with a lot of potential and a sizable budget. But I soon discovered their vision was too small. Despite the area's diverse population, the church had only a handful of nonwhite members.

The church hired a consulting firm to provide a demographics report of the neighborhood. They found out many East Asians lived near the church. At a staff meeting, a debate ensued over whether we should minister to the Chinese people around us. No, I'm not kidding. One other staff member and I posed little threat to the overwhelming majority opposed to the idea. The head of our benevolence ministries warned that we simply did not have funds or knowledge to reach out to "Orientals."

By the time we voted, I was trapped somewhere between befuddled and apoplectic. Why are we voting whether to welcome our Asian neighbors? Our vocal minority lost the vote, and my tenure there was short-lived.

From that church's viewpoint, welcoming "them" posed a problem to "us." Could "they" adjust to "our" tradition? Learning another cultural perspective seemed too complicated for the church. "Perspective" might sound abstract, even poetic or philosophical—that is, until we see things from another person's perspective. Perspective then becomes very practical. We realize perspective is about people.

AN EASTERN PERSPECTIVE ON PAUL'S LETTER

If we so easily misunderstand people around us, how do we expect to see the world through the eyes of Paul and his readers? When we meet someone from another culture, we perceive how different they are from us. Overcoming these differences requires intentionality. Do we show similar intentionality when it comes to understanding the perspective of people who lived over two thousand years ago? This is a far more challenging task, and it requires as much humility and perseverance as intellect.

It is difficult for us to traverse the historical distance between us and the societies of the Bible. In many respects, contemporary readers have more in common with each other than people from ancient biblical cultures. When studying the Bible, we swim in different areas of the same pool and can only imagine that ocean called "the ancient world." We have much to learn about the ancient Mediterranean world of the Bible. Fortunately, ancient biblical societies, as we'll see, have several similarities with East Asian cultures.

After two millennia, few people read Romans with Eastern eyes. Even in Asia, Christians largely interpret Paul's letter from a Western perspective. To be sure, no single "Western" culture exists, yet certain characteristics persist in Western cultures throughout history. Western views, like all perspectives, are limited. In fact, "the idea that one can achieve an acultural theology [is a] 'fundamentalist fallacy.'"[1] Therefore, this book demonstrates how we might read the Bible with a broader cultural lens.[2] By reading Romans with Eastern eyes, we can discern key ideas and applications often overlooked or underemphasized by Western interpreters. An Eastern lens equips readers to see the significance of honor and shame in Paul's message and mission.

Eastern perspectives are not necessarily superior, just as not all Western views are mistaken. Any monocultural lens is myopic. However, a crosscultural reading of Romans helps recover key insights that are often overlooked or underemphasized. Thanks to the internet, modern travel, and multiculturalism, a more culturally balanced perspective is far more possible now than ever before. Our knowledge of other cultures is not exhaustive, yet it has expanded. As a result, more people have multicultural perspectives, which provide potential advantages for biblical interpretation.

THEOLOGY IN THE CONTEXT OF MISSION

Ancient Romans, like us, had cultural blind spots. This is one reason Paul wrote his letter. He wanted the Roman church's support for his mission to Spain. This meant more than patting Paul's back along the way. Paul's team needed to trek on foot over a thousand miles past the Southern Alps and Pyrenees mountains. Travel by ship was just as harrowing. Prayer was needed, but so were money and coworkers. Unfortunately, he could *not* assume their support.   *clever*

This book considers how Paul's gospel exposed cultural blind spots and challenged many problems confronting the Roman church. His adroit use of honor and shame reoriented the values and assumptions of his readers. We will consider the significance of these themes for Paul's message and the church's ongoing mission.

Today, we struggle with issues that are similar to those addressed in Paul's letter. How do we motivate churches to join in God's mission to all nations despite apathy and feelings of cultural superiority? How might we challenge the almost-imperceptible forces that divide churches, including economics, gender, political affiliation, ethnicity,

---

[1]David K. Clark, *To Know and Love God: Method for Theology* (Wheaton: Crossway, 2003), 18.
[2]On using contemporary cultures to interpret the Bible, see Jackson W., *One Gospel for All Nations: A Chinese Contextualization of Salvation through Honor and Shame* (Pasadena: WCL, 2015), 183-98.

and tradition? Even for those outside traditional "honor-shame" cultures, the prolifer-ation of social media in the West creates a "fame-shame" culture.[3] Studies show that people with strong desires for recognition or feelings of disconnection have increased levels of social media use, yet the chase for fame often exacerbates their problems.

HONOR AND SHAME IN ROMANS

This book is not a commentary. Instead, it makes a modest scholarly contribution by considering how East Asian culture can help us interpret Romans. I focus on ways that Romans both reflects and remains significant for cultures that emphasize honor, shame, collective identity, and hierarchy, among other related themes. Rather than debate whether Paul's letter and theology have a "center"—justification, God's righteousness, or something else—this study explores Paul's message from an honor-shame perspective. How did Paul's theology serve the purpose of his mission within an honor-shame context?

Chapter one provides an "Eastern" lens through which to read Romans. Given suffi-cient experience and effort, most readers can have an Eastern perspective, even people who are not from East Asia. To rebut accusations of "orientalism" or stereotyping, I draw from multiple disciplines to explain what can be called an "Eastern" worldview. As a result, it contains a heavier portion of footnotes than other chapters. Many simi-larities exist between people in traditional East Asian cultures and the ancient biblical world. Accordingly, we have good reason to expect reading Romans with Eastern eyes will yield fresh insights today.

Chapter two considers why Paul wrote Romans. Paul, like many East Asians today, was mindful to nurture his budding relationships. Therefore, he framed the letter both to blunt the force of his implicit criticism as well as encourage the Roman church's support for his Spanish mission.

Chapters three through six explore several debated questions from Romans 1–4. Chapter three shows why Paul's view of sin carries far more honor-shame overtones than is often recognized. Chapter four highlights the importance of collective identity for understanding Paul's letter and the problems that confront both Jews and the Roman church. In chapter five, we explore why God's reputation is at stake in Paul's letter: if Christ did not die, God would be dishonored. Chapter six suggests that Paul in Romans 4 primarily answers the question, *Who* are Abraham's offspring? and secondarily, How is one justified? By reading Romans 4 this way, we can better understand the relationship between the gospel and justification.

---

[3]Andy Crouch, "The Return of Shame," *ChristianityToday.com*, March 2015, www.christianitytoday.com /ct/2015/march/andy-crouch-gospel-in-age-of-public-shame.html.

In chapters seven through nine, we turn to Romans 5–8. Chapter seven presents Christ as a "filial" son. He faithfully restores honor to God's kingdom and restores the human family. Chapter eight challenges common interpretations of Romans 7 that emphasize individual guilt but unwittingly foster shame among readers. Chapter nine shows how honor and shame influenced Paul's understanding of salvation.

Finally, chapters ten through twelve answer questions and provide applications following from Paul's message. Chapter ten considers how honor and shame influence the Old Testament texts Paul used, especially in Romans 9–11. In so doing, we can better grasp what he meant by saying those who trust in the Lord "will not be put to shame." In chapter eleven, we look at a few ethical implications of Paul's collectivist theology. Particularly, how should the church see itself and therefore respond to outsiders? Chapter twelve concludes with a survey of Romans 14–16, where Paul applies the gospel to the Roman church. He demonstrates how a proper perspective of honor and shame helps the church be a "harmonious society" and thus glorify God.

NOTE TO READERS

Although I expect most readers of this book will be Westerners (or people strongly influenced by Western thinking), I will sometimes make applications to non-Western contexts. I do this for two reasons. First, I do not wish to give the impression that Eastern cultures are more ideal compared to Western societies. Second, I want to demonstrate how we might also apply the message of Romans within non-Western cultures. After all, a fair number of readers will certainly live or work in non-Western contexts.

By reading Romans with Eastern eyes, we are taking advantage of a contemporary cultural perspective that resembles those of ancient biblical cultures. In the process, we will see how many recurring themes complement traditional interpretations, which sometimes overemphasize the individual and guilt at the expense of the church, honor, and shame.

This book seeks to offer a biblically faithful reading of Romans through Eastern eyes. How will we know whether the book achieves its purpose? On the one hand, I will present several ideas congruent with Western theology. Some people will say, "Couldn't I have gained this insight despite not living in East Asia?" My answer is simple: Yes. There is nothing supernatural about any cultural vantage point. What's more, we should be suspicious of so-called "cultural interpretations" that radically diverge from the church's witness throughout history. Some degree of continuity is expected.

On the other hand, different cultural perspectives incline us to ask particular questions and observe details often missed. While reading this book, many people will sense they have a fresh understanding of Romans. Several interpretations will feel new. In fact, we do not cast aside the brilliant insights of Western scholars, who are indispensable conversation partners. Yet, with a new cultural lens, we become more sensitive to portions of Romans that are sometimes overshadowed by a mountain of tradition.

1

HOW to READ
with EASTERN EYES

Circumstances that form the setting

M any people are wary of "contextual" interpretations of the Bible. I completely
understand the concern. More than a few "contextual theologies" co-opt
Scripture for political or social purposes. Such readings seem more like applications
than interpretations. This might be one reason people refer to "African theology,"
"Indian theology," or "Korean theology," whereas "Western theology" is simply
called "theology."

Theologians increasingly recognize that all theology is contextual, since everyone
reads the Bible from some cultural perspective. However, few people agree about the
practical implications of this insight. Should contextual theologies use different interpretation methods? If context does affect biblical interpretation, how might we need
to rethink our traditional methods of reading the Bible?[1] This book suggests a
way forward.   *Environment*

Writing this book is risky. On the one hand, many readers will be nervous about
potentially mixing the Bible with culture. On the other hand, some people are uncomfortable speaking about an "Eastern" perspective. In today's cultural milieu, such
broad descriptions are sure to be criticized. Paradoxically, ethnicity and culture are
household conversation topics that many people talk about with slight trepidation for
fear of offending others. But for the sake of the gospel and the nations, though, we
need to take risks.   *A non-common opinion*

WHO CAN READ THE BIBLE WITH "EASTERN" EYES?

Sports broadcaster Mike Tirico is known for being the first black broadcaster of a
major PGA golf tournament. In an interview, however, he said, "I am not black," because he has two white parents and grew up in an Italian neighborhood. He told the

---

[1]I do not advocate a reader-response method or "eisegesis," whereby one inserts ideas foreign to the Bible
into our interpretation. Instead, this book simply heeds the constructive insights from books such as
E. Randolph Richards and Brandon J. O'Brien, *Misreading Scripture with Western Eyes: Removing Cultural
Blinders to Better Understand the Bible* (Downers Grove, IL: InterVarsity Press, 2012).

Being 'Black' - An American definition to describe a culture, denying individuality & being. Being identified As 'Black' means nothing And tells you nothing About that person [handwritten annotation]

New York Times, "Why do I have to check any box? … If we live in a world where we're not supposed to judge, why should anyone care about identifying?"[2]

What does it mean to be "black"? Ironically, this is not a black-and-white question. Consider comments by Rodney Harrison, an NBC sports analyst and former NFL player. Harrison said about fellow former NFL player Colin Kaepernick, "He's not black."[3] However, by conventional standards (that is, skin color), both men are considered "black."

By contrast, megastar rapper Eminem has been dubbed a "white negro," who "may have been born *white* but he was socialized as *black*, in the proverbial hood."[4] Todd Boyd, a black man who holds an endowed chair for the study of race and popular culture at the University of Southern California, is more candid, saying that "Em is potentially more *Black than* many of the middle-class and wealthy Black people who live in mainstream White society today."[5]

How do these examples relate to having an "Eastern" perspective? Much in every way. Although Americans have long thought about what it means to be "black" or "white," many still have difficulty defining who in particular is "black." These examples illustrate a point: in some respect, being "black" is about more than skin color.

In the same way, people do not have an Eastern perspective simply because of nationality, skin color, or even ethnic ancestry. Although a counterintuitive idea, this chapter will demonstrate why readers from Alabama, Berlin, or Nairobi can use an Eastern lens to interpret the Bible. Along the way we'll answer a few key questions, like: What is an "Eastern" perspective? Do categories like "Eastern" and "Western" merely play on worn stereotypes? And how do Westerners adopt this perspective? We will first consider why anyone can read the Bible with Eastern eyes.

WHAT MAKES INTERPRETATION POSSIBLE

The ability to assume multiple cultural perspectives is essential for biblical interpretation. Scholars try to understand the Bible from the perspective of its original writers and readers. However, contemporary readers have never lived in the ancient Near East (ANE). Despite this significant limitation, biblical interpreters are confident they can understand an ancient text's meaning.

---

[2]Juliet Macur, "Mike Tirico Would Like to Talk About Anything but Mike Tirico," *New York Times,* July 15, 2017, https://www.nytimes.com/2017/07/15/sports/mike-tirico-olympics-nbc-korea-race.html.

[3]Harrison's comments can be found at "Rodney Harrison Says Kaepernick Doesn't Understand What Black People Face," *SportsTalk 790,* August 30, 2016, http://sports790.iheart.com/onair/the-proper-gentlemen-of-sports-52356/rodney-harrison-says-kaepernick-doesnt-understand-15059009/.

[4]Carl Hancock Rux, "Eminem: The New White Negro," in *Everything But the Burden,* ed. Greg Tate (Harlem: Broadway Books, 2003), 21.

[5]Todd Boyd, *The New H. N. I. C.: The Death of Civil Rights and the Reign of Hip Hop* (New York: NYU Press, 2002), 128.

when asked: Tell me About Alecha Ordinance / Alecha: To Answer "she is Black" is taking Away [handwritten annotation]

Although it is impossible to directly experience biblical cultures from 2,000 to 3,500 years past, we *can* move countries or neighborhoods to gain the firsthand experience needed for a more diverse worldview. Westerners are far more equipped to understand a *contemporary* Eastern perspective than grasp how *ancient* people felt and thought. They are more likely to develop cognitive empathy for East Asians and grow sensitive to their feelings.[6]

To say Westerners cannot have an Eastern perspective effectively nullifies all biblical interpretation. After all, crossing contemporary cultures is exceedingly easier than traveling through time. Furthermore, by rejecting the idea that anyone can read the Bible with Eastern eyes, one seemingly clings to deterministic and rigidly stereotypical views of ethnicity. If people cannot broaden their cultural perspective, no one can grow beyond the narrow box of their ethnicity. - *And read the word of God through the eyes of God*

THE MATTER OF PERSPECTIVE

People are not born with cultural perspectives. They are learned and adjusted over a lifetime. Various experiences and relationships shape one's view of the world. Parents and local environment have a disproportionate influence. Also, people belong to multiple social groups and subcultures. Each contributes to forming one's worldview. So, no cultural perspective (whether Eastern, Western, etc.) is uniform in nature.

Who best represents an "Eastern" perspective? A Japanese grandmother or a twenty-two-year-old Chinese college student? A Taiwanese monk or a Singaporean businessman? A Korean missionary or a Malaysian-born Chinese laborer? These people have views that differ at many points. Each provides only a partial glimpse at what we call an "Eastern perspective."

What if someone spends significant time in the West? To what extent does an American-born Chinese or Korean have an Eastern rather than Western perspective? A scene from *The Karate Kid* (2010) illustrates the point. A mom and her son, Dre, board a plane en route to China, where she will begin a new job. The mother lectures Dre to practice his Mandarin with an Asian man sitting across the aisle. Grudgingly, Dre asks, "*Ni hao ma? Ni jiao shenme mingzi?*" ("How are you? What is your name?") Surprised, the Asian man responds, "Dude, I'm from Detroit." Dre simply replies, "Oh . . . uh . . . S'up?"

What are we to conclude from these observations? First, we can gain cultural perspective if given sufficient experience and effort. Second, no one has a perspective that

---

[6]Daniel Goleman defines cognitive empathy as "the ability to understand another person's perspective." See his "The Focused Leader," *Harvard Business Review* 91, no. 12 (Dec 2013).

+ seeing dismissing my humanity.

entirely represents all East Asians. Within a contemporary, multicultural milieu, this is particularly true since people increasingly interact with others from different cultural backgrounds. Just like a Chinese man who grew up in Houston can have a more Western than Eastern perspective, so a Western woman might have distinctly Eastern viewpoints after living much of her life in Tokyo.

AN "EASTERN" INTERPRETATION OF THE BIBLE?

Is there an Eastern approach to interpreting the Bible? No *and* Yes.

No theology describes the views of all East Asian theologians. Some see the West as oppressive to Asians and propose ideas quite contrary to traditional Western theology. Deng Fucun says "[Western] conservative theological thinking" that separates Christians from non-Christians "places church above the country" and "negates rational thinking."[7] Not all Japanese theology is represented by Kazoh Kitamori's *Theology of the Pain of God* nor Korean Christianity by Minjung theology. One also finds drastic differences between evangelicals like Simon Chan, Paul Lim, and Sam Chan.

Having East Asian heritage also does not necessarily imply one reads the Bible with Eastern eyes. Numerous Asian thinkers have theologies with deep Western roots. For example, many Chinese theologians from the government-sanctioned Three-Self Church are strongly influenced by Marx, Barth, or Rahner. Are they German rather than Chinese theologians? Also, how do we assess Sino-Christian theologians who "seldom quote the Bible in their theological writing," raising the question whether "Sino-Christian theology [is] to be recognized as a Christian theology at all."[8] In short, Asian theologians do not necessarily have an "Asian" rather than a "Western" theology.

Nevertheless, a distinct East Asian perspective does exist.[9] Richard Nisbett surveys empirical studies that highlight definite patterns of thinking among East Asians, by which he means "China and the countries that were heavily influenced by its culture, most notably Japan and Korea." He defends the "East Asian" label in this way:

> Some generalizations are justified despite the myriad differences. An analogy can be drawn to the study of language groups. Indo-European languages differ from one another in countless ways, and East Asian languages differ at least as much. Nevertheless,

---

[7]Deng Fucun, "The Basis for the Reconstruction of Chinese Theological Thinking," in *Christianity and Chinese Culture*, ed. Miikka Ruokanen and Paulos Huang (Grand Rapids: Eerdmans, 2010), 299-300.
[8]Pan-chiu Lai, "Sino-Christian Theology, Bible, and Christian Tradition," in *Sino-Christian Theology*, ed. Jason Lam and Pan-chiu Lai (New York: Peter Lang, 2010), 165.
[9]Ying-Yi Hong, "The Dynamics of Multicultural Identities," in *Social Categories in Everyday Experience*, ed. Shaun Wiley, Tracey Revenson, and Gina Philogène (Singapore: American Psychological Association Press: 2011), 6.

generalizations about the differences between Indo-European languages and East Asian languages taken as a group are possible and meaningful. And, as will be seen, some of those high-level generalizations are remarkably similar to some of the differences in perceptual and thought processes examined in this book.[10]

Zhu Bo lists some characteristics that describe East Asians' ideals or "desired values." They include past-time orientation, respect for hierarchy, interdependence, group orientation (collectivism), face, modesty, and harmony with others.[11]

Despite disparate theological views, Asian theologians share underlying concerns that reflect an Eastern perspective. For example, Enoch Wan states,

> The message of the Gospel within the Chinese cultural context should be characterized by the emphasis on honor, relationship, and harmony, which are at the core of traditional Chinese cultural values. It should be different from [traditional Western theology]'s overemphasis on the forensic nature of the Gospel, the legal dimension of Christ's penal substitution and divine justification.[12]

Simon Chan says a "grassroots Asian theology" not only builds on the themes of honor and shame; what's more, "Asian Christians are better positioned to appreciate the corporate and relational nature of life, both as sinner and as Christians."[13] Tan Hann Tzuu argues that relationship (*guanxi*), harmony, and filial piety are essential issues to be addressed when contextualizing the gospel among Chinese.[14] *Respect for parents, elders and Ancestors*

---

[10]Richard Nisbett, *The Geography of Thought: How Asians and Westerners Think Differently . . . and Why* (New York: Simon & Schuster, 2003), 19.

[11]Zhu Bo, "Chinese Cultural Values and Chinese Language Pedagogy" (master's thesis, Ohio State University, 2008), 24-30. One finds scholarly consensus across academic and professional disciplines. Compare Kwang-Kuo Hwang, *Foundations of Chinese Psychology: Confucian Social Relations* (New York: Springer, 2012); Catherine Tien-Lun Sun, *Themes in Chinese Psychology* (Singapore: Cengage Learning, 2008); and Andrew Kipnis, *Producing Guanxi: Sentiment, Self, and Subculture in a North China Village* (Durham, NC: Duke University Press, 1997); Chinese Cultural Connection, "Chinese Values and the Search for Culture-Free Dimensions of Culture," *Journal of Cross-Cultural Psychology* 18, 2 (June 1987): 143–64; Oliver Yao, "Chinese Cultural Values: Their Dimensions and Marketing Implications," *European Journal of Marketing* (December 1988): 44-57; William B. Gudykunst, Tsukasa Nishida, "The Influence of Culture and Strength of Cultural Identity on Individual Values in Japan and the United States," *Intercultural Communication Studies* 9 (1999–2000): 1-18; Xing Lu and Gui Ming Chen, "Language Change and Value Orientations in Chinese Culture," *China Media Research* 7 (3), 56-63; Alvin M. Chan and John R. Rossiter, "Construction of a Chineseness Values Scale and a Chineseness Ethnicity Scale," *Asia Pacific Advances in Consumer Research* 3 (1998): 61-67; James McCullough, Chin Tiong Tan, and John Wong, "Effects of Stereotyping in Cross Cultural Research: Are the Chinese Really Chinese?," *Advances in Consumer Research* 13 (1986): 576-78.

[12]Enoch Wan, "Practical Contextualization: A Case Study of Evangelizing Contemporary Chinese," *Global Missiology* 1, no. 1 (Oct 2003), http://ojs.globalmissiology.org/index.php/english/issue/view/27.

[13]Simon Chan, *Grassroots Asian Theology* (Downers Grove, IL: IVP Academic, 2014), 81-90.

[14]Hann-Tzuu Tan. *The Chinese Way: Contextualizing the Gospel for the Chinese* (self-published, 2012).

Likewise, Three-Self Church leaders and Sino-Christian scholars have collectivistic theologies. Some contend the gospel "transcends the personal" and should be a force for social and national change.[15] Others think Christianity, like Confucianism, should focus on "this world," "rationality," and "responsibility," and emphasize "the priority of community over individuals."[16] Ethnicity often defines one's collective identity. For K. K. Yeo and C. S. Song, ethnic tradition seems decisive in their theology.

We can conclude from this brief survey that while East Asian cultures and thinkers are neither static nor uniform, this diversity does not eradicate the existence of an "Eastern perspective." Throughout East Asian cultures, a common pattern of thinking or set of values shapes daily life and social interactions. This perspective makes living in East Asia unlike living elsewhere.

These observations highlight patterns without being overly rigid. We could say that cultures are like oceans. Their behavior differs depending on the place. Its waters crash upon different shores in different ways and times. Still, consistent patterns exist within and across oceans, such as large water currents, rising and falling tides, and common life forms. Likewise, to speak of cultures as organic systems does not lock people into strict stereotypes.

COMPARING EASTERN AND ANCIENT WORLDS

Although contemporary Eastern and ancient perspectives are not identical, their similarities are noteworthy. Multiple scholars have taken notice. For example, Simon Chan asks,

> How might our understanding of the Scripture in light of the social environment of honor and shame impact the theology we are trying to develop in Asia? First, Asian Christians would discover that their world is not too far removed from the world of the Bible; on the contrary, it has deep affinities with the biblical world . . . Second, Asian Christians are better positioned to appreciate the corporate and relational nature of life, both as sinners and as Christians.[17]

Dan Wu adds, "As someone who was born and raised in a western context (Australian), but with eastern heritage (Chinese), I find the new appreciation of honor and shame concepts a welcome move. I also agree with Green and Baker that recognising the importance of these concepts moves us closer to the Bible."[18]

---

[15]Compare Huiliang Ni, "Sinicizing Jesus in the First Half of the Twentieth Century: How Chinese Christians Understood Jesus." (PhD diss., Claremont Graduate University, 2008), 131-54.

[16]Pingye Li, "How Do Social and Psychological Needs Impact the Existence and Growth of Christianity in Modern China?" in *Christianity and Chinese Culture*, ed. Mikka Ruokanen and Paulos Huang (Grand Rapids: Eerdmans, 2010), 216-18.

[17]Chan, *Grassroots Asian Theology*, 86.

[18]Daniel Wu, "Honor, Shame, and Guilt: Social Scientific Approaches to the Book of Ezekiel" (PhD diss., University of Sydney, 2013), 272.

In this section, I summarize three major aspects of ancient biblical cultures that share significant affinity with contemporary East Asian cultures. Whatever their specific differences, fundamental values and patterns of thinking in these cultural contexts are similar. Though a generalization, the preponderance of people in East Asia and in the ANE share an honor-shame perspective. For simplicity, I will call them "honor-shame cultures." Again, the goal is *not* to force an East Asian context into the Bible. We want to understand the Bible on its own terms. But while having the biblical text, we do not have direct access to the world of its writers. Therefore, we compare similar cultural contexts that we can more easily understand. This positions us to approximate concerns or themes that were important to the Bible's original readers.

"Honor-shame cultures" refer to contexts where people have a heightened sensitivity to honor-shame dynamics. After all, elements of an honor-shame perspective exist everywhere. Honor and shame are built into the human experience. I simply refer to patterns within cultures. The difference between traditional Eastern and Western cultures is one of degree.

An honor-shame perspective has at least three distinguishing emphases. These cultures particularly stress *tradition, relationship, and hierarchy*. These three factors shape a person's social status or "face."

SOCIAL STATUS: REPUTATION AND "FACE"

A major priority for people in honor-shame cultures is securing recognition and respect from others. While everyone prefers honor over shame, they do not have the same controlling influence in the modern West as in Eastern and ancient cultures.

Shame among East Asians is not merely a negative psychological phenomenon; it also influences moral behavior: "In Chinese culture, if a person is perceived as having no sense of shame, that person may be thought of as beyond moral reach, and therefore is even 'feared by the devil.' Thus, shame to the Chinese is not a mere emotion, but also a moral and virtuous sensibility to be pursued."[19] Moreover, "Research consistently shows that Asian-Americans report a greater propensity to experience shame, compared to their Non-Asian-American counterparts."[20]

In the same way, those in ancient Mediterranean cultures prioritized honor far more than contemporary Westerners. Ancient Romans would steal a person's identity not for money but honor.[21] John Barclay comments on Paul's cultural context,

---

[19]Jin Li, Lianqin Wang, and Kurt W. Fischer, "The Organisation of Chinese Shame Concepts?" *Cognition & Emotion* 18, no. 6 (Oct 2004): 767-97.

[20]June Price Tangney and Jessica L. Tracy, "Self-Conscious Emotions," in *Handbook of Self and Identity*, ed. Mark R. Leary and June Price Tangney (New York: Guilford Press, 2011), 463.

[21]Joseph Hellerman, *Embracing Shared Ministry* (Grand Rapids: Kregel, 2013), 58-59.

The multiple criteria for honor—wealth, ancestry, age, education, legal status, physique, character, and virtuous action—made the quest for honor ubiquitous across the social scale, while the very diversity of these marks of value ensured that strength in one dimension could be challenged by criticism of weakness in another. And challenge was, indeed, the very essence of this culture. Honor was derived from comparison, from placing oneself (or being placed by others) higher on some hierarchical scale, in which one person's superiority means that another is comparatively demeaned.[22]

Many Greco-Romans believed with Aristotle that honor was the greatest external good. Cicero claimed, "By nature we yearn and hunger for honor, and once we have glimpsed, as it were, some part of its radiance, there is nothing we are not prepared to bear and suffer in order to secure it."[23] Dio Chrysostom asked, "What is more sacred than honor?"[24] Likewise in ancient Israel, honor and shame shaped various aspects of daily life and even functioned to enforce moral standards.

Broadly speaking, a person's honor or "face" is one's perceived worth according to the agreed standards of a particular social context. Every group holds certain ideals and assumptions. An implicitly affirmed value system determines how people gain, lose, or protect "face."[25]

People are reckoned worthy of honor (or shame) in two ways. It is *both* achieved *and* ascribed. Social standing depends on performance as well as position. Western societies often lay greater stress on the former; hence the expression, "You are what you do." Emphasizing achieved honor leads to increased levels of competition, individualism, and fear of failure.

Many societies are particularly sensitive to ascribed honor. People are honored (or shamed) because of job title, gender, ethnicity, or family name. Such "face" depends on one's relationship to others. Even if people personally disagree with a country's president, they speak to that leader with formality and respect. Also, being friends with a famous person can get one "face."

Of course, having face in one group means *not* having face in other groups. Key leaders and athletes are honored in their own group yet are less esteemed by competing groups. Members of a political party give "face" to their candidates but not

---

[22]John Barclay, *Paul and the Gift* (Grand Rapids: Eerdmans, 2015), 433-34.

[23]Marcus Tullius Cicero, *XVIII Philosophical Treatises: Tusculanae disputationes, Tusculan Disputations*, J. E. King (trans.), LCL (Cambridge, MA: Harvard University, 1927), 2.24.58.

[24]Dio Chrysostom, *Discourses, 31-6.* Translated by J. W. Cohoon and H. L. Crosby (Cambridge, MA: The Loeb Classical Library, 1939), 31.37.

[25]Interestingly, ancient Greeks and Romans integrated "face" with legal language. The phrase "having a face" (ἔχων πρόσωπον) indicated one had a legal identity and social status. See Bruce W. Winter, *Divine Honours for the Caesars: The First Christian Responses* (Grand Rapids, MI: Eerdmans, 2015), 244-47.

AD: Anno Domini; 'in the year of Christ
BC: Before Christ
How to Read with Eastern Eyes   15

opponents. When controversies force you to "pick a side," your choice will elicit contrary opinions that influence your relative honor (or shame) in others' eyes.

Since all cultures have ascribed and achieved honor (or shame), how do we distinguish Eastern and Western honor-shame? We compare the relationship between ascribed and achieved honor in each context. For example, consider a woman named Irene whose fiancé, Jerry, says it is acceptable for husbands to have mistresses. Irene comes from a poor family. Jerry has an advanced degree and a promising future. His professor is well-connected. Friends urge Irene not to marry a man who is routinely indifferent to her, but Irene brushes off their objections.

Although she has earned a master's degree from a prestigious university, Irene says, "It does not matter if I have a good degree. My family doesn't have *guanxi* [connections]. So, others always get hired before me." Jerry is her ticket to security and social position. She achieved honor due to her academic success. But her own accomplishments only matter if she first borrows (that is, is ascribed) honor from Jerry and his professor.

In many ways, East Asians prioritize ascribed honor over achieved honor. If they do not already have ascribed honor, achieving honor is far more difficult. Therefore, Easterners vigorously seek ascribed "face" (through *guanxi*) as a precondition for greater social status.

In Western contexts, the situation is often reversed. If you already have ascribed honor, it can be difficult to achieve honor because others might say you were "born with a silver spoon in your mouth." If someone has ascribed honor, he must eventually reach some level of achievement to maintain respect. He cannot maintain ascribed honor apart from personal achievement.

In the West, ascribed honor minimizes the value of achieved honor. People even disparage individuals whose advantages are based on ascribed honor from things like the reputation of family members. President George W. Bush was criticized for riding the coattails of his father, the forty-first president. Similarly, many balked when Barack Obama won the 2009 Nobel Peace Prize despite spending most of the previous year running for president.

Americans celebrate the lone hero who overcomes the crowd to accomplish a goal. This popular narrative magnifies praiseworthy actions done independently of others, apart from ascribed honor. By contrast, dependence is frowned upon. Individuals must earn what they get. In individualistic cultures, each person implicitly competes with groups for authority and honor. Consequently, ascribed and achieved honor are in constant tension.

By contrast, ascribed and achieved honor are far more complementary in Eastern cultures. Ascribed honor does not minimize the value of one's achievements, nor does achieved honor detract from ascribed worth. Ascribed honor is prioritized because people are socially shamed if they do not conform to group norms. Achieved honor is capped by the standards of ascribed honor.

Different cultural values underlie distinct views of honor. One perspective sees conformity as humble and virtuous, as honoring the group and its elders. Nonconformity is insolence and pride. Yet a Western perspective regards conformity as mindlessness, as weakness veering toward enslavement.

No society can endure while forsaking community. Therefore, individualists take alternative approaches to collective identity. Perhaps a person identifies with the smallest possible social group needed for survival, like a family or clan, or one might have a fluid sense of group identity. Like voluntary clubs, groups unite based on utility or interest. Because these ties are fragile and temporary, loyalty is a luxury and even harmful to self-interest. Individuals switch groups as necessity or convenience demands. Group loyalty is only as strong as it benefits the individual. Principles, not people, bind groups together.

In the West, even racism is tied to achieved honor. Historically, whites boasted in cultural achievements that seemingly validated ideas about white "progress" such that other ethnicities were deemed "weaker." With time, these assumptions were entrenched as prejudice against anyone from nonwhite groups. Many Westerners essentially used social Darwinism to justify racism based on *achieved* honor-shame.

Ascribed honor and achieved honor are interconnected. They shape who we become. We might identify ourselves based on gender, family, or common interests. Likewise, our sense of identity stems from personal achievements, failures, or other idiosyncrasies. A teacher is ascribed honor based on her title, yet attaining that position requires achieving certain honor. Identity is shaped by our differences as well as similarities.

Honor-shame cultures are not ignorant of or unconcerned with law. However, laws cannot save "face" and relationships. People are willing to suffer injustice rather than lose face by exposing problems in court. For ancient Romans, verbally "abusing one's opponents was a normal feature of litigation." In fact, "Merely to be involved in a lawsuit, then, must have been mortifying for a reputable Roman."[26] In the Bible, Job says innocence matters little if he must still suffer disgrace (Job 10:15; compare 1 Corinthians 6:1, 4-8).

---

[26]J. M. Kelly, *Studies in the Civil Judicature of the Roman Republic* (Oxford: Clarendon, 1976), 94, 98.

TRADITION: STABILITY AND PRACTICE

Honor-shame societies emphasize tradition. Conventional ways of living become authoritative standards for what is good, right, and pure. These cultures characteristically prefer constancy, uniformity, order, and balance. Such values foster ongoing harmony. Many traditional honor-shame societies draw inspiration from the natural world. Nature not only says *what is*; it suggests *what should be*. Bloodline, not personal belief, defines one's fundamental relationships.

People who prioritize relationships tend to have practical, ethical orientations. For instance, Easterners focus more on concrete, ethical ideas above abstraction and doctrine. In Confucian thinking, "self-cultivation of a person must be conducted in the context of developing social relationships."[27] Chinese care more about "this life" than the next. Dilin Liu notes, "The major Chinese philosophies all attach great importance to the physical aspects of life."[28] Likewise, religious and ethical thinking in ancient Mesopotamia and Rome was practical, focused on maintaining social order.

In short, tradition is a boundary marker orienting one's sense of value, identity, and worth. Ancestral rituals guide people toward what is right. Thus, what is normal becomes what is normative.

RELATIONSHIPS: COLLECTIVISM AND SOCIAL IDENTITY

One's "face" is the fruit of cultivating personal relationships. Our standards of honor-shame determine the groups to which we belong. Conversely, groups greatly shape our personal sense of honor-shame. Who do we want to give us "face"? Our answer reveals our group identity or the group we want to belong to. Collective identity provides a sense of morality. In relationships, we gain our perspective of right (that is, honorable) and wrong (that is, shameful). The ways we distinguish "insiders" and "outsiders" will affect our moral sensibilities. Identity brings with it various obligations. We treat insiders differently than outsiders. A person has responsibilities to her own family that don't exist with strangers. People must prioritize their relationships.

Loyalty is a fundamental value in group-oriented cultures. That doesn't mean people always live up to this ideal. Yet the principle remains. People understand "we" trumps "me." Truly autonomous individuals do not exist. Everyone needs relationships. Harmonious relationships require loyalty and reciprocity. Favors beget favors.

---

[27]Chung-Ying Cheng, "The Concept of Face and Its Confucian Roots," *Journal of Chinese Philosophy* 13 (1986): 337.

[28]Dilin Liu, *Metaphor, Culture and Worldview* (Lanham, MD: University Press of America, 2002), 64.

Overt disloyalty breaks relationships and forfeits any future hope of benefiting from those connections.

In a "face economy," personal and collective identity are closely wed together. Face is like "social currency." It is given, received, and shared. If my family or friends have bad reputations, I too come under suspicion by others. Conversely, when children get good grades or attend a prestigious university, parents enjoy their friends' admiration.

Why are collectivist cultures more likely reckoned as "honor-shame" cultures? One reason is increased sensitivity to ascribed honor. In addition, "shame is more conspicuous in collectivist cultures in part because the norms are more commonly shared and widely enforced."[29]

HIERARCHY: POSITION AND AUTHORITY

Humans are sensitive to social hierarchy. All groups have formal or informal authorities who enjoy respect and influence. Social rank depends in part on one's relationship to others in the social hierarchy.

Leaders praise (or criticize) those of lower status based on whether they loyally conform to group expectations. Symbolic actions like saluting, bowing, and wearing certain clothes show respect. Diverse customs not only convey allegiance and group membership; they express social rank. At Chinese banquets, pointing a fish's head toward a leader expresses honor. Those with stronger relational networks (thus "face") reap advantages as they climb the social ladder. For example, one of my previous students received his master's degree although he rarely attended class, failed every test, and had an obvious mental disability; yet, his mother was a high-ranking official in the province.

Authorities seek the community's honor. What happens when a company's CEO makes publicly offensive comments? They often lose their position. If leaders shame themselves, those around them also lose face. Good leaders win honor in order to share it with others.

Like those in the ANE, East Asians navigate traditional social hierarchies. Both contexts prioritize the father-son relationship. In Chinese culture, "this form of patriarchal authority closely resembles that found in ancient Mediterranean cultures."[30] Besides patriarchy, ethnocentrism and patronage affect social stratification in both

---

[29]Jennifer Jacquet, *Is Shame Necessary? New Uses for an Old Tool* (New York: Vintage, 2016), 36.
[30]Jiing-Lih Farh and Bo-Shiuan Cheng, "A Cultural Analysis of Paternalistic Leadership in Chinese Organizations," in *Management and Organization in the Chinese Context*, ed. J. Li, A. Tsui, and E. Weldon (New York: St. Martin's Press, 2000), 100.

Eastern and ancient contexts. Ancestry, clothing, titles, and customary expressions of deference both determine and signify social rank.

J. E. Lendon notes, "Honor is a public thing; it is not a consequence of opinion merely, but of opinion expressed."[31] Loyalty and group identity require outward, public expressions. No one says to a king or spouse that they only want to be loyal *in private*. Thus, personal identities are formed by "the ways in which the individual follows a certain moral order, takes action, or reacts to others' actions in systems of social relationships. [This identity construction happens] with reference to the cultural logic, rules, and values, as well as their own recognition of reality."[32]

Ironically, respect for authority and tradition is one reason many East Asians are slow to develop theologies with distinct East Asian characteristics. I've personally heard Christians in China affirm countless ideas I present in this book but then say they are nervous to teach them because such ideas are not "traditional." Sadly, they often assume Westerners have greater insight into the Bible simply because so much of church history is located in the West.

In summary, tradition, relationships, and social hierarchy are key criteria determining social status in both East Asian and ancient biblical cultures. The concept of face "provides a shared basis for a social order."[33] Face "acts as a type of social glue, bonding people by securing relationships through mutual respect and maintenance of harmony (solidarity face). In more collectivist cultures, care for the face of others may form a basic axiom of social ethics."[34]

WESTERN HONOR AND SHAME

Honor and shame exist in Western societies. In American culture, says Ryan Brown, honor "affects so many aspects of our lives together, from how we interact with competitors, strangers, and family members, to who we find attractive, to our mental health, to how we vote, to how and when we choose to die." Most seriously, honor influences "mental health and suicide, risk-taking and bravery, domestic violence and sexual objectification, reactions to terrorism, presidential decisions to go to war, and how parents name their babies, just to cite a few examples."[35]

---

[31]J. E. Lendon, *Empire of Honour: The Art of Government in the Roman World* (Oxford: Clarendon, 2002), 54.

[32]Hwang, *Foundations*, 125, 193.

[33]R. Penman, "Facework in Communication: Conceptual and Moral Challenges," in *The Challenge of Facework: Cross-Cultural and Interpersonal Issues*, ed. Stella Ting-Toomey (Albany: State University of New York Press, 1994), 25.

[34]Christopher Flanders, "Face," in *Global Dictionary of Theology* (Downers Grove, IL: IVP Academic, 2008), 309.

[35]Ryan Brown, *Honor Bound: How a Cultural Ideal Has Shaped the American Psyche* (New York: Oxford, 2016), introduction.

Western collective identity takes different forms than does Eastern collective identity. Zealous sports fans don clothing with their favorite team logo and talk about the team's accomplishments using "we." An excited fan is not on the team, but he shares the team's collective honor via public identification. Other examples where people have a strong sense of group belonging include the military, churches, gangs, and companies. However, Westerners can quickly change teams or leave groups when dissatisfied. Individualism tempers group loyalty.

Some studies suggest honor-shame thinking in the United States is most evident among American Southerners. Researchers explain higher rates of violence in the South, deemed a "culture of honor." Southerners participate in "face contests" where they feel the need to defend their honor with retribution when insulted.

The way people seek attention is another example of how honor-shame can work in the West. On social media, people seek face/honor by receiving "likes" on their Facebook posts or by posting videos on YouTube. They also do it through other means like making good grades or wearing stylish clothing.

HONOR AND SHAME IN THE BIBLE

In the Bible, these twin themes do not exist only where the words "honor" and "shame" appear. Characters and actions also express these ideas. The following graph contains many biblical words used to convey honor or shame.[36]

Even a cursory look at this list highlights a few points. First, we should *slow down* when reading the Bible. It tells a story about God's work among people in history. We need time for its message to penetrate our minds and hearts. Second, *metaphors matter*. People from every age and culture think in metaphors. They create webs of meaning that are dependent on context. Third, *context determines meaning*. The significance of words and ideas cannot be separated from concrete historical circumstances. The Bible's grand story forms an integrated whole. When we enter and embrace that story, the Bible changes our worldview. It draws from a range of images that are not easily systematized.

The various themes and motifs in the Bible are complementary and should not be played against one another. If we do, we will neglect major themes that God revealed and intends to be communicated to all nations. Honor and shame are among those themes. They serve as important lenses for understanding other biblical images.

---

[36]Werner Mischke, *The Global Gospel: Achieving Missional Impact in Our Multicultural World* (Scottsdale, AZ: Mission One, 2015), 18.

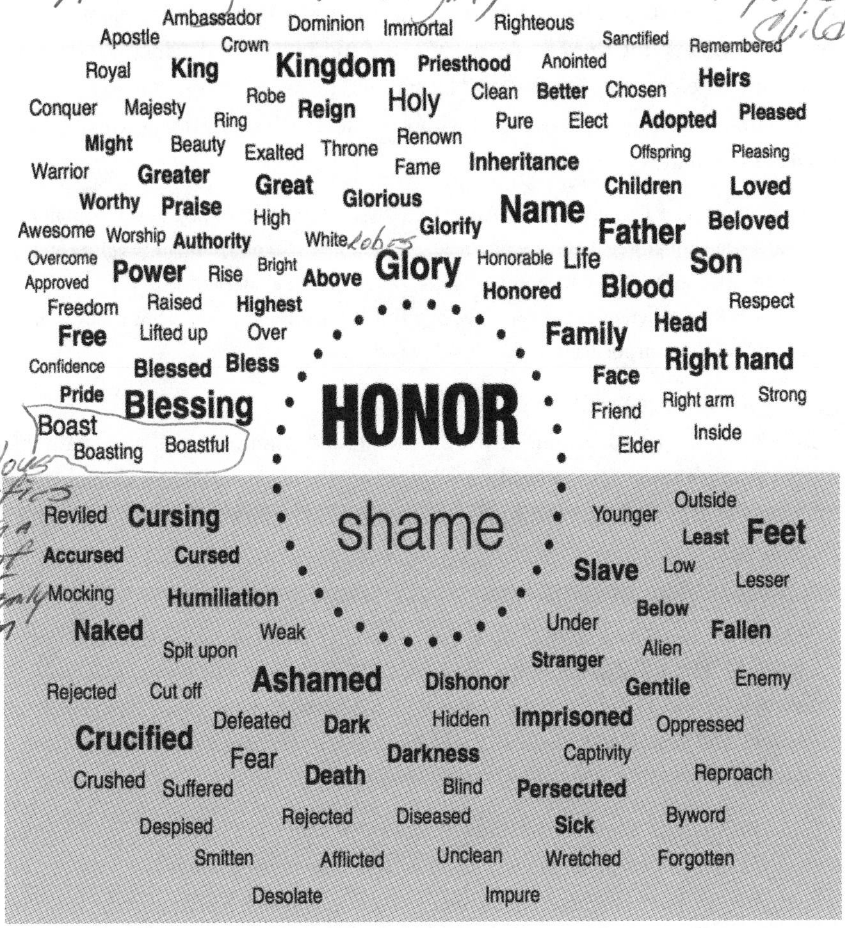

[handwritten: Saying "Yes" to God]

[handwritten: Honoring God Almighty as His Adopted Children.]

Ambassador　Dominion　Immortal　Righteous
Apostle　Crown　　　　　　　Sanctified　Remembered
Royal　**King**　**Kingdom**　**Priesthood**　Anointed　　**Heirs**
　　　　　Robe　　　　　Clean　**Better**　Chosen
Conquer　Majesty　Ring　**Reign**　**Holy**　Pure　Elect　**Adopted**　**Pleased**
Might　Beauty　Exalted　Throne　Renown
Warrior　**Greater**　**Great**　Fame　**Inheritance**　Offspring　Pleasing
Worthy　**Praise**　High　**Glorious**　**Children**　**Loved**
Awesome　Worship　**Authority**　White *lob es*　Glorify　**Name**　**Father**　**Beloved**
Overcome　　　　　　　　　Honorable　Life　**Son**
Approved　**Power**　Rise　Bright　**Above**　**Glory**　Honored　**Blood**　Respect
Freedom　Raised　**Highest**　　　　　　**Family**　**Head**
Free　Lifted up　Over　　　　　　　　　**Right hand**
Confidence　**Blessed**　Bless　　　　　　Face
Pride　　　　　　　　　　　　　Friend　Right arm　Strong
Boast　**Blessing**　　**HONOR**　　Elder　Inside
Boasting　Boastful

[handwritten left margin: Zealous Glorifier. Being a Part of sub?nsly plan]

Reviled　**Cursing**　**shame**　Younger　Outside
Accursed　Cursed　　　　　　Least　**Feet**
Mocking　**Humiliation**　　**Slave**　Low　Lesser
Naked　Weak　　　　Under　Below　**Fallen**
Spit upon　　　　　Alien
Rejected　Cut off　**Ashamed**　**Dishonor**　Stranger　**Gentile**　Enemy
Crucified　Defeated　**Dark**　Hidden　**Imprisoned**　Oppressed
Crushed　Fear　**Death**　**Darkness**　Captivity　Reproach
Despised　Suffered　Rejected　Diseased　Blind　**Persecuted**　Byword
Smitten　Afflicted　Unclean　**Sick**　Wretched　Forgotten
Desolate　　Impure

Figure 1. Biblical words used to convey honor or shame

[handwritten: Shame comes from the power of sin, satan and death. Gen. 3:7 "Saying No to God"]

"GLORY" IN ROMANS

For example, what is the "glory of God" in Romans? How does it relate to humanity's glorification (or lack of glory)? Several scholars have recently discussed these historical and exegetical questions, and here I will briefly summarize some of these key insights. As we will see, this background contains many of the honor-shame elements discussed above.

A significant study comes from Haley Goranson Jacob.[37] She explains how scholars tend to overlook the diverse ways biblical writers use glory language. Jacob lays a

[handwritten: Exegetical — interpretive questions]

[37]Haley Goranson Jacob, *Conformed to the Image of His Son: Reconsidering Paul's Theology of Glory in Romans* (Downers Grove, IL: IVP Academic, 2018).

foundation by first examining the Greek Septuagint (LXX), which Paul quotes extensively in Romans. The word δόξα ("glory"), and specifically God's glory, does not primarily indicate "splendor" or the "visible, manifest presence of God." Instead, she says, "God's glory is commonly associated with his status or his identity as king."[38] With respect to humanity, *Same root word from different languages*

> First, glory (and its cognates) primarily bears its denotative meaning of status/honor *Literal* associated with power, authority, character, or riches. . . . Second, humanity's glory and glorification as exalted status or possessed honor is often associated with the person's status as king, ruler, or person of authority. Third, glorification of a person is never indicative of the transformation of a person's sanctity.[39]

Paul applies this perspective of glory in Romans.

Mikko Sivonen's treatment of the *"doxa* [honor] motif in Paul" is invaluable for gaining a robust understanding honor and shame of Romans. Christ is the *Point / Honor / kings / Support* fulcrum for grasping the relationship between God's glory and humanity's glory. He explains,

Glory

> Paul describes Christ's identity as the intrinsic identity of the *doxa* of God *and* as the derived identity of the *doxa* of God. On the one hand, Christ shares the essential identity of God as the Lord of *doxa*. On the other hand, Christ shares the identity of the image and *doxa* of the (second and better) Adam, who represents humanity, the eschatological Servant, and Israel in order to fulfill the eschatological expectations of the Jewish Scriptures. For Paul, Christ is the one who glorifies God.[40]

Ek katology / 'End of history

Paul in Romans demonstrates how humanity's honor is inextricably interwoven with God's glory. Therefore, Sivonen summarizes, "The vindication of the doxa of God, namely His intrinsic character and divine presence, through Christ and the transformation into likeness of the doxa of Christ, is the narrative structure that undergirds Paul's doxa motif."[41]

Jacob explores the meaning of the phrase "conformed to the image of his Son" (Romans 8:29), which parallels humanity's glorification in 8:30. She demonstrates the importance of Genesis 1:26-28 and Psalm 8 for interpreting Romans. In Psalm 8, humanity is given dominion over creation, being "crowned him with glory and honor" (Psalm 8:5).

This fact is linked closely with Genesis, where humans are "image bearers and thus caretakers of creation in Genesis 1:26-28, a fact that also leads to the noncoincidental

---

[38]Jacob, *Conformed to the Image*, 256.
[39]Jacob, *Conformed to the Image*, 256.
[40]Mikko Sivonen, "The *Doxa* Motif in Paul." (PhD diss., University of Helsinki, 2018), 197.
[41]Sivonen, "The *Doxa* Motif in Paul," 203.

overlap of δόξα ['glory'] and εἰκών ['image'] throughout Paul's letters."[42] Thus, humanity's glorification refers to "being placed in an exalted status or status of honor associated with a position of authority or rule, and that status is the Firstborn Son's as the Messiah and new Adam."[43]

With respect to human glory, Berry adds, "believers experience both a present transformation into glory and a future, consummated share in glory."[44] In the future, they will have bodies resurrected with glory. In the present, they "are free from the powers of sin and death and have received the Holy Spirit, the firstfruits of their adoption."[45] Berry explains,

> Glory is also *functional*. Believers will be conformed to the image of the Son of God so that they might reign with Christ as image-bearing servant-kings. Thus, they will fulfill God's purpose of filling the earth with his glory through image-bearers who reflect his character and kingship in their exercise of God-like authority and responsibility over the new creation.[46]

Bible interpreters frequently underemphasize this present aspect of glory.

In summary, humanity's glorification is relational, ethical, and eschatological. Those who are united with Christ have glory in their new identity as adopted children, heirs, and servant rulers. Therefore, they are responsible to glorify God among all nations. Their whole life is to be "an affirmation of [the divine] nature."[47] These responsibilities are conducted in hope of a future resurrection.

The following chapters will not rehearse these scholarly arguments with respect to glory in full. The purpose of this book is instead to offer an integrated look at honor and shame throughout Romans. The specialized studies of biblical scholars are essential contributions, yet we must still combine their insights with research from other disciplines. In doing so, we will better appreciate the significance of Romans.

HOW DO WE READ THE BIBLE WITH "EASTERN EYES"?

As we've seen, having "Eastern eyes" primarily stems from one's experience and perspective (not ethnicity). Someone raised in Asia or by traditional Asian parents more *likely* sees through an Eastern lens. However, the basic emphases that make up an

---

[42]Jacob, *Conformed to the Image*, 258; compare Donald Berry, *Glory in Romans and the Unified Purpose of God* (Eugene, OR: Pickwick, 2016), 5, 79.

[43]Jacob, *Conformed to the Image*, 222; compare 79-81.

[44]Berry, *Glory in Romans*, 95.

[45]Jacob, *Conformed to the Image*, 237; compare 264-65.

[46]Berry, *Glory in Romans*, 193.

[47]Gerhard Kittel, "Δοκέω, Δόξα, Δοξάζω, Συνδοξάζω, Ἔνδοξος, Ἐνδοξάζω, Παράδοξος," in *Theological Dictionary of the New Testament*, ed. Gerhard Kittel, Geoffrey W. Bromiley, and Gerhard Friedrich (Grand Rapids: Eerdmans, 1964–), 2:244.

honor-shame perspective are not unique to China, Japan, or elsewhere. People from many backgrounds can have viewpoints that closely resemble a traditional Asian worldview.

With intentionality, people can read the Bible with "Eastern eyes." At a basic level, readers who want to do this must first understand and begin to internalize key elements of East Asian culture. Neither reading books nor living cross-culturally alone guarantees one will see the world through an Eastern lens, yet both are critical for those whose upbringing is further removed from a traditional Asian context.

My own story serves as a helpful illustration. I was not born in Asia. "Jackson W." is a pseudonym. I am not of Chinese descent. Nevertheless, I grew up in a family and cultural context steeped in honor-shame. My mother became pregnant with me at age fifteen. She never again saw my biological father, who was married to another woman. My mother's family told her to abort me. They refused to support her, so she was forced to leave school.

Shame tattooed my childhood. Our family's finances were as volatile as my step-father's temper. An account of my childhood could make an episode of *The Jerry Springer Show*. It was not uncommon to see or hear of divorce, jail, adultery, drugs, suicide, and violence in our family. I suffered various types of abuse and so tried to escape the pain by excelling in academics and sports. After becoming a Christian at age fifteen, I quickly grew in my faith . . . and in my hypocrisy. The fear of exposure was constant. I lacked a true sense of belonging to a group. The seeds of despair eventually grew into near-fatal depression.

Ambition was my drug of choice. I earned a full scholarship to a prestigious college. When someone asked me why I chose that school, I replied, "I want to be great." Honor soon gave way to resentment. Growing up, my parents were generally apathetic about my grades, yet they seized my success as an opportunity to win their friends' applause for raising an honorable son. An influential teacher also heaped on pressure, telling me I carried our hometown "on my back."

By the end of freshman year, I reached the precipice of humiliation. I transferred schools, yet my community, ignorant of my reasons for leaving, assumed the worst— that I was a failure. Mere public perception can precipitate shame. To those around me, the truth didn't matter.

This brief glimpse into my story shows a collage of experiences that prepared me to understand how honor and shame work both intuitively and formally. As a young adult, I read John Piper and Jonathan Edwards, whose writings magnify God's glory above all things. At that time, I lived in East Asia, a culture similar to yet different from my own. In graduate school, I studied philosophy and then theology from a Chinese perspective. In that process, I realized honor and shame, at a basic level, work the same in East Asia as they did in my childhood context. The specific cultural rules differ but the underlying framework is the same.

My worldview now is a fusion of multiple perspectives due to my years in East Asia. Through both accident and intentional effort, I've gained the intuition that comes with an East Asian perspective. At the same time, my Western background helps me see things within the culture that others might overlook.

CONCLUSION

By reading Romans with Eastern eyes, we can better understand the message and significance of Paul's letter. Using an "Eastern perspective" does not mean we force modern cultural assumptions into the Bible. Rather, the simple and unavoidable fact is that we all read the Bible through some sort of lens. Our personal and cultural backgrounds influence what we observe and what we overlook. While the content of the Bible does not change, our perception or understanding of it does.

We have seen in this chapter that Asian cultures are diverse. Nevertheless, we can speak of an "Eastern perspective" without falling into stereotypes. In addition, we saw traditional East Asian societies share much in common with ancient biblical cultures. While not identical, their comparable perspectives equip us to ask better questions about the biblical text. Reading with Eastern eyes, we can make observations that would not be possible if we only used a conventional Western perspective.

2

Why Paul wrote Romans

PAUL'S MISSION FRAMES HIS
MESSAGE (ROMANS 1, 15)

In Christopher Nolan's 2010 film *Inception*, Dom Cobb (Leonardo DiCaprio) is a "dream expert" who wants to plant an idea into a wealthy tycoon's mind. To avoid detection, Cobb goes deep into the man's subconscious, entering layers of the businessman's dreams embedded within multiple other dreams.

Nolan's film uses a "frame story," a literary structure that places one or more stories within a larger narrative. Well-known works of literature use frame stories, including Homer's *Odyssey*, Chaucer's *Canterbury Tales*, and Mary Shelley's *Frankenstein*.[1] The strategy allows audiences to assume multiple perspectives within one overarching story. The effects are subtle but significant. Kate Prudchenko captures the benefit of this approach: "A frame may expand or shrink the distance between the reader and the story, change the reader's sense of what is and what is not important, or imply certain sociological, political or ethical consequences that reach beyond the text into the outside world."[2]

Though Romans is a letter, not a narrative, it has a similar shape. Paul presents multiple problems at once, and his approach is so integrated that quick readings cause us to miss Paul's subtlety. His missionary agenda is embedded within a pastoral concern for the Romans, which is couched in the larger narrative of Israel's history.

This chapter explains why Paul's strategy suits his objectives for writing Romans. He shows an acute sensitivity to honor and shame. Paul had never visited Rome (Romans 1:10; 15:23), yet he and the Roman Christians share several mutual friends (Romans 16:3-23). These factors influence how he communicates. Inasmuch as Paul wishes to address problems in the church, he prefers an indirect method of communicating. Ancient Mediterranean cultures, like East Asia today, are generally regarded

---

[1] Other recent examples of frame stories in popular movies include *The Princess Bride, Titanic, The Notebook, Slumdog Millionaire,* and *Life of Pi.*

[2] Kate Prudchenko, "What Are the Effects of a Frame Narrative?" *Pen & the Pad,* accessed August 25, 2018, https://penandthepad.com/effects-frame-narrative-1733.html. For a scholarly treatment, see Gregory O'Dea, "Framing the Frame: Embedded Narratives, Enabling Texts, and *Frankenstein,*" *Romanticism on the Net* 31 (August 2003), www.erudit.org/revue/ron/2003/v/n31/008697ar.html.

as "high-context" cultures. Practically, this means people in these cultures are proficient in communicating indirectly. Information is not always stated explicitly because context allows people to "read between the lines."[3]

By seeing it as a "framed" letter, interpreters can link strands of thought that shed light on the purpose of Romans. Two views are common. According to one, Romans primarily stems from Paul's own sense of identity as an apostle to the Gentiles, and so it serves as a mission support letter. A second view argues Romans mainly responds to the church's local situation (for example, division, relationship to political authority). Interpreters then struggle to relate the letter's beginning and end to its large middle section. Each bookend clearly focuses on concrete matters like Paul's ministry plans and the Roman church. Between them, a lengthy theological argument covers several substantive issues.

These seemingly disparate views make sense from an East Asian perspective. Paul crafts his message using indirectness to achieve multiple objectives. "Indirect" does not imply "unclear" or lacking conviction. Indirect communication is a way of preserving others' "face" and thus relationships. High-context cultures are accustomed to giving and receiving information in this way. A familiar example might be a mother who says to her child, "Did I not tell you to clean your room?" The mother is not asking a genuine question; rather, she is giving an implicit instruction, which the child understands as a directive.

Paul's approach blunts the force of his implicit criticisms. By using Israel's story, he alludes to history and the ways of their true ancestor (Abraham) and king (Jesus). His potpourri of honor-shame language appeals to "pivotal values in the ancient Mediterranean world."[4] In this way, he prepares Roman readers to accept his solicitation for support despite their not yet having met.

CALLING, CHURCH, COVENANT, AND CHRIST

Here it will be helpful to summarize how Paul frames his letter, embedding his points one within another (see figures 2 and 3). Paul's overarching aim is pragmatic. As apostle to the Gentiles, he seeks the Roman Christians' assistance on his way to Spain (Romans 1:5, 13-14; 15:18-28; 16:26). His letter is both introductory and preparatory. Paul anticipates a few interrelated problems that might encumber his efforts.

---

[3]Donghoon Kim, Yigang Pan, and Heung Soo Park, "High-versus Low-Context Culture: A Comparison of Chinese, Korean, and American Cultures," *Psychology & Marketing* 15, no. 6. (Sept 1998): 507-21; Rebecca Merkin, "Cross-cultural Communication Patterns-Korean and American Communication," *Journal of Intercultural Communication* 20 (May 2009): 5-15.

[4]Jerome Neyrey, *Honor and Shame in the Gospel of Matthew* (Louisville: Westminster John Knox, 1998), 8.

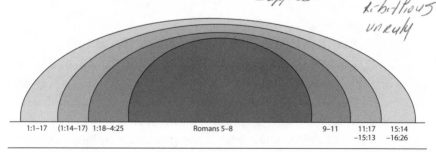

Paul knew his audience

Social divisions undermine the church's understanding of the gospel and its mission. Romans reckoned themselves cultural "Greeks" who looked down on "barbarians," whom Greeks regarded as foolish and uncivilized. The church's sense of cultural superiority would likely stifle enthusiasm for Paul's journey west.

Paul takes a tactful and artful approach. He shows wisdom not to stir undue contention. He leads readers to assume the perspective of Jews who use the word *Gentiles* as a derogatory term. Israel presumed God's special favor, having received the Mosaic law from God. Christ, however, exposes Israel's boasting as foolishness. Israel is blessed. God graciously elected Abraham's family, yet the Jews misconstrue what distinguishes "insiders" and "outsiders." Anyone who gives allegiance to Christ—including Gentiles— belongs to God's people.

Israel's error is far more serious than a theological miscalculation. If justification is restricted to law observers, Gentiles are effectively compelled to become Jews. *Practically*, Jewish group-centrism denies God's righteousness. After all, God promised to bless *all nations* through Abraham's offspring.

Paul's survey is an extended rebuke of Greco-Roman pride. The Roman Christians similarly risk behaving like Jews who exclude Gentiles. When Greeks disregard barbarians, they equally dishonor God. Paul implants his critique within the gospel story to subvert a conventional Roman perspective.

The sting of his warning is fully felt when readers place themselves within Paul's *implied / indirect* implicit narrative. The Roman Greeks are mere *Gentiles*, former outsiders to God's covenant. Historically, prominence of place belongs to Jews, an unpopular minority in the Roman Empire. Paul's message challenges the presumption and recalcitrance fostered by misplaced collective identity. *Probable / suppose*   *Resisting Author* *rebellious* *unruly*

| 1:1–17 | (1:14–17) | 1:18–4:25 | Romans 5–8 | 9–11 | 11:17 –15:13 | 15:14 –16:26 |

Figure 2. The structure of Paul's embedded arguments

Positively, Romans serves as a grand reorientation of cultural values around Christ. Romans 5–8 reframes and so relativizes competing cultural narratives. God through Christ accomplishes what was foreshadowed in Israel's exodus from Egypt. These chapters are a key pivot for Paul, who begins to address his readers more directly.

Romans 9–15 unpack the implications of Romans 5–8. His message resolves tension concerning God's righteousness and the Jew-Gentile relationship. Readers then return to the imminent issue of Paul's Spanish mission.

Observing the panorama of Romans, we see how Paul achieves his purposes. He *dAcES* supplants national and ethnic pride. He helps Roman Christians see God's glory is at *2:24* stake in all they do. Their honor before God depends on accepting Paul's message and mission. Accordingly, Paul expects to enjoy their company and support on the way to Spain.

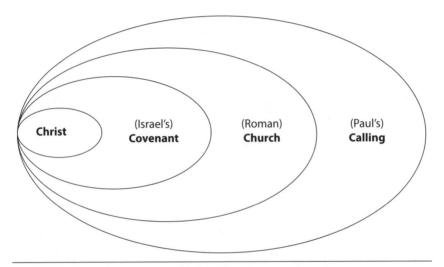

Figure 3. Application of Paul's message to distinct parties

PAUL'S CALLING TO THE GENTILES

Paul is a "servant of Christ Jesus, called to be an apostle, set apart for the gospel of God" (Romans 1:1). The density and length of Paul's gospel summary show why it marks his identity. The gospel determines his theological, pastoral, and missiological agenda. From the moment Paul puts stylus to paper, his tone and message sharply contrast with Greco-Roman honor-shame standards.

How does Paul see himself in light of the gospel? Paul calls himself a "servant" or "slave."[5] His expression is startling given he has never visited this church (Romans 1:10). This introduction differs remarkably from conventional greetings and effectively makes him "lose face." Nowadays, people commonly mention job titles or education to position themselves in conversation, especially with someone they wish to please. If they lack

---

[5]Compare the same word (*doulos*) in Matthew 6:24; Romans 6:16; and 1 Corinthians 7:21.

high social position, they might adjust their job description. Rather than "secretary," we say we are an "administrative assistant." Instead of a "garbage collector," we work in "waste management."

Paul's opening confronts standard measures of honor-shame. While most of us are not politicians or CEOs, we usually try to find some small pond in which we can become big fish. This might be a local church, company, or club. Christians face temptations in church subcultures, which revere titles like "pastor" and "teacher."

Paul also calls himself an "apostle," which denotes a messenger, envoy, or authorized representative. Within a royal context, it can refer to an ambassador, a description Paul applies to himself elsewhere.[6] He has received a mission from God. He gives allegiance to a new king, Christ Jesus. This calling drastically reorients his entire worldview. He assumes a role without social honor. The gospel radically transforms his honor-shame perspective.

Why does Paul see himself this way? He is a man under God's authority and not an ordinary servant/slave. He belongs to Christ, whom the Creator God raised up as the world's king (Romans 1:4; 15:12). Few seek to be slaves, but Paul knows the great honor of being *this* king's slave. He dubs fellow believers "slaves of God" and "slaves of righteousness" who inherit honor, not shame (Romans 6:19-22). Paul, therefore, urges his readers "not to think of himself more highly than he ought to think, but to think with sober judgment, each according to the measure of faith that God has assigned" (Romans 12:3).

Though Paul's identity is defined relative to certain groups, his relationship to others is not independent of his relationship to God. The latter determines his relationship with people. God graciously calls Paul "in the priestly service of the gospel of God, so that the offering of the Gentiles may be acceptable, sanctified by the Holy Spirit" (Romans 15:15-16). This commission transcends social barriers, yet it does not free him from obligations to people. Paul is indebted "both to Greeks and to barbarians, both to the wise and to the foolish" (Romans 1:14). He is identified by his God-given responsibility to others.

Paul's calling does not eradicate his cultural identity. In fact, he says, "Inasmuch then as I am an apostle to the Gentiles, I magnify my ministry in order somehow to make my fellow Jews jealous, and thus save some of them" (Romans 11:13-14). Paul stresses concern for his "kinsmen according to the flesh" (Romans 9:2-3; 10:1). Multiple times, he reminds readers of his heritage: "I myself am an Israelite, a descendant of Abraham, a member of the tribe of Benjamin" (Romans 11:1; compare 4:1, 12; 9:10; perhaps 3:9).

Unlike many people today, Paul does not see himself as an autonomous individual whose identity is independent of others. As Romans 16 attests, he recognizes his dependence on his church family. Being a member of the church does not change his identity

---

[6]See 2 Corinthians 5:20; Ephesians 6:20. Compare P. W. Barnett, "Apostle," in *Dictionary of Paul and His Letters*, ed. Gerald F. Hawthorne, Ralph P. Martin, and Daniel G. Reid (Downers Grove, IL: InterVarsity Press, 1993), 45-51.

as a Roman subject (Romans 13:1-7). He belongs to multiple communities. His collective identity shapes both his theology and practice.

Paul presents a similar view to the Romans, saying that *our view of the church—our collective identity—shapes our sense of mission*. The way the Romans see themselves (as Greek or Jew) and outsiders (like barbarians) determines whether they glorify God by participating in his mission to the nations. This idea pervades every major section of Paul's letter. By conveying this point, he can motivate the church to support the Spanish mission, guard against various divisions, uphold God's righteousness, and equip the church to respond to social authorities. More broadly, Paul expands his mission among Gentiles, clarifies Christ's gospel, and so reorients his readers' worldview.

Paul roots Christian identity in the Scriptures. Notice the dual function of Romans 15:8-12:

> For I tell you that Christ became a servant to the circumcised to show God's truthfulness, in order to confirm the promises given to the patriarchs, and in order that the Gentiles might glorify God for his mercy. As it is written, "Therefore I will praise you among the Gentiles, and sing to your name." And again it is said, "Rejoice, O Gentiles, with his people." And again, "Praise the Lord, all you Gentiles, and let all the peoples extol him." And again Isaiah says, "The root of Jesse will come, even he who arises to rule the Gentiles; in him will the Gentiles hope."

On the one hand, the string of Old Testament citations supports the exhortations preceding 15:8 (concerning church unity for God's glory). On the other hand, they propel Paul to expound his missional vision in Romans 15:14-33. By the grace given to Paul, he "glorifies" (Romans 11:13) or "boasts" (Romans 15:17) in his ministry, specifically what Christ has accomplished through him (Romans 15:15, 18). Drawing on Isaiah 52:15, he adds, "I make it my ambition to preach the gospel, not where Christ has already been named" (Romans 15:20). This explains his visit to Rome. Another observation also suggests the unity of the two sections. Romans 15:13, 33 both serve as prayers for peace in the church. "Peace" is precisely what Paul seeks in the previous chapter (14:17, 19; compare 1:7; 2:10; 8:6).

He seems to demonstrate in practice what he teaches in the letter. Paul interjects that he must first go to Jerusalem, which is in the opposite direction (Romans 15:25-27). The church's health is so vital to his sense of mission that he feels compelled to assist the saints in Israel. His explanation has added weight in view of the preceding discussion.

In summary, the theology of Romans makes sense within the context of Paul's ministry and identity. Paul in close succession reiterates his plans to go to Spain (Romans 15:24, 28). He repeatedly stresses his calling to the Gentiles (1:1, 5, 14; 11:13; 15:15-20). These observations prepare us for the following section.

THE ROMAN CHURCH BECOMES AN OBSTACLE TO OUTSIDERS

How writers begin and end their letters is a clue to their purpose in writing. How do Paul's introduction and conclusion relate to the rest of Romans? Given his expansive theological discourse, why does he give such concentrated attention to his calling and mission? To answer this question, notice how Paul transitions *from* his opening greeting and then *to* his concluding section.

First, compare Romans 1:16-17 and 15:8-9 in light of the major themes of Romans.

> For I am not ashamed of the gospel, for it is the power of God for salvation to everyone who believes, to the Jew first and also to the Greek. For in it the righteousness of God is revealed from faith for faith, as it is written, "The righteous shall live by faith." (1:16-17)

> For I tell you that Christ became a servant to the circumcised to show God's truthfulness, in order to confirm the promises given to the patriarchs, and in order that the Gentiles might glorify God for his mercy. As it is written, "Therefore I will praise you among the Gentiles, and sing to your name." (15:8-9)

Each text acts as a summary statement of Romans. Romans 15:8-9 expounds the broad ideas in Romans 1:16-17. Both passages highlight God's character (his power, righteousness, truthfulness, and mercy). They illustrate how God's work is promised or revealed in the Old Testament. Like Christ, Paul is a servant who is not ashamed of the gospel (Romans 1:1, 16) since it glorifies God. Finally, both texts highlight the scope of God's work: the gospel of Christ saves both Jew and Greek (Romans 1:16).

Paul's rewording in 15:8-9 is intriguing. The phrases "the circumcised" and "the patriarchs" represent Jews. Yet *Gentiles* replaces the narrower term *Greek*. This leads to a second set of observations on Romans 1. Verses 14-17 form a single sentence in Greek. Verses 16-17 support the sentence's main idea in 1:14.

Romans 1:14-15

I am under obligation both to Greeks and to barbarians, both to the wise and to the foolish.
So I am eager to preach the gospel to you also who are in Rome.
For I am not ashamed of the gospel, for it is the power of God for salvation to everyone who believes, to the Jew first and also to the Greek.

First, Paul's theological thesis serves as *support* for his calling. Second, he inexplicably alternates how he classifies people. After twice using "Gentiles" (Romans 1:5, 13), he further differentiates two groups of Gentiles—Greeks and barbarians—who typify "the wise" and "the foolish," respectively. The same sentence then refers to "the Jew first and also to the Greek."

Why does Paul distinguish Greeks from other Gentiles?[7] Most interpreters regard this as a relatively inconsequential question. Curiously, some scholars mistranslate "Greek" (*hellēn*) as "Gentile."[8] Others summarily dismiss the distinction. Concerning Romans 1:16, N. T. Wright claims, "'Greek' here is a way of saying 'Gentile.'"[9] Consequently, some commentators trivialize Paul's wording in Romans 1:14, which says, "I am under obligation both to *Greeks* and to *barbarians*." Others sweepingly conclude 1:14 refers to "Gentiles" or simply "everyone."[10]

Paul's references to "Greeks" seem random; however, multiple clues suggest he is intentional. The chart below notes where Paul mentions "Greeks."

Table 1. Paul's references to "Greeks"

Romans 1:14	I am under obligation both to *Greeks* and to barbarians, both to the wise and to the foolish.
Romans 1:16	For I am not ashamed of the gospel, for it is the power of God for salvation to everyone who believes, to the Jew first and also to the *Greek*.
Romans 2:9	There will be tribulation and distress for every human being who does evil, the Jew first and also the *Greek*.
Romans 2:10	but glory and honor and peace for everyone who does good, the Jew first and also the *Greek*.
Romans 3:9	What then? Are we Jews any better off? No, not at all. For we have already charged that all, both Jews and *Greeks*, are under sin.
Romans 10:12	For there is no distinction between Jew and *Greek*; for the same Lord is Lord of all, bestowing his riches on all who call on him.

Although Paul normally talks about *Jews* and *Gentiles*, at times he strategically distinguishes Greeks from Gentiles. Greeks are one kind of Gentile; not all Gentiles are Greeks. Romans 1:14 distinguishes Greeks from barbarians. His cultural contemporaries deemed the former "wise" and the latter "foolish," so Paul subtly adapts how he speaks of Greeks. In Romans 1:16 and 2:9-10, he prioritizes Jews, putting "Greeks" in the second position. Without explanation, Paul again shifts his wording, comparing Jews and *Gentiles*. The only exceptions are found in Romans 3:9 and 10:12, where Paul abruptly reinserts "Greek" instead of "Gentile."

---

[7]For an in-depth study of this question, see Jackson W., "Paul Writes to the Greek First and also the Jew," *JETS* 65, no. 4 (Dec 2013): 765-79.

[8]Among others, see Ben Witherington III and Darlene Hyatt, *Paul's Letter to the Romans: A Socio-Rhetorical Commentary* (Grand Rapids: Eerdmans, 2004), 46.

[9]N. T. Wright, "The Letter to the Romans," in *The New Interpreter's Bible* (Nashville: Abingdon, 2002), 424. Others hold similar views.

[10]Craig S. Keener, *Romans: A New Covenant Commentary* (Eugene, OR: Cascade, 2009), 26; James D. G. Dunn, *Romans 1–8* (Dallas: Word, 1988), 33; Robert Mounce, *Romans*. New American Commentary (Nashville, TN: B&H, 1995), 69.

Paul's original readers would have distinct responses to these terms. "Greek" carried honorific connotations. Greeks were regarded as culturally astute. In contrast, "barbarians" describes non-Greeks, including Jews. As Jewett explains, the term "is the 'N-word' in Greco-Roman culture. When paired with its ideological opposite, 'Greeks,' it denotes the violent, perverse, corrupt, uncivilized realm beyond."[11] From the Jewish perspective, "Gentile" was a derogatory expression used to refer to non-Jews. Thus, "Paul's references to 'Jews' and 'Greeks' must be viewed against the backdrop of a history of interethnic (*not* interreligious) conflict between people who defined themselves as 'Jews' and 'Greeks' in the cities of the eastern Mediterranean basin."[12] Ancient authors report reoccurring conflicts between "Jews" and "Greeks," even when fighting did not serve their interests.[13]

Romans 3:9 and 10:12 shed light on Paul's thinking. In each, Paul's conclusions have a universal scope. Without distinction, Jews and Greeks have sinned and find salvation in Christ. These verses effectively summarize their respective sections. Likewise, Romans 1:16 and 2:9-10 also capture an overarching idea within the context. Furthermore, Romans 2:11 says God shows no partiality. Finally, "Greeks and barbarians" include *all* Gentiles (Romans 1:14).

In Romans, Paul addresses his readers by their collective social identity. As he did in 1 Corinthians 1–2, Paul seeks to humble Greeks who boast in wisdom. He challenges Greco-Roman pride, recounting God's dealings with the Jews to undermine the Greeks' own sense of cultural superiority. Greeks likewise looked down on "barbarians," the very people Paul wants to serve in Spain.

Paul anticipates some degree of indifference, perhaps antipathy to his plans to preach among Spanish "barbarians." One does not naturally expect Roman Greeks to support Paul's mission. Their prejudice stems from the way they partition the world according to cultural values. They ascribe social worth based on language, education, and wisdom.

Paul's gospel can overcome the Greeks' culture-centrism. His Jew-Gentile discussion is a fitting analogy for the Greek-barbarian relationship. Historically, Jews disdained Gentiles, so he undermines feelings of cultural superiority among Jews by showing how Israel makes the same error. Paul's shifting language in Romans 1–2 is intended to humble his audience. He subtly reminds Greeks they are mere *Gentiles*. Historically, they are outsiders to God's people. Paul doesn't want to shame the Roman believers; he wants them to perceive how honored they are for belonging to Christ's kingdom.

---

[11]Robert Jewett, "Honor and Shame in the Argument of Romans," in *Putting Body and Soul Together: Essays in Honor of Robin Scroggs*, ed. Virginia Wiles, Alexandra R. Brown, and Graydon F. Snyder (Valley Forge, PA: Trinity Press International, 1997), 264. Likewise Dunn, *Romans 1–8*, 32-33.

[12]Christopher Stanley, "'Neither Jew Nor Greek': Ethnic Conflict in Graeco-Roman Society," *Journal for the Study of the New Testament* 64 (1996): 124.

[13]As with Josephus's account (in *Antiquities* 16) of Greek persecution of Jews in Asia Minor. See Stanley, "Neither Jew Nor Greek," 106-8.

Despite receiving God's mercy, Roman Greeks were in danger of acting proud like certain Jews. At this point, Paul's subtle comparison is quite "bold" (compare Romans 15:15). Many ancient Romans looked down on Jews. Around the time Romans was written, "Claudius had commanded all the Jews to leave Rome" (Acts 18:2).[14] Jerry Daniel summarizes, "The Jewish people were classed as barbarians and, along the Syrians, as 'nations born to be slaves.' The Greek and Roman attitude toward them [Jews] was more one of contempt than of hatred."[15] Paul's comparing Greeks with Jews is provocative. By humbling the Roman Greeks, he hopes to motivate them to support his Spanish mission.

To contextualize his message, Paul uses "wisdom," a basic value in ancient Greek culture. Aside from 1 Corinthians, Paul appeals to "wisdom" in Romans more than any of his letters. When talking about human wisdom, he gives humbling warnings (Romans 1:22; 11:25; 12:16; 16:19; compare 1:14). He says of unrighteous people, "Claiming to be wise, they became fools" (Romans 1:22). Likewise, he tells is audience, "Never be wise in your own sight" (Romans 12:16). By contrast, Paul uses "wisdom" more positively when describing God (Romans 11:33; 16:27). He exults, "Oh, the depth of the riches and wisdom and knowledge of God! How unsearchable are his judgments and how inscrutable his ways!"

Paul's gospel undercuts Greek ethnocentrism by usurping conventional notions of honor-shame. He doesn't do away with honor-shame; he reorients them. Rather than boasting in human wisdom, God's people boast in his wisdom. When Christ is the measure of glory, faith is the identity marker transcending every culture. Collective identity is redefined such that Greeks can even consider "barbarians" insiders.

Paul is not an individualist who disregards collective identity. By confronting ethnic and national identities, he simply relativizes their importance. In describing God's people, he says each one belongs to the church as a member of Christ's body.

Table 2. Human wisdom and God's wisdom

HUMAN WISDOM	
Romans 1:14	I am under obligation both to Greeks and to barbarians, both to the *wise* and to the *foolish*.
Romans 1:22	Claiming to be *wise*, they became *fools*.

---

[14]In the first century, the Jews twice were expelled from Rome. See Suetonius, *Claudius* 25; *Tiberius* 36; Josephus, *Antiquities* xiii 5, 5. Compare Dio Cassius 60.6.6.

[15]Jerry Daniel, "Anti-Semitism in the Hellenistic-Roman Period," *Journal of Biblical Literature* 98 (1979): 53. He quotes Cicero, *De provinciis consularibus* 10.

Romans 11:25	Lest you be *wise* in your own sight, I do not want you to be unaware of this mystery, brothers: a partial hardening has come upon Israel, until the fullness of the Gentiles has come in.
Romans 12:16	Live in harmony with one another. Do not be haughty, but associate with the lowly. Never be *wise* in your own sight.
Romans 16:19	For your obedience is known to all, so that I rejoice over you, but I want you to be *wise* as to what is good and innocent as to what is evil.
GOD'S WISDOM	
Romans 11:33	Oh, the depth of the riches and *wisdom* and knowledge of God! How unsearchable are his judgments and how inscrutable his ways!
Romans 16:27	to the only *wise* God be glory forevermore through Jesus Christ! Amen.

By reading Romans with Eastern eyes, we become more sensitive to issues related to collective identity. A coherent unity emerges between different sections of Paul's letter. Ultimately, his purpose for writing is practical. The church's missional ambition is undermined when believers use culture to define insiders and outsiders.

Paul recognizes the relationship between the gospel and group identity. The gospel declares Christ as king of all nations, not merely Jews. The scope of Christ's kingship expands the size of potential "insiders." His kingdom includes people from every ethnic and social group. As we'll see, this view of Romans reveals applications that might otherwise be overlooked.

Paul does not write to individuals but to groups. His readers see themselves not as individuals but as people in community. The entire letter is highly contextualized for people sensitive to collective identity. In the ancient world—as in many places today— ethnic or national identity says more about someone than individual distinctions.[16] If we read Romans with individualistic Western eyes, we will more likely overlook the importance of group identity and miss much of Paul's meaning.

CHRIST REORIENTS AND REDEFINES

Romans 5–8 forms a theological pivot in Paul's framed argument. Having challenged Jewish presumption in previous chapters, he now reorients all of human history in light of Christ. Rather than dividing the world into Jews and Gentiles, he reckons people either "slaves of sin" or "slaves of righteousness" (Romans 6:17-19). This is possible because of Christ. Because of his death and resurrection, Christ defeats sin and death. The reign of a new king brings a fundamentally new worldview. Within Paul's fresh interpretation, people are ascribed new identities not based on national or ethnic distinctions.

---

[16]While concepts like "ethnicity" and "nationality" are anachronistic, I use them for simplicity to describe what typically is the largest group with which one identifies.

As will be seen later, Romans 5–8 recontextualizes Israel's history. All people are subject to sin, a master whose wage is death. Christ is the king who leads God's people out of slavery through the waters of baptism. They do not seek the fading glory of Rome; rather, all those in Christ shall receive God's Spirit, confirming their adoption by God (Romans 8:15-17). This perspective not only redefines collective identity but also their understanding of worth. Their view of other people and their sense of mission stem from a new honor-shame perspective.

Throughout history, writers have recontextualized their national history to shape people's worldviews. In essence, Paul's theological retelling in Romans 5–8 serves a similar function. He reorients human history around Christ. His letter is well suited for a people concerned with honor. Haley Goranson Jacob explains that "throughout the letter there is an implied narrative of glory, a narrative that begins with humanity forsaking the glory of God, that is, humanity's purposed identity and vocation (Rom 1:23; 3:23) and God's people receiving again the glory of God (Rom 2:7, 10; 5:2; 8:17, 21, 30; 9:23)."[17] Naturally, Paul's theological narrative effectively reconstructs readers' collective identity, view of ethics, and sense of mission.

The outline below summarizes the general flow discussed thus far. I put parentheses around Romans 1:14-17, where Paul comments on Greeks, barbarians, and Jews. These verses briefly foreshadow his train of thought. In the second half of the letter, Paul is more direct about his concerns.

Paul's **Calling** to the Gentiles (1:1–17)
  (Roman **Church**, 1:14–17)
    Redemptive History from Perspective of Israel's **Covenant** (1:18–4:25)
    Reinterpretation of Humanity's Salvation in **Christ** (5–8)
    Implications concerning God's Plan for Jews and Gentiles (9–11)
    Applications for Roman Church (11:17–15:13)
  Paul's Mission to Spain (15:14–16:26)

Figure 4. Summary: outline of embedded contexts

THEOLOGY FOR THE SAKE OF MISSION

James and Sunny were fortunate to find someone to care for their one-year-old daughter, Grace. After moving to China, they needed to learn Mandarin. Their helper ("Ayi") watched Grace while the couple attended class at a university. Grace and Ayi bonded immediately. Ayi treated the little girl like her own child. A year later, James and Sunny found Ayi and Grace at their normal meeting spot after class. Unfortunately,

---

[17]Haley Goranson Jacob, *Conformed to the Image of His Son: Reconsidering Paul's Theology of Glory in Romans* (Downers Grove, IL: IVP Academic, 2018), 98.

they didn't recognize their child. Feeling Grace's hairstyle did not fit the weather, Ayi had chopped off the girl's long golden hair.

Being Americans, James and Sunny were aghast at Ayi's audacity. In America, not even grandparents typically assume the right to cut a child's hair to such an extreme. Their tutor translated their concern, explaining Ayi's decision was inappropriate. Though stunned, Ayi received the criticism. But James and Sunny were unsure they communicated clearly, so they asked their tutor to reiterate their grievances to Ayi.

Within hours, Ayi quit her job despite her desperate financial need. The tutor explained to James and Sunny that they had caused Ayi to "lose face." Although she loved Grace dearly and intended well, Ayi felt their criticism was too direct. She couldn't continue working with the couple.

This story illustrates how easily we can offend people with direct speech. This is especially true for people we don't know well or who have different backgrounds. In any relationship, showing respect (or giving "face") is critical. When conflicts arise, people often use indirect ways of communicating. This approach preserves relationships by honoring others. Also, it is frequently more persuasive because people do not feel disrespected or shamed.

Romans is a demonstration of this kind of practical wisdom. Paul first embeds his message in Israel's narrative and then within a retelling of redemptive history in Christ. He thus addresses several serious issues in the Roman church. Concerned as they were for their good reputation, cultural pride and prejudice toward outsiders threatened their willingness to support Paul's Spanish mission. Meanwhile, he tries to reconcile groups divided by controversy. Paul's letter reminds us that collective identity is a sensitive issue for people across the world. It quickly becomes a major stumbling block in relationships and ministry.

Unlike James and Sunny, Paul grasped how culture influences those with whom we communicate. To thrive in high-context cultures, our knowledge must go beyond the basic facts of a culture or person. Worldviews have subtle but significant effects on us. People depend on countless assumptions to share and interpret information. These include beliefs about what is shameful and the proper way to honor others. But Paul's desire is not merely to teach doctrine. He addresses fundamental issues about how Romans see the world, including their views about "insiders" and "outsiders."

Paul uses Israel's story to reframe the problems that need solving. By changing his readers' perspective, he allows them to see the world with a different set of eyes. Indirectly, Paul reinterprets the Roman Christians' history and experience. Likewise, contemporary Christians need to discern the Bible's overarching but implicit narrative. In this way, we, like Paul, can do theology for the sake of mission.

3

DISHONORING GOD
and OURSELVES (ROMANS 1–3)

American revolutionary Patrick Henry was neither Chinese nor Korean. If he were, he probably wouldn't have said, "Give me liberty or give me death." After all, there are far more important things than personal liberty and legal justice. Who cares about laws and liberty when one's reputation is at stake?

Many people would prefer injustice and even death to allowing their families or themselves to suffer shame. For example, victims of domestic abuse often do not report the problem to authorities. One woman explains, "People would look down on me and my family. We would lose face and be embarrassed. No one would marry my younger sisters because of the scandal. I would not be valued in my community. I feel ashamed of myself."[1] In several countries, students commit suicide "when they are falsely accused of stealing a classmate's money or when they cannot maintain excellent school work. They prefer death to dishonour for fear that they may disgrace the family's good name."[2]

In fact, the distinction between lawbreaking and losing face is often blurry. In the ancient Chinese Tang Code, (grand)children could be put to death for accusing their (grand)parents of a crime. Younger generations were obligated to hide an elder's criminal infractions and were even allowed to help family members "evade legal sanction."[3] This is both an ancient and modern phenomenon. In 2013, a Thai man was sentenced to ten years in prison because in Thailand it is "a crime to defame, insult or threaten the king, queen, heir to the throne or regent."[4] Bahrain

---

[1] "Experiences of Human Trafficking and Related Exploitation: Victim/Survivors' Stories," *Research and Public Policy Series* (April 2015): 121-40. https://aic.gov.au/publications/rpp/rpp124/experiences-human-trafficking -and-related-exploitation-victimsurvivors-stories.

[2] Kun-Ok Kim, "What Is Behind 'Face-Saving' in Cross-Cultural Communication?" *Intercultural Communication Studies* 3, no. 1 (1993): 42. Similarly, Andrew Lam, "Asian-Americans' Rising Suicide Rates: Three Students Take Their Lives," *New America Media*, Aug 13, 2009.

[3] Dora ShuFang Dien, *The Chinese Worldview Regarding Justice and the Supernatural: The Cultural and Historical Roots of Rule by Law* (New York: Nova Science Publishers, 2007), 5.

[4] Thomas Fuller, "Thai Court Gives 10-Year Sentence for Insult to King," *New York Times*, January 23, 2013, www.nytimes.com/2013/01/24/world/asia/thai-court-gives-10-year-sentence-for-insult-to-king.html.

and Turkey have similar laws.[5] Until recently, insulting the French president was also a crime.

In countless contexts, honor and shame are serious concerns. "Losing face" is a matter of life and death. From an Eastern perspective, Patrick Henry's famous quote might perhaps be rephrased, "Give me face or give me death!" What does the Bible say to people for whom shame is a living death?

ARE YOU A CRIMINAL?

When translating the Bible into new languages, certain words require special attention. "Sin" is one example. If people don't understand the meaning of sin, they can hardly grasp many other ideas. Our word choices carry theological significance.

Consider the Chinese Union Version (CUV), the most common Bible translation in China. Some nickname it the "Chinese King James Version." In the early twentieth century, a team of missionaries and Chinese Christians translated the CUV. Their translation decisions have since had an incalculable effect on Chinese believers.

The CUV translates "sin" using the word for "crime" (罪, *zui*). When average people hear they are "sinners," they actually hear, "You are a criminal." Not surprisingly, this news shocks listeners and instantly draws protest: "I haven't stolen anything!" or "I haven't broken any law."

Typically, Christians explain that God made a law and we've all broken it. They often follow up by explaining Adam and Eve. Because our first ancestors ate fruit from a tree, they broke God's law. Since they are "criminals" and we are their children, we too are criminals. Consequently, we join in their crimes and deserve God's eternal punishment.

This evangelistic presentation confuses people. Many reject it immediately as irrelevant or foreign. Christians then have no choice but to move on from the conversation, assuming the listener's reaction is nothing more than evidence they have a hard heart.

THE PROBLEM OF "SIN"

How we define a problem determines how we try to solve it. We can easily understand why translators chose to translate sin as "crime." After all, God is a judge who declares people guilty or innocent. At one level, their description of sin is correct. At another

---

[5]Suzan Fraser, "Turkish Teen Release: His Crime? Insulting the President," *Christian Science Monitor*, December 26, 2014, www.csmonitor.com/World/Latest-News-Wires/2014/1226/Turkish-teen-release-His-crime -Insulting-the-president; Suzanne Plunkett, "Bahrain Toughens Penalties for Insulting King," *Reuters*, February 5, 2014, www.reuters.com/article/2014/02/05/us-bahrain-law-idUSBREA140KX20140205.

level, we also see how they compromised their translation by settling for a meaning that is *merely* true.

Why do I say "merely" true? Many biblical metaphors explain sin. The CUV is not necessarily wrong. Rather, it overly constricts "sin" to a single image or motif favored by Western theologians. By default, the translators implicitly elevated legal metaphors above all other expressions for sin.

This translation decision has ripple effects, influencing our understanding of other biblical ideas. If we narrowly define sin as crime, we'll have more difficulty explaining other doctrines in ways that both make sense and remain faithful to the Bible's original intention.

Translating sin as "crime" creates an unbalanced understanding of God. Chinese Christians confess that God is a "Father," yet the CUV forces them to speak about God and sin in awkward ways. For example, they "break a law" when disobeying the heavenly Father. But no one naturally says a three-year-old commits a "crime" when he throws a fit for not getting his way. If we mix the language of law and family like this, listeners/readers are easily confused about our meaning. No doubt, the CUV's translators had good intentions. Yet their inability to discern the influence of Western Christian history makes it difficult for many Chinese to understand humanity's basic problem.

We easily forget the basic fact that we all have a worldview. That is, all people have assumptions about the world that shape how they see and experience life. The cultures we live in naturally influence our view of the world. If we are not careful, we assume that all people—including the biblical writers—basically think like us. Consequently, we might unwittingly force our cultural perspective about sin onto the text as if our views were equivalent to those in Scripture.

We all have blind spots. Mistakes might stem from a lack of awareness or perhaps humility. Whatever the case, we now turn again to Paul's own words. His discussion concerning sin provides a fuller, more biblical perspective.

WHAT IS GOD ANGRY ABOUT?

Romans 1:18-32 is the longest discussion about sin in the letter. For now, I'll use the word "sin" to describe humanity's most fundamental problem, but ultimately, we want to give Paul a chance to speak for himself. Remarkably, Paul never mentions the word "sin." Nor does he talk about "law."

In verse 18, Paul summarizes the human problem. He says, "The wrath of God is revealed from heaven against all ungodliness and unrighteousness of men, who by their unrighteousness suppress the truth." Christians routinely interpret "unrighteousness" almost exclusively in legal terms. Instead of assuming this meaning, though, let's first survey the surrounding context. We need to slow down and ask, "What does the Bible say?"

First, observe that "unrighteousness" is defined in relation to God (Romans 1:18-23). God clearly reveals his glory to humanity. However, their response to God evokes wrath:

> For although they knew God, they did not honor him as God or give thanks to him, but they became futile in their thinking, and their foolish hearts were darkened. Claiming to be wise, they became fools, and exchanged the glory of the immortal God for images resembling mortal man and birds and animals and creeping things. (Romans 1:21-23)

God is the measure of righteousness. "Right" and "wrong" are not relativistic concepts that change between cultures. I say this because too many people mistakenly assume an honor-shame perspective inevitably results in theological or moral relativism.

Second, Paul uses honor-shame language to explain how God sees "unrighteousness." Humanity "did not honor him as God or give thanks to him" (Romans 1:21). To make matters worse, people valued created things above the Creator. They "exchanged the glory of the immortal God" for idols (Romans 1:23). People are not simply naive. No, people "claim to be wise," thus become "foolish" (Romans 1:21-22).

Verses 24-28 use honor-shame to both describe their error and express God's angry response:

> Therefore God gave them up in the lusts of their hearts to impurity, to the dishonoring of their bodies among themselves, because they exchanged the truth about God for a lie and worshiped and served the creature rather than the Creator, who is blessed forever! Amen. For this reason God gave them up to dishonorable passions. For their women exchanged natural relations for those that are contrary to nature; and the men likewise gave up natural relations with women and were consumed with passion for one another, men committing shameless acts with men and receiving in themselves the due penalty for their error. (Romans 1:24-28)

Paul again highlights humanity's essential problem: they exchange the truth of God for a lie because they worship the creature, not the Creator. Verses 26-27 clarify the fact that we honor one creature above all—ourselves!

WHOSE GLORY DO THEY EXCHANGE?

This theme of "exchanging" God's glory echoes multiple Old Testament passages. Verse 23 particularly draws from Psalm 106:20 and perhaps Jeremiah 2:11 (compare Deuteronomy 4:16-18). The psalmist recalls the Israelites' idolatry at Horeb, saying, "They exchanged the glory of God for the image of an ox that eats grass." However, modern translations of Psalm 106:20 obscure an important insight. Neither the

Hebrew text nor the Greek Septuagint (LXX) has the phrase "of God." They simply say the Israelites "exchanged their glory." Paul in effect interprets the Old Testament's meaning. The Israelites exchanged God's glory.

The contrast between the Old Testament and Paul's wording adds a dimension to Paul's message that could otherwise go unnoticed. The "glory of God" in Romans 1:23 has a dual reference. Paul does not primarily speak of God's inherent glory. Nor does he simply say people do not enjoy God's glory via worship. In light of Psalm 106:20, we see that *God's glory is also their glory.* If ever people had reason to rejoice (or "boast"; compare Romans 5:2-3), it was the Jewish people, whom God chose to be his means of blessing the world. However, they lost sight of the reason for rejoicing and boasting.[6]

For example, consider Jeremiah 2:11 in context:

> Has a nation *changed its gods*, even though they are no gods? But my people have *changed their glory* for that which does not profit. Be appalled, O heavens, at this; be shocked, be utterly desolate, declares the Lord, for my people have committed two evils: they have forsaken me, the fountain of living waters, and hewed out cisterns for themselves, broken cisterns that can hold no water. (Jeremiah 2:11-13)

The phrase "changed their glory" is equivalent to "changed their gods." The language of worth is evident by both the mention of "profit" (2:11) and the imagery of 2:13. The Lord asks, "What wrong did your fathers find in me that they went far from me, and went after *worthlessness*, and became *worthless*?" (Jeremiah 2:5). God is Israel's true claim to honor. By forsaking God's glory, they in fact forfeit their own glory.

THE GLORY OF HUMANITY AND ISRAEL

What is the specific nature of this glory? The answer lies in understanding Paul's allusions to Israel and Adam. Donald Berry summarizes the relationship between the two: "Israel was to be a corporate Adam, a people who knew God, to whom he would reveal his glory, and through whom he would display his glory to the world. The entire world was to be blessed through Israel, as God had promised Abraham. But Israel found out that it too was in Adam."[7]

In what specific way is Adam/humanity to glorify God? Haley Goranson Jacob demonstrates a correlation between image and glory in Genesis 1:26-28 and Psalm 8:5-8.[8] The psalmist writes about humanity:

---

[6]Both words translate the same Greek term. Compare Romans 2:17, 23; 3:27; 5:2-3, 11.

[7]Donald Berry, *Glory in Romans and the Unified Purpose of God* (Eugene, OR: Pickwick, 2016), 65.

[8]Haley Goranson Jacob, *Conformed to the Image of His Son: Reconsidering Paul's Theology of Glory in Romans* (Downers Grove, IL: IVP Academic, 2018), 95. Compare 75-98.

Yet you have made him a little lower than the heavenly beings
    and crowned him with glory and honor.
You have given him dominion over the works of your hands;
    you have put all things under his feet,
all sheep and oxen,
    and also the beasts of the field,
the birds of the heavens, and the fish of the sea,
    whatever passes along the paths of the seas.

In Romans 1, humanity forsakes its vocation to rule over creation as God's image
bearers. Instead, they serve the creature rather than the Creator (1:25). Brendan Byrne
notes, "Idolatry represents the summit of 'futility' (v. 21) in that it has human beings
submitting themselves in worship to the creatures over which they were meant to rule."[9]
Paul interweaves Adam and Israel's story in Romans 1. Jacob observes that

> Israel is described as becoming subject to the nations (Jer 2:14-16; Ps 105:41-42, 46 LXX)
> because of their "exchange of glory" (i.e., worship of idols). . . . Israel's glory was their
> honorable position as rulers over the land they were to possess (Lev 20:24; Num 33:53;
> Deut 5:31-33; see esp. Deut 28:63-64; 30:5, 16-18; Josh 23:5). Israel forsook that created
> purpose by submitting themselves to idols and thus to other nations (see Sir 49:5). As
> with that of all humanity in Adam in Romans 1:23, the nature of Israel's glory was their
> honorable status associated with dominion and authority.[10]

What was true of ancient Israel is true for the rest of humanity. Although God originally vested the human family with honor, all lack the glory of God. Paul forces readers
to ask the question, "In what or whom do we seek our honor?" God confers humanity
with the glory of servant-kings, yet all who forsake that call bear the shame of slaves.

IMPURITY AND SHAME BEFORE GOD

What results from people's unrighteousness? God "gives them up" to "dishonorable
passions" and "shameful acts." Romans 1:29-32 clarifies the impure nature of their
behavior. Intriguingly, shame is both the *cause* of God's anger and the *consequence*
of disregarding him. Because people do not honor God, he gives them over to self-
inflicted shame.

Honor and shame are not mere subjective, psychological feelings. God ultimately
determines what is worthy of honor or shame. Theologically, honor and shame express
one's objective value. This observation is important. Writers often misunderstand

---

[9]Brendan Byrne, *Romans*, 2nd ed. (Collegeville, MN: Liturgical Press, 2007), 68.
[10]Jacob, *Conformed to the Image*, 106. On page 82 she writes that "it is no coincidence that in certain key passages where Paul uses δόξα ["glory"] in Romans it is in close proximity to his use of εἰκών ["image"] (Rom
1:23-25; 8:29-30; see 1 Cor 11:7; 15:40-49; 2 Cor 2:7–4:6; Col 1:11, 15, 27; 3:4-10)."

honor and shame as if they were relative, in contrast to an objective law. Now, it is true that different cultures possess contrasting views about honor and shame. However, it is also true the Bible itself uses honor-shame language to describe the unchanging standard for all humanity—God himself.

Paul's emphasis on sin in Romans 1:18-32 differs from traditional Western theology. "Sin" means dishonoring God and thus acting shamefully. Sin is self-exaltation. We think of ourselves more highly than we ought (compare Romans 12:3). The passage nowhere mentions "law." When speaking of humanity's problem, Paul instead uses honor-shame language.

SIN AND "LOSING FACE"

Human sin makes God lose "face." Some people recoil and reply, "God cannot lose face!" The objection misunderstands the nature of "face," which is an Eastern way of talking about honor and shame. "Face" has both objective and subjective connotations.[11] "Face" can even have a moral dimension. For instance, in Chinese culture, the phrase "*ni bu yao lian*" ("You do not want face") is an insult because it conveys a person's immoral lack of regard for others. It can indicate one's shameful behavior, ill repute, or psychological state.[12] In saying God "loses face," we simply mean that sin publicly dishonors God.

How can "face" have both an absolute and relativistic standard? God ultimately decides what is honorable and shameful. I once heard a conference speaker state it this way: "All truth is relative . . . *relative to God*." In other words, when Christians say something is "absolutely" true or good, we mean it is true or good relative to God.

Before knowing Christ, sinners do not share God's perspective on glory. We treat God as if he were not infinitely precious, wonderful, and praiseworthy. At best, we treat him as ordinary. At worst, we publicly express contempt for him. The sins listed in Romans 1:29-32 simply express humanity's shameful disregard for God. The non-Christian is ashamed of the gospel because it sounds like foolishness. They treat God as though he had no face.

Consequently, they lose face before God. By contrast, those around them applaud their sin (1:32). In other words, sin gives them face by the standards of the culture. The actions in Romans 1:29-31 simply reveal one's honor-shame standard. To win approval (that is, face) from the world, people will lose face in the eyes of God and his people.

---

[11]Compare Jackson W., "Have Theologians No Sense of Shame? How the Bible Reconciles Objective and Subjective Shame" *Themelios* 43, no. 2 (2018): 205-19.

[12]For a detailed discussion of "face" and its implications for morality and theology, see Jackson W., *Saving God's Face: A Chinese Contextualization of Salvation Through Honor and Shame* (Pasadena: WCIUP, 2013), 151-77.

SEEKING FACE BY PEOPLE PLEASING

People must choose which "face" they want. Whose approval do they seek? In Romans 2, Paul reinforces the view of sin found in Romans 1 by turning his attention to the person who compares himself to others. Paul exposes the absurdity of thinking that true honor comes through such relative means. God condemns them because they misjudged whose opinion really matters (Romans 2:1-5).

Romans 2:6-11 use honor-shame to present sin and judgment in objective terms.

> He will render to each one according to his works: to those who by patience in well-doing seek for glory and honor and immortality, he will give eternal life; but for those who are self-seeking and do not obey the truth, but obey unrighteousness, there will be wrath and fury. There will be tribulation and distress for every human being who does evil, the Jew first and also the Greek, but glory and honor and peace for everyone who does good, the Jew first and also the Greek. For God shows no partiality.

Paul appears to set up a legalistic framework (whether actual or hypothetical). Upon a closer look, though, Paul's specific wording undermines this view.

Verses 7-8 explain 2:6. The main verb in 2:7 is "seek" (*zētousin*). What does one seek? "glory and honor and immortality." How does one seek these things? "by patience in well-doing." Notice the relationship between honor and good works. One's actions are a *means of seeking honor*. They express a person's honor-shame perspective. The unrighteous in 2:8 manifest "self-seeking" *through* their disobedience. Contrary to modern expectations, Paul urges readers to pursue honor. Rather than denounce achieved honor, he redefines its basis. Furthermore, Paul magnifies the importance of works when he relates them to a righteous desire for honor.

DISHONOR BEFORE DISOBEDIENCE

Romans 2:23-24 is a central passage for explaining sin relative to honor-shame and law. Paul begins, "You who boast in the law dishonor God by breaking the law." Notably, the main verb in 2:23 is "dishonor" (*atimazeis*). In fact, the prepositional phrase "by breaking the law" modifies the main verb "dishonor." Hence, "breaking the law" explains how the Jews dishonor God. Their main problem concerns honor and shame. "Breaking the law" is just one way someone dishonors (that is, sins against) God.

Verse 24 confirms Paul's stress on dishonor, grounding his prior statement. Paul recalls Isaiah 52:5, "For, as it is written, 'The name of God is blasphemed among the Gentiles because of you.'" The essential problem is obvious. Paul's opponents publicly shame God's name in the eyes of the nations.

One more passage underscores the point that Paul does not use the lawbreaking metaphor to define sin. In Romans 5:12-14, he says,

Therefore, just as sin came into the world through one man, and death through sin, and so death spread to all men because all sinned—for sin indeed was in the world *before* the law was given, but sin is not counted where there is no law. Yet death reigned from Adam to Moses, even over those whose sinning was not like the transgression of Adam, who was a type of the one who was to come.

What is the relationship between "sin" and the "law"? He differentiates them in sequence: "sin indeed was in the world *before* the law was given." For Paul, sin is not defined fundamentally by the law. Sin existed before the law. In addition, sin existed even when no one directly disobeyed a command: "Yet death reigned from Adam to Moses, even over those whose sinning was not like the transgression of Adam" (5:14).

Why does sin exist apart from the "law?" Paul refers to the Mosaic law. Although this observation seems obvious, some readers might be tempted to generalize "law" such that Paul is referring to a universalized human law. As a metaphor, sin can be understood as breaking God's law. However, readers should not settle for what is merely metaphorically coherent. These verses clearly distinguish primary and secondary metaphors. Honor and shame are central to understanding the evil of "sin." Emphasis is also a part of the author's original meaning.

LACKING THE GLORY OF GOD

Paul presents sin in this way throughout the letter, saying that one does not fully live in a way that truly honors God. Whether Jew or Gentile, "none is righteous, no, not one; no one understands; no one seeks for God" (Romans 3:10-11). Consequently, they have all become worthless (Romans 3:12). Why? "There is no fear of God before their eyes" (Romans 3:18). In short, people belittle God. Despite being God's image bearers, humans do not reflect his worth.

Romans 3:23 says that "all have sinned and lack the glory of God."[13] What does it mean for humanity to lack the glory of God? Scholars have long observed the close link between Romans 1:23 and 3:23. These verses "describe humanity's *intended* identity and purpose as God's vicegerents by describing its exchange of and thus loss of God's glory—the glory that the son of man in Psalm 8 is intended to possess."[14] Paul's allusion to Adam and humanity's call to reign over creation is far more explicit in Romans 5. Therefore, Jacob concludes, "Adam/humankind ultimately abdicated his

---

[13]"Lack" translates *hystereō* better than "fall short." Because 3:23 is so well known, it is mystifying that people do not give more attention to honor-shame as a major motif in Romans and the Bible in general.
[14]Jacob, *Conformed to the Image*, 101.

God-given throne and invited sin and death to reign in his stead (explicit in Rom 5:12, 17, 21). He rejected his created role as God's vicegerent over creation."[15]

Humanity's lack of glory is the natural consequence of sin, that is, not glorifying God. Our lack of glory is rooted in a lack of faith. In Romans 14:23, Paul makes the sweeping claim that "whatever does not proceed from faith is sin." Why is faith significant for understanding sin? Paul elaborates on Abraham's faith: "No unbelief made him waver concerning the promise of God, but he grew strong in his faith as he *gave glory to God*, fully convinced that God was able to do what he had promised" (Romans 4:20-21). Genuine faith in God magnifies his worth. By faith, we honor him.[16]

Readers should not see a false dichotomy between honor-shame and law as a result of this chapter. After all, the Mosaic law is a royal law by which God reigned as Israel's king. The most direct way to dishonor a king is to disobey him. As rebels, sinners become "slaves to sin," thus "slaves to impurity and to lawlessness" (Romans 6:19). Even so, the "law" metaphor describes just one way in which humans dishonor God.

People are cloaked in the honor of those things they glorify, boast about, and rejoice in. All that Paul says about sin stems from this idea. When people seek honor by means other than Christ, they exchange true honor and bring shame on themselves. Sin does not reflect God's worth or glory. Our disregard or even disdain for God's honor brings shame upon his name. We do not ascribe to God the glory due him.

What must happen for humanity to recover the glory we long for yet lack? The one true God must also show himself worthy of honor. Humans can only reflect the glory of him whose image we bear. As Sivonen states, "God's intrinsic *doxa* is displayed *derivatively* in His image, in humanity."[17] Accordingly, Paul will later defend God's honor (for example, his righteousness). In so doing, he explains why "hope does not put us to shame" (Romans 5:5).

How might these insights shape our lives and ministry? If Paul wrote today, what might he say?

CHASING A NAME

People frequently use social media to publicly shame those who break social rules of morality. In the internet age, the court of public opinion determines guilt and innocence. If individuals do not protect their reputation online, they suffer social rejection, losing friends or even careers. Writing to North American readers, Andy Crouch says that "large parts of our culture are starting to look something like a postmodern fame–shame culture. Like honor, fame is a public estimation of worth, a powerful currency

---

[15]Jacob, *Conformed to the Image*, 103-4.
[16]Other commands use honor-shame language (e.g., Romans 13:7; 15:7). Disobedience dishonors God.
[17]Mikko Sivonen, "The Doxa Motif in Paul" (PhD diss., University of Helsinki, 2018), 196.

of status. But fame is bestowed by a broad audience, with only the loosest of bonds to those they acclaim."[18]

What moral problem do people face in this environment? It's not legalism. Few people try to earn God's favor through moral law keeping. They care more about winning praise and acceptance. Previous generations worried about hell, but today people fear the shame of exclusion. How people talk about morality has shifted. Crouch observes, "In a fame–shame culture, the only true crime is to publicly exclude—and thus shame—others. Talk of right and wrong is troubling when it is accompanied by seeming indifference to the experience of shame that accompanies judgments of 'immorality.'"[19]

In light of this cultural change, the church should rethink how we talk about "sin." We should not adopt the relativistic standards of a fame-shame culture, but we should not overlook the opportunity afforded to us in this context. Particularly, we can speak more directly about the heart issues beneath the desire for fame and fear of shame.

In Romans 2:29, Paul commends the person whose "praise is not from man but from God." What motives lie beneath our actions and words? Whether heathens or hypocrites, people often do what they do because they want others' approval. The natural desire to please others becomes distorted and destructive. Both business executives and pastors are susceptible to people-pleasing and vain ambition. The allure of praise drives us to overwork, overspend, and overlook our families.

These observations sometimes lead people to think "face" is virtually synonymous with pride. But seeking glory is not inherently sinful. Remember, Paul even says we *should* pursue glory and honor (Romans 2:6-11). How so? By first seeking "face" from God (2:29).

Whose approval do you seek? This question applies equally to believers and nonbelievers. Paul's words challenge us to examine our hearts to identify those whose opinions matter most to us. Who, with a single comment, can make or break our day? Who can most easily change our mind or crush our spirit? These questions reveal our motives and our moral compass. How we look at other people also shows our standard of honor and shame. Whom do we criticize or praise, and why?

Shame is usually associated with nonconformity, yet conformity also can be an expression of sin. As long as we satisfy social expectations, we can handpick certain sins to condemn while we ignore others. So long as we gather with people who agree with us, we can overlook our own vices. We face the subtle temptation to use tradition, custom, and history to justify behaviors or attitudes as normal and right. Community, denomination, and culture mask our injustices and insecurities.

---

[18]Andy Crouch, "The Return of Shame," *Christianity Today*, March 2015, www.christianitytoday.com/ct/2015/march/andy-crouch-gospel-in-age-of-public-shame.html.
[19]Crouch, "The Return of Shame."

We scarcely hear the voice of conviction amid the applause of a crowd. Those in the church might confuse social conformity and godly character. We secure good reputations by following social rules. At the same time, those norms can blind us to sin. No one is free from sin simply because other people do not know about it. Greeks boasted in wisdom, yet this is precisely why they excused prejudice toward "foolish barbarians."[20]

As with wisdom, many of God's gifts can become reasons for shame. Romans 1–2 illustrate this fact in different ways. In Romans 1:18-32, people worship God's good creation. Paul condemns the unrighteousness of sinners who "exchanged the truth about God for a lie and worshiped and served the creature rather than the Creator" (1:25). As a result, humans are given over to idolatry and shame (1:23-31). Likewise, sex is not sinful in Romans 1:26-27. It becomes idolatrous when one worships the gift instead of the Giver.

Today, we use God's gifts to gain social status but not true glory. We might buy a luxury vehicle when cheaper cars will do. We justify the extra expense in the name of safety when in fact we enjoy the image it projects. Parents spend exorbitant amounts of money and time so their kids might win sports scholarships. Busyness is a badge of honor for other parents. I've heard numerous Asian children complain because their parents send them to special academic classes both after school and on weekends. They hardly know their parents, who would lose "face" if their own child—unlike other children—did not also spend an extra thirty hours weekly in special tutoring sessions. When chasing a name, we are prone to stumble in shame.

In 1:21, Paul suggests one root of human shame. He says, "For although they knew God, they did not honor him as God or *give thanks to him.*" Rebecca Konyndyk DeYoung develops this insight:

Vice misdirects glory to the wrong end: ourselves. . . . Our goodness is genuinely good, but it is not, ultimately, only ours. That is the point of using gift language. If the goodness is a gift from God, and glory rightly attaches to that good gift when it reflects back to the Giver, then making glory self-referential rather than relational misses the main point.[21]

Gratitude is an effective strategy to combat idolatrous glory seeking. Genuine gratitude reveals a person's delight in the Giver of grace. Such gratefulness focuses on the glory of the Giver (compare Romans 14:6; 1 Corinthians 10:30-31; 2 Corinthians 4:15; 9:11-13). It spurs praise and faith. This is not the response of pride or fear.

The person who thanks God in this way truly honors God *as God.* When we recognize God's character, our attention can look forward to the fulfillment of his

---

[20]See chapter 2 above.
[21]Rebecca Konyndyk DeYoung, *Vainglory: The Forgotten Vice* (Grand Rapids: Eerdmans, 2014), 124.

promises (compare Hebrews 11:6). Fostering gratitude in community builds faith that overcomes sin and gives glory to God, fully convinced God is able to do what he had promised (Romans 4:20-21).

We've just seen the importance of Romans 2 for understanding Paul's view of sin. In the next chapter, we will explore how he develops some of the themes mentioned above. Although God gave the law as a gift to Israel, ironically it became the means by which the Jews dishonored God. They boasted in their obedience to God's law. This marked them as insiders. Nevertheless, Paul says mere outward conformity does not win God's praise.

4

DISTINGUISHING "US"
and "THEM" (ROMANS 2–3)

In 1862, Garnet Wolseley explained why British forces destroyed the Summer Palace, the Chinese Emperor's sacred grounds:

> The great vulnerable point in a Mandarin's character lies in his pride, and the destruction of Yuen-ming-yuen was the most crushing of all blows which could be leveled at his Majesty's inflated notions of universal supremacy. . . . It serves to undeceive all Chinamen in their absurd conviction of their monarch's universal sovereignty.[1]

From a Chinese perspective, these words epitomize the hubris that produced China's "century of national humiliation." Beginning with the Opium Wars, China endured a hundred years of serial conflict and colonization by "foreign devils." In reaction, Chinese leaders sought ways to fortify people against foreign influence. In the early 2000s, to strengthen national solidarity, they began to celebrate "National Humiliation Day."[2] Education reforms were enacted to ensure that "students were taught to 'never forget national humiliation.' . . . Textbooks were rewritten. The Practical Dictionary of Patriotic Education included a 355-page section on the details of China's humiliations."[3] These actions send a clear message to the country: to restore our honor, we must remember our shame.

China's recent history helps us appreciate ancient Israel's experience. At the time of the Babylonian exile, foreigners oppressed Israel. Gentiles sacked Jerusalem, destroyed the temple, enslaved Jews, and occupied their homeland. Outside their homeland, Jews were mocked due to their extreme poverty. The Old Testament prophets describe Israel's exile as a time of shame and dishonor.[4] For many, "exile" included the period after the captives returned to their land yet were enslaved by

---

[1]Garnet Wolseley, *Narrative of the War with China in 1860* (London: Longman, Green, Longman, and Roberts, 1862), 281.

[2]See William C. Callahan, "History, Identity, and Security: Producing and Consuming Nationalism in China," *Critical Asian Studies* 38, no. 2 (June 2006): 179-208.

[3]Evan Osnos, *Age of Ambition: Chasing Fortune, Truth, and Faith in the New China* (New York: Farrar, Straus and Giroux, 2015), 140.

[4]Jeremiah 2:26, 36; 9:19; 14:4; 15:9; 20:11; 51:51; Ezekiel 16:27-61; 44:7-13; Joel 1:11; Hosea 10:6; Zeph 3:19; compare Neh 1:3; 2:17. In Apocryphal works, see 1 Esdras 8:71-76; Tobit 3:4; 1 Maccabees 1:28; Baruch 1:15; 2:6.

foreign powers.[5] Gentile domination was regarded as the consequence of Israel's unfaithfulness to God.

Naturally, many Jews responded to this crisis by urging a stricter adherence to the Mosaic law. God would vindicate Israel only when she became faithful to his covenant. The law was the perceived means of Israel's justification whereby God would demonstrate his righteousness by saving his people and judging their Gentile enemies. By separating from Gentiles, Jews hoped God would finally fulfill his promises to exalt Israel. Modern readers who forget this background may lack sympathy and instead feel only perplexed by the Jews' blatant prejudice. To the Jews, their use of the law seemed a natural corrective to their past unfaithfulness.

WORTH AND WORKS

Romans 2 introduces the concepts of "works" and "law" in Paul's letter. The traditional perspective on Paul (TPP) sees "works" as representative of one's moral efforts to earn God's approval. For those who hold this view, the law primarily signifies God's commands for his people.[6] The TPP emphasizes the relationship between salvation, "works," and "law." The new perspective on Paul (NPP) generally interprets "works" more narrowly as boundary markers like circumcision, food laws, and Sabbath keeping. Obedience in these areas distinguished Jews from Gentiles.[7] The NPP highlights the sociological implications of "works" and "law" in Paul's letter. Naturally, these are generalizations. Theologians routinely adopt elements from both views.

The TPP and NPP are "both right, just not at the same time."[8] Each camp emphasizes different sections of Paul's letters. They do not sufficiently account for how Paul develops his thoughts to address the distinctive circumstances facing various churches. His earlier letters deal most directly with the Jew-Gentile divide and more frequently speak about justification. Later writings lack these emphases and stress "salvation," a broader idea that includes justification.

---

[5]Nehemiah 9:36; compare 5:5; Ezra 9:9. See N. T. Wright, *Paul and the Faithfulness of God*, vol. 1 (Minneapolis: Fortress, 2013), 139-96.

[6]Proponents of the TPP include Stephen Westerholm, *Perspectives Old and New on Paul: The "Lutheran" Paul and His Critics* (Grand Rapids: Eerdmans, 2004); John Piper, *The Future of Justification: A Response to N. T. Wright* (Wheaton, IL: Crossway, 2008).

[7]Although NPP disagree at various points, representative works include James Dunn, *The New Perspective on Paul* (Grand Rapids: Eerdmans, 2008); N. T. Wright, *Justification: God's Plan and Paul's Vision* (Downers Grove, IL: IVP Academic, 2009). For an introduction to both perspectives, see Kent L. Yinger, *The New Perspective on Paul: An Introduction* (Eugene, OR: Cascade, 2011). A scholarly middle position is Michael Bird, *The Saving Righteousness of God: Studies on Paul, Justification, and the New Perspective* (Waynesboro, GA: Paternoster, 2007).

[8]Garwood Anderson, *Paul's New Perspective: Charting a Soteriological Journey* (Downers Grove, IL: IVP Academic, 2016), 379. The following summary reflects Anderson's thinking. See 373-77.

"Works of the law" are closely linked to justification and the Mosaic law, a dividing line between Jew and Gentile. However, Paul increasingly uses "works" in a general sense as churches move beyond debates about whether Gentiles must keep the law to belong to God's people. This development explains why Paul commends "good works" more frequently in later letters, once readers were less likely to confuse "works of the law" and "works" more broadly understood.

Contemporary readers often flatten the contrast between grace and works such that gift givers do not expect recipients to return favors in kind. By nature, grace is "free" and so does not imply reciprocity. However, this view oversimplifies, even distorts, how ancients perceived grace. Ancient gift-giving typically entailed reciprocity from the recipient such that exchanging gifts brought people together in relationship. Ancient Romans

> were explicit and completely unapologetic about the fact that gifts create ties of obligation. . . . For this reason, they also insist that the donor must judge the *worth* of the recipient: one does not tie oneself to the disreputable, ungrateful, or otherwise worthless beneficiary.[9]

For Jews, this perspective extended to God. Pious Jews gave to the poor in part because they expected reciprocation (that is, reward) from God.[10] In summary, ancient readers felt the worth of a gift should reflect the recipient's worth.

Jews used the law as a measure of worth. John Barclay says,

> On my reading, "works" represent not human initiative but the display of human worth as defined by criteria other than God's. Thus, the central question is not "do we trust in God or in our own efforts?" but "is God's saving action given to those who define the worthy, or without regard to worth?"[11]

"Worth" simply describes the honor (or shame) ascribed to people based on culturally assumed "criteria of worth." Barclay summarizes, "Thus, the foil to Paul's theology is not a human self-righteousness that attempts to earn salvation but the natural assumption that when God acts in saving benevolence, he distributes his gifts to those we consider fitting or worthy."[12]

Law keeping brought honor, whereas disobedience brought shame. Since God gave the law to the Jews, they thought God was partial to Israel. He would honor Jews and shame Gentiles. Accordingly, the law distinguishes insiders from outsiders, and obeying the law brings honor from God (Romans 2:10). Likewise, people gained

---

[9]John Barclay, *Paul and the Gift* (Grand Rapids: Eerdmans, 2015), 39.
[10]Barclay, *Paul and the Gift*, 43-44. Compare Matthew 6:1-6.
[11]Barclay, *Paul and the Gift*, 541.
[12]Barclay, *Paul and the Gift*, 541.

acceptance from fellow Jews. The community praised those whom they expected God to reward. We begin to see the problem with Paul's Jewish opponents. In effect, their sin is "the perverse spirit of competition for honor that has turned the law into a system of status acquisition."[13]

Assuming the law measured a person's worth in God's eyes, Jews regarded Gentiles as shameful outcasts. Their only hope was to give allegiance to the Lord and observe the commands of Moses. One was thus justified by keeping the law. Those reckoned righteous were deemed worthy of divine honor.

THE ETHICS OF ETHNIC IDENTITY

Certainly, "works of the law" had moral value since they came from God. Such works simultaneously served as social boundary markers and moral actions. They had ethnic and ethical significance. In short, law keeping and thus being Jewish had implications for society and salvation. Salvation was not individualistic; it entwined with social identity.

Circumcision carried positive *ethical* implications within a distinct *ethnic* community. In Israel, circumcision signified one's identity and entailed obligations for God's people. Conversion reoriented Gentiles' national or ethnic identity. Doing works of the law symbolized allegiance to Israel's God and thus identified his people.

Honor and shame play key roles in personal *and* collective identity. In effect, the TPP emphasizes achieved honor, focusing on individual distinctions or merit. The NPP lays stress on ascribed honor based on relationships, social status, and identity. Ascribed and achieved honor (or shame) exist everywhere, yet cultures are not equally sensitive to each kind. Typically, Easterners are more cognizant of ascribed honor than Westerners, for whom achievements generally define identity. The former intuitively link honor with collective identity.

From Israel's perspective, Gentiles were ascribed honor from God once they joined Israel by obeying the law. Ethnicity alone did not determine justification. The native-born Jew could forfeit honor by disregarding the law (that is, achieved shame). In so doing, covenant breakers effectively forsook the honor-shame standards that marked God's covenant people. The covenant-breaking Jew—like Gentiles—did not prove himself worthy of God's gift, that is, the law.

Although collective identity is a critical theme throughout Romans, it is especially prominent in Romans 2–3, where Paul considers *who* truly are God's people. As he does this, Paul undermines ancient Jewish ethnocentrism/nationalism. People with a

---

[13]Robert Jewett and Roy D. Kotansky. *Romans: A Commentary.* ed. Eldon J. Epp. Hermeneia (Minneapolis: Fortress, 2007), 462.

sense of cultural superiority inevitably divide the world into insiders and outsiders. For Paul, the theological implications are treasonous. In effect, they "colonize" the world over which Christ is king.

INSIDERS AND OUTSIDERS

Paul's discussion of justification is meant to address the question, Who are insiders and outsiders? It appears that he uses justification to underscore collective identity, not merely individual salvation.[14] He not only speaks of his Gentile mission (1:6, 13), he uses social labels that would raise the eyebrows of his original readers. He intentionally distinguishes Greeks and barbarians, the wise and foolish, the Jew and Greek. After Romans 2:9-10, "Greeks" are provocatively labeled "Gentiles," whom Jews scorned as "dogs."

Romans 2:1-11
Therefore you have no excuse, O man, every one of you who judges. For in passing judgment on another you condemn yourself, because you, the judge, practice the very same things. [2] We know that the judgment of God rightly falls on those who practice such things. [3] Do you suppose, O man—you who judge those who practice such things and yet do them yourself—that you will escape the judgment of God? [4] Or do you presume on the riches of his kindness and forbearance and patience, not knowing that God's kindness is meant to lead you to repentance? [5] But because of your hard and impenitent heart you are storing up wrath for yourself on the day of wrath when God's righteous judgment will be revealed.   [6] He will render to each one according to his works: [7] to those who by patience in well-doing seek for glory and honor and immortality, he will give eternal life; [8] but for those who are self-seeking and do not obey the truth, but obey unrighteousness, there will be wrath and fury. [9] There will be tribulation and distress for every human being who does evil, the Jew first and also the Greek, [10] but glory and honor and peace for everyone who does good, the Jew first and also the Greek. [11] For God shows no partiality.

heated/ conversation partner

Although the implied interlocutor in Romans 2 is Jewish, we should not assume Paul is addressing specific Jewish readers in Rome. The expression "O man" in 2:1, 3 is a standard way of addressing a more generalized or imagined reader who fits a broad description and is not limited to immediate readers.[15] Romans 2 does not criticize specific Jewish Christians in Rome just as 1:18-32 does

---

[14]I do not imply justification is merely social, as though Paul is only concerned about church membership. *Who* belongs to God's people is inextricably tied to questions about *how* one is justified. Collective identity is about salvation as much as ecclesiology.

[15]Compare Romans 9:20; 1 Timothy 6:11; James 2:20; Proverbs 8:4 (LXX).

not censure the behavior of Rome's Gentile Christians. Paul's rhetorical strategy fits the larger structure of Romans. That is, he rehearses Israel's history and views of Gentiles to address specific issues in the Roman church, like Greek prejudice against barbarians.

In Romans 1:14–2:10, Paul uses common cultural classifications only to relativize their value before God. God "will render to each one according to his works" without partiality to any social group (2:6, 11). Eternal life is granted to any "who by patience in well-doing seek for glory and honor and immortality" (2:7).[16] The wording and repetition in 2:9-10 foreshadow the argument Paul is getting ready to make. All people will either suffer tribulation or gain honor according to what they do, *not* according to their culture or ethnicity. "Jew" and "Greek" unambiguously signify two types of collective identity. These terms would certainly evoke pride in each group. By underscoring ethical works, Paul undercuts ethnic pride.

Next, he rebuffs Jewish presumption. National identification justifies no one. Paul exposes how narrowly the Jews (and Greeks) understood collective identity. God does not distinguish "insiders" and "outsiders" via worldly, unrighteous standards. When ethnic and national categories primarily determine social identity, they contradict the gospel.

Romans 2:12-16

For all who have sinned without the law will also perish without the law, and all who have sinned under the law will be judged by the law. [13] For it is not the hearers of the law who are righteous before God, but the doers of the law who will be justified. [14] For when Gentiles, who do not have the law, by nature do what the law requires, they are a law to themselves, even though they do not have the law. [15] They show that the work of the law is written on their hearts, while their conscience also bears witness, and their conflicting thoughts accuse or even excuse them [16] on that day when, according to my gospel, God judges the secrets of men by Christ Jesus.

Paul introduces the law in 2:12. At this same point, Paul begins to contrast "Jews" and "Gentiles." This is not incidental, and we must not confuse the contrast between Jew/Greek with that of Jew/Gentile. A Greek is a Gentile, but a Gentile is not necessarily Greek. Whereas "Greek" connoted honor, Jews used "Gentile" derisively.

[16]In the LXX, the word pair "glory and honor" appears thirteen times. Grindheim concludes, "To seek glory and honor and immortality is to look for God and to yearn for God's personal presence. . . . This people share in God's glory, therefore, not by virtue of their inherent qualities but by virtue of the fact that they serve as a demonstration of God's mercy." See Sigurd Grindheim, "A Theology of Glory: Paul's Use of Δόξα Terminology in Romans," *Journal of Biblical Literature* 136, no. 2 (Summer 2017): 462, 465.

In Romans 2:12-14, the law distinguishes Jews and Gentiles. Each sentence builds on the previous one. Verse 12 contrasts two groups to be judged: "all who have sinned without the law" and "all who have sinned under the law." Verse 13 develops the idea but now contrasts "hearers of the law" and "doers of the law." Only the latter are justified. Verse 14 then has a surprising twist. Paul combines phrases from 2:12-13 and applies them to "Gentiles." One would expect only someone "under the law" (2:12) could be a "doer of the law" (2:13). However, in 2:14, Paul twice emphasizes Gentiles "do not have the law" (using 2:12's contrast). He effectively defines "Gentile" as one without the law. Paul then says they "do what the law requires" (borrowing from 2:13).

A few observations may clarify Paul's implication. First, the law defines each group that Paul contrasts (2:12-14). Second, he simultaneously introduces the law and re-introduces the term "Gentiles," having used "Greek" four times since last mentioning "Gentiles" in Romans 1:13. "Gentile" better represents all non-Jews, while "Greeks" signifies only a small subset. Thus, the law specifically marks Jewish "insiders" as distinct from Gentile "outsiders," from a Jewish perspective.

A common mistranslation masks a significant detail. The ESV translates 2:14, "For when Gentiles, who do not have the law, *by nature* [*physis*] do what the law requires, they are a law to themselves, even though they do not have the law." Grammatically, *physis* can modify either what comes before (not having the law) or the following verb (doing the law). Traditionally, interpreters have chosen the latter, saying Gentiles *by nature* obey the law's requirements.

However, context favors the alternative. *Physis* explains why Gentiles do not have the law.[17] Romans 2:27 provides clarity: "He who is *physically* [*physis*] uncircumcised but keeps the law will condemn you who have the written code and circumcision but break the law." Both verses use *physis* and belong to the same stream of thought. Inexplicably, many versions translate the same word differently. In 2:27, *physis* cannot mean "by nature" since all males are born with foreskin. If *physis* is translated "by nature" in 2:27, the sentence and its contrast make no sense. No one is circumcised *by nature*.

Galatians 2:14-16 uses *physis* in a manner similar to Romans 2. There Paul writes,

> But when I saw that their conduct was not in step with the truth of the gospel, I said to Cephas before them all, "If you, though a Jew, live like a Gentile and not like a Jew, how can you force the Gentiles to live like Jews?" We ourselves are Jews *by birth* [*physis*] and not Gentile sinners; yet we know that a person is not justified by works of the law but through faith in Jesus Christ, so we also have believed in Christ Jesus, in order to be justified by faith in Christ and not by works of the law, because by works of the law no one will be justified.

---

[17]The following argument draws from N. T. Wright, "The Letter to the Romans," in *The New Interpreter's Bible* (Nashville: Abingdon, 2002), 441-43.

As in Romans, Paul uses *physis* to distinguish Jews and Gentiles. Because Paul and Peter are Jews from birth, they have known the law since childhood. Gentiles in Romans 2:14 were not born into Jewish families. Therefore, they do not "naturally" have the law.[18]

How then can Gentiles keep the law? Verse 15 adds, "They show that the work of the law is written on their hearts." The passage clearly speaks of the Mosaic law, which required circumcision (Romans 2:17-29). "Law" here is not a universal moral code abstracted from history.

In verse 16 Paul speaks of the day when "God judges the secrets of men by Christ Jesus." This judgment refers to justification (2:13). Robert Olson gives Old Testament support for linking honor and glory (2:7, 10) with the justification/judgment of Romans 2:13, 16. He says,

> The term "will be justified" in Rom 2:13 (δικαιωθήσονται) is very possibly an allusion to Isa 45:25, which states that " . . . all the seed of Israel will be justified and will glory." Rom 2:13 and Isa 45:25 are, in fact, the only two places in the LXX and NT in which that precise form of the word occurs.[19]

Verse 16 is a *positive* judgment, when uncircumcised Gentiles are shown to be "inward" Jews (2:25-29). Notably, both 2:16 and 2:29 use the same word, *kryptos*, which the ESV translates first as "secrets" and then as "inward." The praise in 2:29 is the judgment Paul anticipates in 2:16.[20]

Paul's comments in 1 Corinthians 4:4-5 suggest we are on the right track.

> For I am not aware of anything against myself, but I am not thereby *acquitted* [*dikaioō*]. It is the Lord who judges me. Therefore do not *pronounce judgment* [*anakrinō*] before the time, before the Lord comes, who will bring to light the things now *hidden* [*kryptos*] in darkness and will disclose the purposes of the heart. Then each one will receive his *commendation* [*epainos*] from God.

This passage links key words from Romans 2—being justified ("acquitted"), judgment, hidden, and commendation ("praise" in Romans 2:29). Paul awaits the day when God will commend him, having judged or disclosed what is hidden in the heart.

---

[18]Compare Romans 2:28, "For no one is a Jew who is merely one outwardly, nor is circumcision outward and physical." The last phrase, *en sarki* ("physical"), is also found in Ephesians 2:11-12 ("in the flesh"), where it signifies ethnic identity and is functionally equivalent to *physis*.

[19]Robert Olson, *The Gospel as the Revelation of God's Righteousness: Paul's Use of Isaiah in Romans 1:1–3:26* (Tübingen: Mohr Siebeck, 2016), 217. Also, "For 'honor' (τιμή; Rom 2:7, 10) as related the eschatological gift of the presence of God in Isaiah, and so related to 'glory,' compare 11:10; 35:2" (p. 214).

[20]The phrase *dia Christou Iēsou* is consistent with other "union with Christ" language and connotes a positive meaning. The judgment in 2:16 is saving because it is *through Christ*. Thanks to Wendel Sun for this observation.

Although the Mosaic law divides Jews and Gentiles culturally, it does not separate God's people. Rather, they have the law written on their hearts (Romans 2:15, 29). This is proven by the fact that they keep the law as was intended. Romans 2:25-29 unpacks this point more fully. Later, Paul explains how one fulfills the law. He says that "the one who loves another has fulfilled the law" (Romans 13:8; compare 13:10).

Naturally, Gentiles have "conflicting thoughts." After all, some Jews claimed Gentiles should be circumcised and thus become Jews. Many Gentiles believed the gospel and received the Spirit, not circumcision. Yet since this new faith arose from Judaism, Gentile believers felt internal conflict, not knowing what to do. Some doubted whether faith was enough. Should they be circumcised? Does salvation require they change national identity?

Significantly, we see a stark contrast between the two groups of Gentiles in Romans 2:15 and 1:18-32. That Paul highlights the Gentiles' conscience in 2:15 is noteworthy, since those in 1:18-32 show no signs of a properly functioning conscience.[21] Instead, the conscience now has moral discernment *because* the law is written on their hearts.[22]

ESTABLISHING BOUNDARIES

In Romans 2:17-29, Paul combats ethnocentrism by highlighting the Jews' failure to keep the law. Jews used circumcision to signify they were God's people. Coming from God, the Law carries divine (hence moral) authority. We need not choose between ethics and ethnicity. We also should not abstract the Mosaic law to form a set of divine moral principles, as if Paul does not speak particularly to Jews. To do so not only runs against the argument of Romans 2, it also leads to other problems. For example, if Paul refers to a universal moral law, he would not say *twice* in Romans 2:14 that Gentiles do not have the law.[23]

He again contrasts two groups—Jews (2:28-29) and Gentiles (2:25-27), who are "physically uncircumcised but keep the law." However, in Romans 2:26 Paul anticipates a shift in the discussion that will become clear later. He asks, "Will not his uncircumcision *be regarded as* [*logizomai*] circumcision?" He uses the same verb to explain who is "reckoned" righteous in Romans 4. In 2:26, Gentiles are reckoned as "circumcision," a label corresponding to the "inward Jew" of Romans 2:29.

---

[21]Although not in Greek, the ESV adds "while" and "also," which could mistakenly imply a contrast between "the work of the law [being] written on their hearts" and their conscience bearing witness.

[22]Wendel Sun, "Seeking (Exchanged) Glory: The Gentiles of Romans 2," *Journal of Asian Evangelical Theology* 20, no. 2 (2016): 52.

[23]In addition, Romans 5:14 clarifies the meaning of law in 5:13. From Adam to Moses, there was no law, which could not be said if Paul refers to a universal law laid on the conscience of all humans.

Romans 2:17-29

But if you call yourself a Jew and rely on the law and boast in God [18] and know his will and approve what is excellent, because you are instructed from the law; [19] and if you are sure that you yourself are a guide to the blind, a light to those who are in darkness, [20] an instructor of the foolish, a teacher of children, having in the law the embodiment of knowledge and truth— [21] you then who teach others, do you not teach yourself? While you preach against stealing, do you steal? [22] You who say that one must not commit adultery, do you commit adultery? You who abhor idols, do you rob temples? [23] You who boast in the law dishonor God by breaking the law. [24] For, as it is written, "The name of God is blasphemed among the Gentiles because of you."

[25] For circumcision indeed is of value if you obey the law, but if you break the law, your circumcision becomes uncircumcision. [26] So, if a man who is uncircumcised keeps the precepts of the law, will not his uncircumcision be regarded as circumcision? [27] Then he who is physically uncircumcised but keeps the law will condemn you who have the written code and circumcision but break the law. [28] For no one is a Jew who is merely one outwardly, nor is circumcision outward and physical. [29] But a Jew is one inwardly, and circumcision is a matter of the heart, by the Spirit, not by the letter. His praise is not from man but from God.

What distinguishes "insiders" from "outsiders" is not social identity? True "insiders" among God's people have new hearts "by the Spirit," and their "praise is not from man but from God." Put simply, one's identity is determined by whose "face" one seeks.

God does not disregard collective identity; he reorients it. His people have the law "written on their hearts." This is a promise of the new covenant. Jeremiah writes,

> I will put my law within them, and I will write it on their hearts. And I will be their God, and they shall be my people. And no longer shall each one teach his neighbor and each his brother, saying, "Know the LORD," for they shall all know me, from the least of them to the greatest, declares the LORD. (Jeremiah 31:33-34; compare Ezekiel 36:26-27)

Jeremiah 31:34 foreshadows the redefinition of God's people. They will no longer be a spiritually mixed ethnic group, where some are faithful and others not.

THE ADVANTAGES OF COLLECTIVE IDENTITY?

Romans 3:1-4, 9-10

Then what advantage has the Jew? Or what is the value of circumcision? [2] Much in every way. To begin with, the Jews were entrusted with the oracles of God. [3] What if some were unfaithful? Does their faithlessness nullify the faithfulness of God?

> ⁴ By no means! Let God be true though every one were a liar, as it is written, "That
> you may be justified in your words, and prevail when you are judged." . . .
>   ⁹ What then? Are we Jews any better off? No, not at all. For we have already
> charged that all, both Jews and Greeks, are under sin, ¹⁰ as it is written: "None is
> righteous, no, not one."

The questions in Romans 3:1-2 are the exact response one would expect if Romans 2 is about collective identity. "Circumcision" symbolizes Jewish identity. The replies of 3:2-4 suggest Paul and his opponents assume God will somehow be faithful to Israel. The real question is how God manifests his faithfulness.

In Romans 3:9-18, Paul completes his assault on presumption based on group identity. His sudden contrast of "Jews and *Greeks*" once again reminds Roman Greeks that they should heed the criticism leveled against Israel. The pride that overcomes many Jews threatens to swallow Greeks as well.

Verse 9 directly compares "we" and everyone else. The ESV supplies "Jews," though the Greek verb *proechometha* only implies "we." Because of this, some think Paul condemns humans in general, not simply Jews. But the context suggests otherwise. Prior passages center on Israel's privilege and pride. The following Old Testament verses support the negative answer in 3:9. *All* are under sin, *even* Jews. Verses 10-18 are an ironic indictment that only Jews could appreciate. Paul uses the law, the very source of Jewish pride, to humble them.

Romans 3:19-20 summarize Paul's point. Jews suffer from the same problem as non-Jews (see 3:9). The law itself testifies against them. The Jews cannot appeal to history or tradition to prove God is partial to them against Gentiles.

Paul's wording in Romans 3:20 reinforces the preceding argument. The Greek wording says literally, "no *flesh* [*sarx*] will be justified." Not even circumcised flesh brings justification before God. Although all humanity is under sin (Romans 3:9, 23), Paul particularly emphasizes the problem in the hearts of fellow Jews—boasting in group identity.

PATRIOTISM OR PREJUDICE?

For ancient Jews, law keeping was no private matter of morality. It typified Israel's identity as God's people. From childhood, every Jew was taught about the Maccabean revolt against Antiochus Epiphanes IV, who desecrated the temple and forbade Jews from obeying the Mosaic law. It is not surprising, then, that Paul's Jewish opponents insisted Gentiles be circumcised. If Paul is correct, their questions in Romans 3:1 are natural.

Tempers flare when people feel their national symbols are attacked. In August 2016, enraged fans burned jerseys of NFL quarterback Colin Kaepernick. Why? He chose to sit during the national anthem while the American flag was raised. He explained, "I am not going to stand up to show pride in a flag for a country that oppresses black people and people of color." Seething criticism followed. One commentator wrote, "his incendiary gesture . . . smacks of selfishness, a self-absorption. . . . Colin Kaepernick has chosen to engage in an act of hate against the America of 2016."[24] His birth mother said he was bringing *shame* to his country and his family.[25] Meanwhile, others supported and even joined him, claiming Kaepernick's protest embodied the values represented by the flag.

All cultures invest certain symbols with moral value. In response to Kaepernick, David Brooks gives a rationale for acts of national solidarity:

> When we sing the national anthem, we're not commenting on the state of America. We're fortifying our foundational creed. We're expressing gratitude for our ancestors and what they left us. We're expressing commitment to the nation's ideals, which we have not yet fulfilled. If we don't transmit that creed through shared displays of reverence we will have lost the idea system that has always motivated reform. We will lose the sense that we're all in this together. We'll lose the sense of shared loyalty to ideas bigger and more transcendent than our own short lives. If these common rituals are insulted, other people won't be motivated to right your injustices because they'll be less likely to feel that you are part of their story. People will become strangers to one another and will interact in cold instrumentalist terms.[26]

Brooks's appeal sounds more Eastern than individualistic. He cites ancestral values, common rituals, and loyalty. Historically, flags, anthems, and—for Jews—circumcision represent people's collective identity. These symbols recall shared history, revered convictions, and the sacrifices of many. What happens when someone breaks tradition? They are accused of disloyalty and derided as outsiders.

Before becoming the President of the United States, Barack Obama caused a stir by not wearing an American flag lapel pin.

> Shortly after 9/11, particularly because as we're talking about the Iraq war, [wearing a pin] became a substitute for, I think, true patriotism. . . . My attitude is that I'm less concerned about what you're wearing on your lapel than what's in your heart. And you show your patriotism by how you treat your fellow Americans, especially those who

---

[24]Mark Davis, "Kaepernick Anthem Snub Is Not a Free Speech Issue," *Townhall.com*, August 29, 2016, http://townhall.com/columnists/markdavis/2016/08/29/kaepernick-anthem-snub-is-not-a-free-speech-issue-n2211297.

[25]Mark Sanchez, "Colin Kaepernick's Birth Mom Ironically Shames Him on Twitter," *New York Post*, August 30, 2016, http://nypost.com/2016/08/30/colin-kaepernicks-birth-mom-ironically-shames-him-on-twitter.

[26]David Brooks, "The Uses of Patriotism," *New York Times*, September 16 2016, www.nytimes.com/2016/09/16/opinion/the-uses-of-patriotism.html.

served. You show your patriotism by being true to our values and our ideals and that's what we have to lead with is our values and our ideals.[27]

As a result of his decision, critics questioned Obama's love of country. For many, American flag pins are not a "substitute" but signify true patriotism.

Modern controversies like Kaepernick's sitting during the anthem or Obama's not wearing a lapel pin reflect the complexity of Paul's cultural context. It is difficult to separate symbols from substance. Insiders defend identity markers to protect the group's integrity or ideals. How does this desire for purity move from partiality to prejudice?

WHO ARE "WE"?

Paul's comments remind us there is no "me" without "we." Our relationships influence how we see the world, our ethical choices, and the significance we give to actions, symbols, and social identity. Paul causes us to ask, "Who are *we*?" How are we prone to categorize people? Whereas his readers sorted the world into "Greeks/barbarians" or "Jews/Gentiles," people in China are typically classified as "Chinese" or "foreigners."

Westerners use other labels (for example, black/white, male/female, and Republican/Democrat). Other social lines include wealth, education, occupation, ethnicity, neighborhood, religion, sexuality, and so on. Anyone who endures junior and senior high school understands that the criteria for being an "insider" change rapidly, yet the consequences of not conforming can affect people for a lifetime.

What are common symbols of social status in your context? How do you win recognition and become reckoned as an "insider"? To find out, you can ask, "What can I do when I want others to think well of me?" Perhaps you can use big vocabulary words, wear special clothing, clean your house, talk about how busy you are, drop names, or recount past successes.

Christians are not immune to the formal and informal standards that distinguish insiders and outsiders. Some include church size, views on alcohol, and political affiliation. Busyness in ministry can become a status symbol. In missionary subculture, some workers measure "success" by the rapidity or number of conversions and churches they report.

How might we unwittingly foster social tribalism? Christians are sometimes ethnically segregated for reasons other than overt prejudice or official policy, such as when they choose a neighborhood to live in. For some people, moving into a city and sacrificing the status and safety of the suburbs is simply unthinkable. Thus, the desire for social acceptance divides the church.

---

[27]Jeff Zeleny, "Obama's Lapels," *New York Times*, Oct 4, 2007, http://thecaucus.blogs.nytimes.com/2007/10/04 /obamas-lapels.

Christians sometimes identify more with social groups than the church. For example, consider patriotism or nationalism. In history, national and political identity routinely have merged with religious belief. I sometimes ask students, "Are you a Chinese Christian or Christian Chinese?" In certain American circles, people could ask, "Are you an American Christian or Christian American?"

Our world is not entirely different from Paul's. We too can have collective identities grounded more in social convention than Christ. His letter forces us to think about how collective identity should influence gospel ministry, whether in the West or internationally. Those who regard America as a "Christian country" will likely support certain policies. In denominational subcultures, some people have views of ministry that are far too narrow because they say, "We [fill in your denomination] do not do that sort of thing."

Likewise, Paul equips missionaries to serve those who hear slogans like, "To be Malay is to be Muslim," or "To be Thai is to be Buddhist." Morality cannot be separated from group membership. This point contrasts popular interpretations of Paul that claim he opposes ethical legalism (and only indirectly addresses ethnicity). Most Chinese or Japanese non-Christians do not seek merit before God through good works. A typical Easterner sees little value in striving for ethical perfection if that means forfeiting social position. Paul's words apply to people besides merit-seeking moralists; they transform the hope of those who want "face" and family.

OUR GOSPEL REDEFINES OUR RELATIONSHIPS

When sharing the gospel, we should address core life issues that concern people's sense of identity. With whom do they identify? To whom are they loyal? How does their desire for belonging shape their values, conduct, and goals?

Few modern-day gospel presentations address ethnic or national identity. No doubt one reason is that some people think the gospel primarily concerns individual salvation. Issues like racism and church unity seem like mere applications. Perhaps others do not want to blend religion and politics. Whatever the case, Romans contradicts the idea that ethnic conflict is a second-tier concern for the church.

Because Paul proclaims *one* king, Christ, "collective identity" is a gospel issue. His kingdom has no cultural boundaries. God is not a local deity concerned only with the welfare of one social group. Therefore, Paul deconstructs common notions of honor and human identity. This difficult task requires him to disentangle particular cultural symbols from the divine story of the one true God. Although the following quotation appears during a discussion of Galatians, Barclay's summary is apt:

> Since ethnicity, status, and gender are no longer criteria of superior worth (Gal 3:28), and since God pays no regard to the "face" (Gal 2:6) but distributes his grace without

regard for the worth, the normal grounds for competition have lost their significance. The assembly of believers forms a new community of opinion, constituted by the gift to the unworthy. Within this community arises, of course, an alternative system of worth, a new form of "social capital."[28]

Gospel ministry is nothing less than overturning worldviews that effectively divide the world into culture-centric colonies.

The central gospel message is Jesus as the world's true king (Romans 1:1-4). For this reason, the church should take seriously the fact that ethnic and national identities remain significant stumbling blocks to faith. Christ claims kingly authority over every tribe and tongue. People divide God's kingdom when they fundamentally identify with specific social groups above Christ's church.

Our gospel message veers toward individualism when it does not challenge people to redefine their relationships and reevaluate their social identity. Individuals do not exist apart from relationships. The gospel calls people *into* a community, not individuals out of culture. Paul labors to redefine the *community* of God, that is, the church. To rephrase Romans 3:29, is God the God of Western individuals only? Is he not God of every tribe and nation?

How do people follow Christ without forsaking their culture? This is a major concern for many non-Westerners. Some equate being "Christian" with being Western. For countless missionaries, the only Christianity they know is clothed in Western culture. How do crosscultural missionaries help local Christians become disciples in ways that honor but do not idolize the surrounding culture?

In Romans, Paul gives us a few suggestions. First, do not underestimate the significance of cultural symbols and rituals. Do not assume their meaning—whether good or bad—apart from extensive discussion with people from the local context. Crosscultural workers always face two temptations: either they are too optimistic about a culture (excusing its shortcomings) or are overly pessimistic about a culture (assuming the culture contradicts the Bible). Westerners would benefit from greater self-awareness of their own culture.

Second, remind people of the core values behind their traditions. This equips people to make wise decisions about how and whether to participate in certain activities. They can also better communicate their perspective to others. Perhaps certain traditional practices can be adapted.

Third, find a middle way among false alternatives. Paul never forbids circumcision. Still, he does not want people to give it a meaning that contradicts the gospel.

---

[28]Barclay, *Paul and the Gift*, 435.

Finally, help people see how group identity affects their opinions about their culture and traditions. We belong to countless social groups. As believers, we belong first to the *human* family. If people see that they belong to a global and historical church, they have a better perspective on their culture. They will value its uniqueness without embracing its shortcomings.

Although I speak of "their culture," these words also apply to "our culture" (whatever that is). These applications relate to anyone living in a multicultural context, not just crosscultural missionaries. In America, for instance, members of one social group can apply these suggestions when interacting or thinking about people from other groups. The gospel redraws our ethnic and economic lines.

Social distinctions based on anything but Christ lead to constant comparison and competition. We regularly make choices about our social identity, particularly how to express it. The gospel redefines "insiders" and "outsiders" because Jesus is king. By making much of him, we resist temptations to idolize culture, individuality, and whatever leads to ungodly boasting. As my former pastor often said, "Comparison is the thief of joy. Either it discourages us or makes us proud."

5

CHRIST SAVES
GOD'S FACE (ROMANS 3)

Jonathan couldn't contain his anticipation as family gathered to open Christmas presents. His mother knew he wanted an Xbox 360 video game system, but she had a surprise for him. In a video of the moment he opens the present, Jonathan peels back the wrapping, soaking in every second. Everyone urges him to open the green box, its label "Xbox 360" now fully exposed.

But instead of a gaming system, he pulls out multiple articles of winter clothing. A room full of people roars with laughter. His mother had decided to prank her son after discovering Jonathan sneaked a peek at his Christmas presents. Jonathan stares in disbelief. He doesn't have the breath to answer the taunts of his brother, who is shooting the video. As everyone leaves the room, Jonathan is in tears. Viewers are left wondering what lesson Jonathan's mom taught him.[1]

It is true that Jonathan disobeyed by looking at the gifts. Still, was his mom right to do what she did? Did his transgression justify his mother's actions? She raised his hopes on Christmas day only to humiliate him. Is this how moms treat their children?

This story of betrayal gives a glimpse into what must have been the feelings of Paul's Jewish opponents. If what Paul says in Romans 2 is true, many Jews would question God's character. None of them doubted Israel's sin. The exile patently demonstrated their unfaithfulness. However, God raised their expectations with gracious promises. Now, according to Paul's gospel, God seemingly spurns his people but accepts Gentiles. For typical Jews, Paul's teaching would imply that God is unrighteous.

WHY IS GOD RIGHTEOUS?

In Romans 3, more is at stake than ethnic pride and personal salvation. God's own honor is threatened. We must keep in mind the common tradition shared by Paul and his Jewish readers. In Mikko Sivonen's important study on the "*doxa* [glory] motif" in

---

[1] Arthur Williams, "Brother on christmas . . . ," *YouTube*, December 31, 2007, https://youtu.be/VhO-OE931D4.

Paul's writing, he notes that a "distinctive use of *doxa* [glory] in the Septuagint is the anticipated vindication of the *doxa* of the Lord, associated with a hopeful eschatological restoration of Israel and the nations."[2] Accordingly, Paul now explains why his teaching does not in fact undermine this hope of glory.

Verses 1-3 capture the voice of Paul's Jewish opponents. In effect, their objection functions like a *reductio ad absurdum*. They assume an absurd conclusion—God is unfaithful—to expose a presumed fallacy of Paul's thinking.

Romans 3:1-4

Then what advantage has the Jew? Or what is the value of circumcision? Much in every way. To begin with, the Jews were entrusted with the oracles of God. What if some were unfaithful? Does their faithlessness nullify the faithfulness of God? By no means! Let God be true though every one were a liar, as it is written, "That you may be justified in your words, and prevail when you are judged."

The opening questions of Romans 3 are in response to Paul's message in Romans 2. God established various covenants with Israel, but Paul says God is not partial to Jews and even accepts lawless Gentiles. If this is true and physical circumcision does not matter, "what advantage has the Jew? Or what is the value of circumcision?" Despite apparent contradictions, Jews do have unique advantages. Israel was entrusted with God's "oracles," namely his saving promises to Israel.[3] Paul waits until Romans 4 to unpack the content of these covenant promises.

In these verses Paul rejects a possible objection. If the Jews' unfaithfulness means God doesn't distinguish between Jews and Gentiles, is God's faithfulness contingent on the faithfulness of his people? No, Paul says, God's steadfastness doesn't depend on human ability or righteousness. He shows himself "true" even while people lie.

In Romans 3:4, Paul cites a psalm to support his conclusion. Psalm 51:4 says God will be "justified"; that is, God is declared or proven righteous despite his people's unrighteousness. In context, God's righteousness in Romans 3:4 is another way of saying he is "faithful" and "true" (3:3-4).

Many readers suppose God's righteousness in 3:4 refers to his punitive justice against sin.[4] God shows his righteousness because he punishes sin. However, this view does not follow from Romans 3:1-2. Nor does it explain the advantage of Jews over Gentiles.

---

[2]Mikko Sivonen, "The *Doxa* Motif in Paul." (PhD diss., University of Helsinki, 2018), 40.
[3]Thomas Schreiner, *Romans*, Baker Exegetical Commentary on the New Testament (Grand Rapids: Baker Academic, 1998), 149; John Murray, *The Epistle to the Romans* (Grand Rapids: Eerdmans, 1997), 94.
[4]For example, Douglas J. Moo, *The Epistle to the Romans* (Grand Rapids: Eerdmans, 1996), 190.

Other interpreters argue God's righteousness refers to his covenant faithfulness, which brings salvation.[5] But these interpreters tend to be inconsistent in applying this view. They still assert 3:5 speaks of God's punitive righteousness and claim God's righteousness in Psalm 51:4 refers to God's right to punish David's sin. If so, Paul seemingly misapplies David's original meaning.

GOD'S GLORY IS REVEALED APART FROM THE LAW

Any interpretation of Romans 3:4 should satisfy two criteria. First, it must fit the immediate context. Second, it must cohere with David's original meaning in Psalm 51. How might we resolve the apparent tensions? After all, God's honor is at stake.

> **Psalm 51:1-4**
>
> Have mercy on me, O God, according to your steadfast love; according to your abundant mercy blot out my transgressions. [2] Wash me thoroughly from my iniquity, and cleanse me from my sin!
> [3] *For* I know my transgressions, and my sin is ever before me. [4] Against you, you only, have I sinned and done what is evil in your sight,
> *so that* you may be justified in your words and blameless when you are judged.[6]
>
> *Adapted from ESV*

If we misunderstand David's expression in Psalm 51:4, we will not grasp Paul's logic in Romans 3.[7] In Psalm 51:4, which Paul quotes, David uses a purpose clause, indicated by "so that" (*lemaan*; LXX, *hopōs an*). However, a problem emerges when connecting the purpose clause with the preceding sentence. It would appear that David sins *in order that* God will get glory.

To make sense of Psalm 51:4, observe David's flow of thought beginning in 51:1-2. He states his petition for salvation in four different ways. The "for" in verse 3 indicates the reason for David's request. The latter half of verse 4 explains a purpose for which God should answer David's prayer. Therefore, verses 3-4 have two subordinate clauses. They depend on or explain the primary petition(s) in verses 1-2.

---

[5]James D. G. Dunn, *Romans 1–8* (Dallas: Word Books, 1988), 134; Brendan Byrne, *Romans* (Collegeville, MN: Liturgical Press, 1996), 109.
[6]I read κρίνεσθαί (50:6 LXX; Rom 3:4b) as passive ("you are judged") rather than middle voice. Thus, the quote's second line explains the first. See Pss. Sol. 2:15; 3:3, 5; 4:9; 8:7, 26, 29-35; 9:3; 17:12; see also Isa 43:6, 26; 45:19-25. Cf. Dunn (1988, 133-134); Longenecker (2016, 348); Watson (2016, 407).
[7]The following summarizes the fuller explanation in Jackson W., "Why Is God Justified in Romans? Vindicating Paul's Use of Psalm 51 in Romans 3:4," *Neotestamentica* 51, no. 2 (2017): 291-314.

The purpose in 51:4 links back to David's request for rescue. People mistakenly assume 51:4 modifies 51:3, where David confesses his sin. Thus, Psalm 51:4 has a different meaning than readers suppose. Rather than extolling God's punitive righteousness, David says God will be justified *through salvation*. When God answers the petition of 51:1-2, people will proclaim God righteous. After all, God made a covenant with David not to forsake him but make his offspring reign forever (2 Samuel 7:13-14). If God breaks this promise, he would be unrighteous!

This interpretation fits the context. Psalm 51:14 says, "Deliver me from blood-guiltiness, O God, O God of my salvation, and my tongue will sing aloud of your righteousness." In essence, David reiterates verses 1-2, 4b, omitting the ground clause of verses 3-4a. If Psalm 51:4 refers to God's retributive righteousness (via punishing David's sin), it's natural verse 14 would carry the same connotation. However, it makes no sense to read the same concept in contrary ways within the same context. In addition, verse 14 is incoherent if David says he'll praise God for his wrath against sin when in fact God saves David.

In this way, Psalm 51 perfectly supports Paul's argument in Romans 3. David emphasizes the same key ideas as Paul. God doesn't delight in works of the law. He rejoices in right hearts. Psalm 51:16-17 states, "For you will not delight in sacrifice, or I would give it; you will not be pleased with a burnt offering. The sacrifices of God are a broken spirit; a broken and contrite heart, O God, you will not despise" (compare Psalm 51:18-19). God wants his people to have new hearts. David prays, "Create in me a clean heart, O God, and renew a right spirit within me. Cast me not away from your presence, and take not your Holy Spirit from me" (Psalm 51:10-11).

David's example confirms that the law does not fundamentally define God's people. Instead, their identity is "a matter of the heart, by the Spirit" (Romans 2:29). Paul thus supports the claim that human unfaithfulness does not nullify God's faithfulness (Romans 3:3-4). David perfectly counters suggestions that a person must keep the law to be reckoned one of God's people. Thus, Romans 3:1-4 explains God will show himself righteous by fulfilling his saving promises. Just as for sinful David, so God will do for faithless Israel.

Likewise, God manifests righteousness in Romans 3:4-5 by saving his people. Human sin is a backdrop against which God's glory is magnified. The impenitent objector of Romans 3:5-7 distorts Paul's meaning. God's judgment consists in saving his people through the condemnation of his enemies. Therefore, the objection lodged against Paul is nonsense—even reprehensible.

Paul uses the law in Romans 3:10-18 to expose the Jews' shame, drawing from a range of Old Testament passages. It's as though Paul is calling his countrymen atheists. After all, "no one seeks for God" (3:11; compare 3:18). The same words applied to the psalmists' enemies are now used against faithless Jews (compare Psalm 14:1-3; 51:1-3).[8]

In fact, Paul's entire way of talking about sin obliterates typical outsider designations.[9] Whereas "sinner" previously referred to a select group of social undesirables, Paul applies the term to *everyone*. This has two consequences. First, Paul effectively levels the social pecking order. The scorned and esteemed alike are equal before God. He reorients readers' perspective of honor and shame. Second, reckoning all people "sinners" magnifies the glory of Christ's victory over sin and death. Everyone should honor the king who saves humanity.

In summary, Paul is here defending God's honor, casting his opponents into the role of "outsiders." Their own Scriptures nullify their claim to have status (or "face") before God. Ironically, the law exposes the futility of human boasting. The law dishonors those who boast in the law.

If Paul is correct, his Jewish opponents are questioning God's righteousness. How is God faithful if he pays no regard to his law? How can he accept Gentiles but reject law-keeping Jews? In Romans 3:1-8, Paul doesn't give a complete answer. But he does offer a potent counterpoint via Psalm 51. Even when David sins, God is faithful to save him.

HOW DOES CHRIST SAVE GOD'S FACE?

In Romans 3:21-26, Paul elaborates how God demonstrates his righteousness apart from the law and national identity. All have sinned and lack the glory of God. The law testifies to humanity's problem and God's solution. It is not the primary way God vindicates his name. Rather, Christ upholds God's honor. Christ saves God's "face" against the shame of human sin.

Romans 3:21-26

But now the righteousness of God has been manifested apart from the law, although the Law and the Prophets bear witness to it— [22] the righteousness of God through faith in Jesus Christ for all who believe. For there is no distinction: [23] for all have sinned and fall short of the glory of God, [24] and are justified by his grace as a gift, through the redemption that is in Christ Jesus, [25] whom God put forward as a propitiation by his blood, to be received by faith. This was to show God's righteousness, because in his divine forbearance he had passed over former sins. [26] It was to show his righteousness at the present time, so that he might be just and the justifier of the one who has faith in Jesus.

[8]Richard B. Hays, *The Conversion of the Imagination: Paul as Interpreter of Israel's Scripture* (Grand Rapids: Eerdmans, 2004), 90.
[9]Paul R. Trebilco, *Outsider Designations and Boundary Construction in the New Testament: Christian Communities and the Formation of Group Identity* (Cambridge: Cambridge University Press, 2017), 133-36, 219-25.

What threatens God's honor? Humanity behaves disgracefully, although they are made in the image of God their Father. Even those who have his law dishonor him. This circumstance creates multiple problems. First, God promises Abraham, "In you all the families of the earth shall be blessed" (Genesis 12:3; 18:18; 22:18). How can God bless the nations when they deserve the curse of death?

Second, God chose Israel as the means for blessing the world. Yet Israel is unfaithful and was exiled. Those who know God best bring ill repute to his name (Romans 2:23-24). Despite God's promises, the Jews are unfit vassals of blessing.

Third, Jews directly opposed the fulfillment of God's covenant with Abraham. God never treated Israel as an end in themselves. Rather, they were chosen to be a means of grace for the world. Whereas God promised to bless all nations, Paul's opponents limited God's salvation to Israel. They supposed one must first become a Jew before being reckoned righteous. Thus, God's blessing could not extend to all nations but only one ethnic group. Tragically, those who claimed to be Abraham's offspring implicitly deny the promise he believed.

Romans 3:24-25a explains how Christ solves the glory problem of 3:23. Paul doesn't develop a full-orbed theology of atonement. Instead, he emphasizes the purpose of Christ's death. Two times, he stresses that Christ's death "was to show God's righteousness" (Romans 3:25-26).

How does God show his righteousness? Romans 3:21, 26 serve as bookends to a coherent unit of thought. In both verses, God's righteousness is manifested *now* or *in the present*. God's righteousness in 3:21 is the same as in 3:26. Since 3:21 refers to God's saving righteousness, so also does 3:26. Many interpreters think God's righteousness in 3:26 is punitive. In fact, God manifests his righteousness through salvation. It is nonsensical to say God's punitive righteousness "has been manifested *apart from the law.*" It is precisely the law that condemns (Romans 2:27) and through which sin is aroused (Romans 7:5).

Observe the parallel logic of Romans 3:20-21, 26:

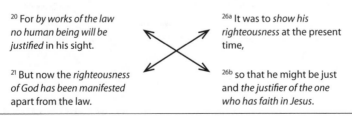

²⁰ For *by works of the law no human being will be justified* in his sight.

²¹ But now the *righteousness of God has been manifested* apart from the law.

²⁶ᵃ It was to *show his righteousness* at the present time,

²⁶ᵇ so that he might be just and *the justifier of the one who has faith in Jesus.*

Figure 5. Parallel logic of Romans 3:20-21, 26

Whereas the law cannot justify, God's righteousness now is revealed. Justification by works of the law contrasts the revealing of God's righteousness (3:20-21). Note also how God's righteousness in 3:26a is manifest in 3:26b. God justifies those who have faith in Christ. With respect to God's righteousness, 3:26b perfectly contrasts 3:20. God would not manifest righteousness if the law were able to justify. He shows it when he justifies people by faith. Paul lays the foundation for a later conclusion: "That is why [justification] depends on faith, in order that the promise may rest on grace and be guaranteed to all his offspring—not only to the adherent of the law but also to the one who shares the faith of Abraham, who is the father of us all" (Romans 4:16). God reveals the glory of his righteousness by faithfully keeping his promise to Abraham.

Paul has not left the argument begun in 3:1-4.[10] Why does God "pass over former sins" and justify people by faith? God in Christ vindicates his honor by demonstrating his righteousness. In this sense, *Christ saves God's face*. Because of the cross, all nations will see God's glory. Fundamentally, atonement is a God-centered act. Jesus dies for God, who through him keeps his covenant promises and enacts righteousness in creation. This plan is revealed in the Law and the Prophets (Romans 3:21).

In part, Romans 3:25-26 concludes the first stage of Paul's overall thesis (Romans 1:16-17). Romans 1:18–3:20 defines a problem akin to David's in Psalm 51:3-4a. Likewise, Paul in 3:21-26 explains how God proves himself righteous. This resembles David's reasoning in Psalm 51:4b. Just as Romans 1:16 proclaims "salvation to everyone who believes, to the Jew first and also to the Greek," so Romans 3:27–4:18 magnifies the breadth of God's people. They come from all nations. They are marked by faith in Christ, who redefines their collective identity.

The argument in Romans 3:28-30 is subtle but unmistakable. Some people, like Paul's Jewish opponents, primarily define their collective identity based on secondary criteria such as ethnicity, nationality, gender, political party, or economic status. These are customary ways of dividing the world into social classes. This human tradition has grievous effects, especially as it concerns God's glory.

Romans 3:27-30

Then what becomes of our boasting? It is excluded. By what kind of law? By a law of works? No, but by the law of faith. [28] For we hold that one is justified by faith apart from works of the law. [29] Or is God the God of Jews only? Is he not the God of Gentiles also? Yes, of Gentiles also, [30] since God is one—who will justify the circumcised by faith and the uncircumcised through faith.

Observe the contrast in Romans 3:27-28, 29-30. The former speaks of "works" and "faith." Paul then changes categories, referring to "Jews" and "Gentiles." If "works" in

---

[10]We will see in Romans 3:27–4:25 how God's righteousness fits within the broader argument that begins in Romans 2.

3:27-28 denote mere ethical behavior, the new terminology is pointless. However, the reason Paul parallels works/faith with Jews/Gentiles is because "works of the law" functionally separate Jews from non-Jews.

We are now ready to connect collective identity and God's honor. If we are justified through works of the law, we must become Jews. But this implies that God is only God of the Jews, not Gentiles (3:29). Paul denies that idea as an affront to Jewish mono-theism. God is God of both Jews and Gentiles "since God is one." Because Jews feel a sense of group superiority, they essentially reduce God to a local tribal deity. They narrow the scope of God's kingdom to one people.

Collective identity reflects our view of God. What happens when we define our-selves by gender, education, language, or other social distinctions? We subtly speak of God as if he is partial to us against others.

There are serious consequences when we blur the lines between belonging to a social group and being Christian. For example, if believers in the United States see themselves as Christian Americans (as opposed to American Christians), they could easily see America as a kind of Israel or promised land. Political ideologies merge indistinguishably with theological convictions. Wars and political policies take on the status of divine mandate.

Likewise, how we determine "insiders" and "outsiders" reveals our standard of honor. Many Americans think it is honorable to be a "self-made" person. They value personal freedom, autonomy, and hard work. This independent mindset can breed a contrary spirit that demands personal rights while not taking responsibility for others' needs. With this perspective, we'll tend to view as outsiders those deemed less suc-cessful or too different. In churches, factions form around personal preference and traditional social values, rather than those of God's kingdom.

The one true God is worthy of unique honor. Because he reigns over the world, God requires the allegiance of all nations. This is the sort of faith by which God justifies his people. In Romans 4, Paul uses Abraham as an illustration of the nature of justifying faith: "No unbelief made him waver concerning the promise of God, but he grew strong in his faith as he gave glory to God, fully convinced that God was able to do what he had promised" (4:20-21). Because he knew the Creator God "gives life to the dead and calls into existence the things that do not exist" (4:17), Abraham's faith mag-nifies the glory of God's sovereignty and faithfulness. Saving faith gives God "face."

THE JUSTIFICATION OF GOD

The nations are not the only ones justified by faith. God also is justified by means of faith (Romans 3:4). However, God is declared righteous in a totally different way than are people.

The justification of God is not a tangent in Paul's theology. He briefly answers the objection of 3:1-2, then continues to discuss Jews, Gentiles, collective identity, and faith. Later, he fully attends to the subject in Romans 9, focusing on God's character and plan.

Paul's argument in Romans 9 echoes Romans 3. In Romans 9:4-5, he recounts Israel's many advantages. As in Romans 3, Paul anticipates a potential objection in Romans 9:6-8. There he says,

> But it is not as though the word of God has failed. For not all who are descended from Israel belong to Israel, and not all are children of Abraham because they are his offspring, but "Through Isaac shall your offspring be named." This means that it is not the children of the flesh who are the children of God, but the children of the promise are counted as offspring.

Once more, God's reputation is tied to collective identity. If we misunderstand who belongs to God's people, we might accuse God of unrighteousness (compare Romans 9:14). Therefore, Paul clarifies collective identity in Romans 9 just as he does in Romans 2–4.

To defend God's honor, Paul rebuffs Jewish presumption. God's election of Israel doesn't imply that he is partial to Jews based on ancestral birth. The Pentateuch itself undermines that assumption. Although Abraham already had Ishmael, God chose Isaac (Romans 9:7). Likewise, God elects the younger Jacob over Esau despite social convention (Romans 9:12).

To clarify who are God's people, Paul engages in what appears to be doublespeak. He previously argued that both Jews and Gentiles are reckoned as "Abraham's offspring." Similarly, Paul challenges typical notions of the term *Israel* in Romans 9:6-8. Christ redefines Paul's understanding of Israel.

What's at stake? In Romans 9:14, Paul asks, "What shall we say then? Is there *injustice* [*adikia*] on God's part?" He replies, "By no means!" Verses 15-18 offer support:

> *For* he says to Moses, "I will have mercy on whom I have mercy, and I will have compassion on whom I have compassion." *So then it depends not on human will or exertion, but on God, who has mercy.* For the Scripture says to Pharaoh, "For this very purpose I have raised you up, that I might show my power in you, and that my name might be proclaimed in all the earth." *So then* [*ara oun*] he has mercy on whomever he wills, and he hardens whomever he wills.

God's covenant promises depend on grace, not nationality or social position. This is Paul's point in Romans 4:16 when speaking of justification: "That is why it depends on faith, in order that the promise may rest on grace and be guaranteed to all his offspring—not only to the adherent of the law but also to the one who shares the faith of Abraham, who is the father of us all."

God is not bound by external measures of justice/righteousness. Cultural norms do not constrain God either to save or condemn. Nor should we think God is only concerned for one expression of righteousness, whether "punitive," "restorative," or "covenantal" righteousness. The Creator does all things for his name's sake. This includes raising up oppressive rulers like Pharaoh (Romans 9:17). Paul reinforces the point in Romans 9:22-24:

> What if God, desiring to show his wrath and to make known his power, has endured with much patience vessels of wrath prepared for destruction, in order to make known the riches of his glory for vessels of mercy, which he has prepared beforehand for glory— even us whom he has called, not from the Jews only but also from the Gentiles?

God does not stake his honor on the passing sensibilities of any culture, denomination, or generation.

God's "face" or reputation depends on context, not culture. That is, because honor and shame are dependent on context and relationship, it is critical that we look at God with a right lens. If we have a narrow, provincial perspective on the Bible and the world, we'll begin to question God's honor.

To vindicate God's name, Paul broadens his readers' perspective. They must recall the biblical grand narrative lest they forget the scope of God's kingdom. He does all things so that his "name might be proclaimed in all the earth" (Romans 9:17). At the same time, Paul speaks of specific people and events. God displays his glory in concrete ways throughout history.

Our observations might also help us respond to another question long debated by biblical interpreters. In Romans, what is the specific nuance of πίστις (usually translated as "trust," "faith" or "faithfulness"), especially in light of Paul's focus on righteousness? While I don't pretend to resolve the debate here, being sensitive to honor-shame dynamics can make us aware of other potential interpretations. In Romans 3-4, Paul intensifies his focus on "faith," yet scholars debate whether phrases like "πίστεως Ἰησοῦ" refer to trust/faith in Christ or Christ's faithfulness. Both are grammatically possible translations. We've already seen that Romans 3:3 frames the coming discussion by raising the question whether God is faithful.

So, does Paul intend to highlight people's faith, God's faithfulness and/or Christ's faithfulness? Later chapters will touch on these topics further. Without diving deep into them here, I suggest a possible way forward. In honor-shame contexts, the practice of patronage and a stress on reciprocity are frequently present. Scores of books and articles have noted the importance of patronage in the ancient world and its potential influence on the Bible, including Romans.[11] Within patron-client relationships, a basic

---

[11]For example, see David deSilva. *Honor, Patronage, Kinship and Purity: Unlocking New Testament Culture* (Downers Grove, IL: IVP Academic, 2000), 95–156.

obligation of patrons was to show themselves faithful or reliable such that clients could trust them. In response to a patron's faithfulness, a client was expected to show loyalty.

In the context of Romans 3-4, Paul likely depicts God as a patron with Abraham and his offspring as clients. Christ appears to serve as a "broker" (or mediator) who stands between patron and client.[12] In different respects, a broker must display both trust and faithfulness in his mediating role. Perhaps then, we need not choose between "trust" or "faithfulness" when translating πίστις in this context. One's role in a patron-client relationship may inform our decision. Accordingly, it would be reasonable to conclude that Paul underscores the faithfulness of God our Patron (as in Romans 3:3), while at the same time he speaks of our faith/trust as clients (compare 3:22b). Thus, we are to show faith in the faithfulness of God (compare 4:20-21).[13] As to whether Paul refers to Christ's faithfulness (3:22a, 26), we shall return to that question later.

If we take the theology of the biblical writers out of their context, we become more likely to speak of God in philosophical terms, in which God's righteousness and glory become abstract theoretical concepts. Or we will take the route of ancient Jews, reducing God's sphere of concern to our own life, family, or nation.

HONOR AND LOYALTY

By contrasting God's faithfulness and human unfaithfulness, Paul magnifies divine honor and our shame. It is not coincidental that Romans 3 introduces "faith" against the foil of works. The Jews thought loyalty to ancestral tradition brought God honor. However, God is the model of true faithfulness (Romans 3:4). He demonstrates righteousness apart from Jewish identity. In the same way, God's people glorify him by giving allegiance to Christ, not by works of the law.

Romans spurs us to rethink our understanding of loyalty, group identity, and honor. Loyalty is an inconvenient virtue. We will hardly esteem loyalty when we stress personal autonomy, self-reliance, and independence. One writer says, "Loyalty conflicts with the prerogative of changing our preferences, since from the standpoint of loyalty, changing preferences is a sign of inconstancy. Blaming betrayal without praising loyalty, we want to be free from loyalty without suffering from its absence."[14] Social media provides many friends and followers who are never there when we close the computer to face real life. Marketers vie for the loyalty of their customers, though

---

[12]See Andrew Kim Seng Tan. "The Rhetoric of Abraham's Faith in Romans 4." (PhD diss., University of Cape Town, 2016).

[13]Also compare Daniel J. McKaughan, "On the Value of Faith and Faithfulness." *International Journal for Philosophy of Religion* 81 (2017): 13-15.

[14]Gladdin J. Pappin, "A Virtue Betrayed, A Review of *Loyalty: The Vexing Virtue* by Eric Felten," *First Principles Journal* 47, no. 1 (2012): n.p., www.firstprinciplesjournal.com/articles.aspx?article=1818.

everyone knows the relationship lasts only so long as we give them money. People divorce their spouses and change churches with the calendar.

In this context, it is hard to grasp how closely loyalty is linked to honor. Breaking from one's people and traditions is not only immoral but shameless. While no one in any culture always lives up to their ideals, many East Asians take loyalty and honor far more seriously than Westerners might imagine.

John Condon gives us the example of suicide in Japan, which, while "often misunderstood in America, is the ultimate means of taking responsibility for having brought shame to one's group. This most personal act is, in Japan, still an act that expresses a supreme concern for what others think."[15] Sam Louie adds, "Taking one's life is seen as an honorable way of atoning for public disgrace and expression of one's deep sense of shame."[16]

When people care about honor and loyalty, they will take relationships into consideration. These basic concerns help people discern right and wrong. In some cultures, wives are murdered in an "honor killing" if they are thought to have committed adultery. By contrast, Diana West comments, "In a shameless culture . . . self-restraint is continually undermined."[17] People are "shameless" when they care too little about relationships and reputation.

This same connection between honor and loyalty pervades the Old Testament. Jeremiah appeals to God, "Do not spurn us, *for your name's sake*; do not dishonor your glorious throne; remember and do not break *your covenant* with us" (Jeremiah 14:21). In Psalm 143, David confesses no one is righteous (Psalm 143:2). He then appeals to God's honor and righteousness. He says, "*For your name's sake*, O Lord, preserve my life! *In your righteousness* bring my soul out of trouble!" (Psalm 143:11; compare 143:1).

In Paul's message, God's honor is central. Paul makes us reexamine assumptions about *how* God demonstrates his righteousness. For many people, the "holy and righteous character of God" is seen as an obstacle to salvation.[18] In fact, salvation is possible *because* God is righteous. Nehemiah plainly states why God rescues his people: "You have kept your promise, for you are righteous" (Nehemiah 9:8).

Furthermore, we should not contrast God's righteousness with his love. Because God righteously seeks the glory of his name, he loves us perfectly.[19] God is not unjust

---

[15]John Condon, *With Respect to the Japanese: A Guide for Americans* (Yarmouth, ME: Intercultural Press, 1984), 30; as cited in Sam Louie, *Asian Honor: Overcoming the Culture of Silence* (Bloomington, IN: Westbow, 2012), 7.

[16]Louie, *Asian Honor*, 7.

[17]Diana West, *The Death of the Grown-Up: How America's Arrested Development Is Bringing Down Western Civilization* (New York: St. Martin's Press, 2007), 96.

[18]Bruce Demarest, *The Cross and Salvation: The Doctrine of God* (Wheaton, IL: Crossway, 2006), 345, 362-63.

[19]See John Piper, "Is Jesus an Egomaniac?" Passion Conference. January 4, 2010, www.desiringgod.org /messages/is-jesus-an-egomaniac.

to save sinners precisely *because* he upholds his own glory. God in wrath opposes sin (Romans 1:18; 2:5, 8; 3:5; 5:9). Still, we should pause to consider whether we talk about God's righteousness and wrath in the same way found in Romans and elsewhere. If we confuse God's righteousness and his wrath, we lose an important way the Bible speaks of God's steadfast love. God generally manifests his righteousness by *saving* his people, yet this requires that God in wrath defeat their enemies (for example, sin and death; Romans 8:3; 1 Corinthians 15:25-26).

How might this perspective affect our view of God? It is common to describe God in abstract terms like *omniscient, omnipotent,* and *omnipresent.* By contrast, Paul focuses on God's work in history in the lives of David and Abraham, and ultimately manifests in Christ's ministry. In this he follows the Old Testament's pattern of presenting God, who reveals himself concretely through relationships in history. In Leviticus 25:38, God says, "I am the Lord your God, who brought you out of the land of Egypt to give you the land of Canaan, and to be your God" (compare Deuteronomy 5:6-7). Likewise, in Exodus 3:14-15, God identifies himself via his relationships:

> God said to Moses, "I am who I am." And he said, "Say this to the people of Israel, 'I am has sent me to you.'" God also said to Moses, "Say this to the people of Israel, 'The Lord, the God of your fathers, the God of Abraham, the God of Isaac, and the God of Jacob, has sent me to you.' This is my name forever, and thus *I am to be remembered throughout all generations.*"

Following Paul's example, our teaching about God should be rooted foremost in biblical theology, not simply systematic theology. Although these two disciplines are never fully separated, their approaches have important differences. At the risk of oversimplification, I will say that in biblical theology, scholars primarily attempt to read the Bible in its original literary, historical, and cultural contexts. They consider the questions and answers of the ancient writer and his audience. Systematic theology synthesizes a variety of (often unrelated) passages in order to address the concerns of a contemporary audience, which are not necessarily the same as the biblical authors'.

Both approaches are valid and helpful, yet systematic theology should be grounded in biblical theology. Otherwise, modern readers are more prone to commit eisegesis, inserting their own meaning into the text. In that case, reader's assumptions guide the study and systemization of the Bible's teaching.[20]

---

[20]This oversimplification does not address an array of issues related to interpretation and theological method. Even in biblical theology, scholars interpret texts in light of assumptions from systematic and historical theology. For now, I stress the importance of defining concepts in light of the writers' original context rather than our cultural contexts.

NEITHER SHAMELESS NOR ASHAMED

In 2011, Congressman Anthony Weiner resigned after admitting he sent sexually explicit pictures to six women over a three-year period. Two years later, Weiner ran for mayor of New York City. One voter asked, "How can I trust you with my family and my community when you can't be trusted in your own family?" Nonplussed, Weiner replied, "Sure, I dishonored my wife . . . but I didn't do anything to you."[21] Weiner's reply divorced honor from authority. To his questioner, though, a shameless leader is untrustworthy. Who wants to follow a shameless person?

According to Romans 2, Jews could raise similar questions about God's honor. God promised to bless Israel, restore her from exile, and raise a Davidic king to rule the nations. But Paul seems to describe an alternative reality. *Gentiles* receive the blessings promised to Israel. If God is unfaithful to his own people, how then can Gentiles trust him?

In Romans 3, Paul raises the stakes and goes beyond social commentary. Cultural traditions and so-called private behaviors have theological significance. They reflect our views about what is worthy of honor and shame. God's reputation is at stake when we make decisions about relating to others, especially our group identity.

God's righteousness upends conventional notions of honor-shame. Christ is faithful to God, even to the point of death. He does not dishonor God. In fact, the cross makes it possible for God to keep his covenant promises and so establish righteousness in creation. The shame of Christ vindicates God's honor. In this sense, Christ's sacrifice saves God's "face."

Accordingly, Christians should reconsider evangelism methods that make much of people but hardly honor God except as a bridge to salvation. God is no means to another end. To alleviate human shame, we must first esteem God. Paul's gospel extols *God's* worth first, and then human value. True, Jesus dies for people. But he dies for God above all.

Romans 3 is perfectly suited to inspire faith. To trust God's promises, we must be convinced he is righteous. He remains true even when we are unfaithful. God's promises are not contingent on our faithfulness. Believers' confidence rests on the fact that God is faithful to uphold his honor, since "if we are faithless, he remains faithful— for he cannot deny himself" (2 Timothy 2:13).

Finally, Paul's teaching has implications for morality. After all, Romans 3 illustrates how God acts righteously. "Righteousness" is not an abstract concept. It is inherently relational. Ultimately, righteousness is understood relative to God's glory. His

---

[21]Meredith Jessup, "Weiner Responds to Voter: 'Sure, I Dishonored My Wife . . . but I Didn't Do Anything to You!'" *The Blaze*, August 1, 2013, www.theblaze.com/news/2013/08/01/weiner-responds-to-voter-sure-i -dishonored-my-wife-but-i-didnt-do-anything-to-you/.

righteousness is the measure for his people. Within this community, honor and shame are redefined. Christians cannot talk about right and wrong without considering the reputation of God and his people. It's no wonder Paul elsewhere says, "So, whether you eat or drink, or whatever you do, do all to the glory of God" (1 Corinthians 10:31).

6

WHO IS WORTHY
of HONOR? (ROMANS 4)

While waiting in line, two middle-aged Chinese women had a lively debate. They could not understand a nearby American family who had a white son and black daughter. The children looked to be about the same age. The women asked themselves, "Why does the girl have black skin but the boy and the parents have white skin?" Finally, one lady had an idea. She asked her friend, "Are they twins?" The parents overheard the conversation and told both women that their daughter was adopted. Surprisingly, it never occurred to those Chinese women that the girl might be adopted.

Adoption is not a concept many East Asians think about. Few people adopt, since perpetuating bloodline is a fundamental concern in cultures that prioritize family name. As a result, "many adoptions in South Korea are concealed from family and friends—and, in many cases, the adopted child. Parents ensure that the baby's blood type matches their own; some mothers even fake pregnancy. All this sends the message that adoption is shameful."[1]

Even Westerners often define identity using bloodline or birth culture. While living in Alabama, David and Heather Platt adopted their son Caleb from Kazakhstan. They are frequently asked whether Caleb knows his family and cultural history. David, resisting the assumption that identity is reckoned according to bloodline or birth culture, summarizes his reply:

> Actually, Caleb does know a lot about his family heritage. . . . Caleb has more family heritage than he knows what to do with, and not just family heritage. . . . We're very intentional about teaching his cultural heritage. He is familiar with cultural literature like *Mr. Brown Can Moo, Can You?* and *Goodnight, Moon*. . . . He knows all about his culture's foods, like barbecue and mac and cheese and watermelon and birthday cake. He's very familiar with cultural music. He probably can't identify a Kazakh song right now, but he knows [our church's] worship CD backwards and

[1] S. C. S., "Why Adoptions Are So Rare in South Korea," *The Economist*, May 27, 2015, www.economist.com /blogs/economist-explains/2015/05/economist-explains-32.

forwards. He may not yet know the Kazakh national anthem, but he has heard *Sweet Home, Alabama.*[2]

Platt says he gets defensive when people ask, "Have you ever met Caleb's real mother?" He replies, "Let me introduce you to her. Her name is Heather."

WHO? VS. HOW?

Who belongs to Abraham's family? This is Paul's basic question in Romans 4. Many interpreters instead focus on the question, "*How* do people join Abraham's family (and so be justified)?" Although interrelated, the distinction between "who" and "how" is important.

Imagine a man boasts, "I can birth a baby." You would correct his misunderstanding by informing him *how* one gets pregnant. The question "who" can give birth is answered by answering the "how" question. Consider another question: "Who is the child's father?" What assumptions influence your answer? Do you first think of biology and culture? Or do you think more broadly about stepfathers and adoptive fathers? The "who" question is distinct from asking how one becomes a father.

In Romans 4, "how" one is justified is important, yet more fundamental is "who" can be justified. In justification, God gathers a people who glorify him though faith. In this chapter, Paul elaborates on Romans 3, where he says God demonstrates his righteousness by justifying Jews *and* Gentiles. The fundamental identity of God's people does not stem from culture or natural relationships. Paul seems to overthrow the law since, as a covenant, it formally marks the relationship between God and his people. Jews therefore reasoned, "Abraham is *our* father, not the Gentiles."

JUSTIFYING SALVATION THROUGH SOCIAL IDENTITY

How do we explain justification from an honor-shame perspective? The word *dikaioō* is typically translated "justify," "declare righteous," or "vindicate." Accordingly, "This verb describes the recognition by God of the worth of a person who has already been transformed by participation in Christ."[3] Those who are justified (and are thus "insiders") are *ascribed* honor. Why?

Justification is a declaration akin to an adoption decree. Kevin Vanhoozer suggests, "Adoption refers to a forensic act. One might even say that adoption *imputes* filial status."[4] Justification can be called a "speech act" whereby one's speech brings some reality into

---

[2]David Platt, "Free as Sons," *Radical.net*, December 21, 2008, www.radical.net/sermon/free-as-sons/.

[3]John Barclay, *Paul and the Gift* (Grand Rapids: Eerdmans, 2015), 376n66.

[4]Kevin Vanhoozer, "Wrighting the Wrongs of the Reformation? The State of the Union with Christ in St. Paul and Protestant Soteriology," in *Jesus, Paul and the People of God: A Theological Dialogue with N. T. Wright*, ed. Nicholas Perrin and Richard B. Hays (Downers Grove, IL: IVP Academic, 2012), 255-56.

existence.[5] A common example is the declaration of a judge or pastor, "I pronounce you husband and wife." Not surprisingly, adoption language is "a vital and central idea" in contexts where Paul discusses justification (Romans 8; Galatians 3–4).[6]

Even so, John Barclay gives a helpful qualification. He states that "it is important to note that acquittal here means that one is shown to be in the right, not that one is forgiven or absolved of guilt."[7] Therefore, being justified entails "being considered a worthy recipient of salvation" or a "fitting beneficiary of divine gift."[8] Justification is not a precondition of salvation but rather the declaration that *"the saving gift has already been given in Christ, without regard to worth."*[9]

Justification in Romans is a way of recognizing a person's honorable status, that is, one's identity as Abraham's offspring. The justified person belongs to Abraham's family because she is "in Christ." Works (of the law) and faith serve as proxies for group honor using different measures of worth. Justification by faith creates a new community whose ascribed honor does not stem from standard social distinctions.[10]

Some readers might suspect I'm overemphasizing the social dimension of justification at the expense of salvation, saying justification is about people and God while social divisions are mere consequences of deeper theological problems. This objection misunderstands the claims in this chapter. It also might presume an unnecessary chasm between "sacred" and "secular." Throughout human history, social identity and practice give concrete expression to religious/theological ideas. To distinguish them is akin to separating body and spirit. While the distinction is *theoretically* possible, detachment is utterly unnatural.

If justification is an aspect of salvation, how can we justify sustaining focus on its social dimension? Put simply, *the fact that God gives the Mosaic law effectively makes sacred Israel's sense of self identity.* This natural inference is based on God's election of Israel. It is not that Jews assumed mere birth or ethnicity guaranteed salvation. After all, "insiders" were reckoned "outsiders" if they did not fulfill the expectations of membership—that is, keeping the law. Presumably, such obedience demonstrates allegiance to God, and in this way fidelity to God and group are merged. Romans 4 illustrates the social and salvific dimensions of justification.

---

[5]Vanhoozer, "Wrighting the Wrongs," 248-49. He cites John Searle's helpful summary: "The speaker in authority brings about a state of affairs specified in the propositional content by saying in effect, I declare the state of affairs to exist." See John Searle, *Expression and Meaning* (Cambridge: Cambridge University Press, 1979), 26.

[6]N. T. Wright, "Response to Kevin Vanhoozer," in *Jesus, Paul and the People of God: A Theological Dialogue with N. T. Wright*, ed. Nicholas Perrin and Richard B. Hays (Downers Grove, IL:IVP Academic, 2012), 259.

[7]Barclay, *Paul and the Gift*, 376n67. His comment describes the use of the verb *dikaioō* in the LXX.

[8]Barclay, *Paul and the Gift*, 377-78.

[9]Barclay, *Paul and the Gift*, 378. Emphasis original.

[10]As we'll see in Romans 5–6, ascribed honor depends on the achieved honor of the faithful Christ. Philip Esler explicitly calls righteousness an "ascribed honor" that affects one's group identity in his *Conflict and Identity in Romans* (Minneapolis: Fortress, 2003), 167, 186-88.

When defending justification, Paul stresses collective identity. Since justification reckons people members of God's kingdom, Paul answers a natural question: *Who* constitutes God's people—only Jews or also Gentiles? Being justified in Romans 4 is a marker of social identity. *How* individuals are justified is an implication of Paul's main point: *who* can be declared righteous.

Here an individualistic perspective puts readers at a disadvantage. We should not ask, "How does justification concern me individually?" but rather "What does justification say about us as a group?" It is possible for Westerners to discern Paul's group emphasis. To do so, however, it is necessary to become sensitive to the fact that identity derives from membership in a community.

"WHO" IS JUSTIFIED?

In Romans 4, then, Paul primarily focuses on identity: *who* can be justified. It is not that Romans 4 completely ignores the "how" question; instead, *that is not the principal problem addressed in the chapter.*

Romans 4:1-8

What then shall we say? Have we found Abraham to be our forefather according to the flesh? [2] For if Abraham was justified by works, he has something to boast about, but not before God. [3] For what does the Scripture say? "Abraham believed God, and it was counted to him as righteousness." [4] Now to the one who works, his wages are not counted as a gift but as his due.

[5] And to the one who does not work but believes in him who justifies the ungodly, his faith is counted as righteousness, [6] just as David also speaks of the blessing of the one to whom God counts righteousness apart from works:

[7] "Blessed are those whose lawless deeds are forgiven, and whose sins are covered; [8] blessed is the man against whom the Lord will not count his sin."*

Adapted from ESV

Verse 1 frames the message of Romans 4. A growing number of scholars agree Paul's question looks something like the translation in the box above.[11] This translation focuses on Abraham's identity: In what sense is Abraham "our forefather"? According to flesh or, implicitly, according to faith?

---

[11] In Greek: *Ti oun eroumen heurēkenai Abraam, ton propatora hēmōn kata sarka?* Common translations obscure the direction of Paul's argument. For example, the ESV translates 4:1, "What then shall we say was gained by Abraham, our forefather according to the flesh?" This rendering centers attention on what Abraham gains. Therefore, it seems Abraham's identity is not the subject of the following paragraphs. Compare Richard Hays "'Have We Found Abraham to Be Our Forefather According to the Flesh?' A Reconsideration of Rom 4:1," *Novum Testamentum* 27, no. 1 (1985): 81; Garwood Anderson, *Paul's New Perspective: Charting a Soteriological Journey* (Downers Grove, IL: IVP Academic, 2016), 81-83.

Consider the answer Paul gives in the chapter. He overwhelmingly emphasizes that Abraham is the father of all by faith, whether circumcised (Jews) or uncircumcised (Gentiles).[12] In short, Paul refutes the idea that Abraham is father only to the Jews "according to the flesh." He answers "no" to the question posed in Romans 4:1. When Paul uses this opening in his letters, the question typically requires an affirmation or denial. Paul most often answers negatively. In fact, even if we assume Paul answers the question of how Abraham was justified, this verse doesn't ask that question nor does Paul directly state anything Abraham gained.[13]

Notice the progression of Paul's thought. In Romans 4:2-8, he contrasts works and faith in means of justification. Neither Abraham nor David were "justified by works." After 4:8, Paul's focus narrows decisively to a different question: Who receives the blessing of justification?

Romans 4:9-12

Is this blessing then only for the circumcised, or also for the uncircumcised?
[9b] For we say that faith was counted to Abraham as righteousness.
[10] How then was it counted to him? Was it before or after he had been circumcised? It was not after, but before he was circumcised.
[11a] He received the sign of circumcision as a seal of the righteousness that he had by faith while he was still uncircumcised.
[11b] The purpose was to make him the father of all who believe without being circumcised, so that righteousness would be counted to them as well,
[12] and to make him the father of the circumcised who are not merely circumcised but who also walk in the footsteps of the faith that our father Abraham had before he was circumcised.

We should distinguish Paul's primary and secondary points. His main argument begins in 4:9a and continues in 4:11b. In 4:9b, Paul adds a "for," making 4:9b-11a a parenthesis supporting his larger idea. Romans 4:11b explicitly highlights *why* Abraham is justified before receiving circumcision: "to make him the father of all who believe without being circumcised, so that righteousness would be counted to them as well." This statement, along with 4:12, answers the question posed in 4:9a ("Is this blessing then only for the circumcised, or also for the uncircumcised?"). Both

---

[12]It is no argument against my interpretation that Abraham is called our forefather *kata sarka* ("according to the flesh"). Verse 2 immediately substitutes a parallel description: *ek erkōn* ("by works"). Paul switches from *kata* to *ek* throughout the chapter. He varies the object of the preposition by using mutually defining descriptors. Instead of *sarka*, he uses *peritomēs* ("circumcision," 4:12) and *nomou* ("law," 4:14, 16); he also applies this construction to *pisteōs* ("faith," 4:16).

[13]One cannot simply answer that Abraham "gained" justification/righteousness. That question is never up for debate, being established in Genesis 15:6. Nor does that answer advance Paul's argument. What is questioned is the nature of his justification.

circumcised *and* uncircumcised receive the blessing. This explains why Paul in 4:9b-11a speaks of faith and works, that is, *how* Abraham is justified.

In Romans 4, as in Romans 3:27-30, faith and works define *who* is justified. The precise mechanics or means of justification are significant here inasmuch as they support Paul's central thesis: *Gentiles* can be justified, not only Jews.

Paul uses the law and faith to highlight people's *collective identity*. Examples from the immediate context include Romans 3:28-30; 4:9, 11-12, 14, 16. Jews are characterized as "the circumcised" and "the adherent to the law." A Gentile is called "uncircumcised." However, faith defines a different group: those who "walk in the footsteps of [Abraham's] faith . . . share in the faith of Abraham," being reckoned as Abraham's offspring.

Romans 2:25-29 further confirms how Paul categorizes two group identities. The one who presumes to be a "Jew" in 2:28-29 is the physically circumcised person of 4:25-27. In Romans 2:17, the same person is described again: "You call yourself a Jew and rely on the law." This way of grouping people goes back to Romans 2:12-14, where "Gentiles" are those "who do not have the law" (compare Romans 15:8-9).

Romans 4:13-18

[13] For the promise to Abraham and his offspring that he would be heir of the world did not come through the law but through the righteousness of faith.

[14] For if it is the adherents of the law who are to be the heirs, faith is null and the promise is void.

[15] For the law brings wrath, but where there is no law there is no transgression.

[16] That is why it depends on faith, in order that the promise may rest on grace and be guaranteed to all his offspring—not only to the adherent of the law but also to the one who shares the faith of Abraham, who is the father of us all, [17] as it is written, "I have made you the father of many nations" —in the presence of the God in whom he believed, who gives life to the dead and calls into existence the things that do not exist.

[18] In hope he believed against hope, that he should become the father of many nations, as he had been told, "So shall your offspring be."

Romans 4:16 decisively shows the function of faith and works in Romans. The key phrase is "to all his offspring—*not only* to the adherent of the law *but also* to the one who shares the faith of Abraham."

Paul divides Abraham's offspring into two groups: "the adherent of the law" and "the one who shares the faith of Abraham." The two groups are separated by "not only . . . but also." The adherents to the law are reckoned as Abraham's offspring, yet this group cannot refer to people who are Abraham's offspring *because of* law keeping.

Otherwise, Paul would be contradicting his entire argument. Paul does not claim two paths to justification: by adhering to the law or by faith.

When Paul contrasts the law and faith in the passage, he ultimately makes a conclusion about Abraham's identity. In Romans 4:11-12, Abraham is circumcised after being justified in order "to make him the father of all who believe without being circumcised . . . and to make him the father of the circumcised." It is noteworthy that 4:12 uses the same phraseology found in 4:16 ("not merely . . . but who also"). In both verses, the phrase describes Jews, who adhere to the law via circumcision. In both instances, the law keeper is reckoned a child of Abraham.

Accordingly, he does *not* contrast law and faith in order to discuss how people are justified. Instead, law and faith (in 4:16) distinguish two types of people in Abraham's family. Both come under one umbrella—those guaranteed the promise by faith (4:12, 16). Faith defines the collective identity of Christ's followers, not ethnicity, tradition, social status, and so on (compare Galatians 3:26-29). Therefore, Andrew Tan concludes,

> Fortunately, ethnicity is not a primordial construct but is a malleable one. Romans 4 represents Paul's discursive strategy for re-constructing the ethnic identity of both Judean and gentile Christians so that both groups have equal honour. To achieve his objective, Paul first removes the Mosaic law as a means to acquiring honour. At the same time, he reconstructs the ethnic identity of Judean Christians without obliterating their present Judean identity which is particularly associated with circumcision and the Mosaic law. The end of Paul's rhetoric is to make Judean Christians Abraham's descendants by trust in their patron, God. He also reconstructs the ethnic identity of gentile Christians that makes them Abraham's descendants by trusting in the same patron, God. In this way, gentile Christians can receive honour by ascription.[14]

In Romans 4:16-18, Paul three times reemphasizes Abraham's *identity* as "father of us all." His family spans the world. Abraham believed God's promise that "he should become the father of many nations" (4:17-18). Even the promise's content does not announce a *means* of justification. He does not say, "If you believe, then you will be justified." His argument does not turn on the "how" question.

The focus in God's promise is the *scope* of Abraham's family. The question of who is justified is no mere corollary of the gospel. Unsurprisingly, the Abrahamic promise is *equivalent* to the gospel in Galatians 3:8, where Paul says, "And the Scripture, foreseeing that God would justify the *Gentiles* by faith, preached the gospel beforehand to Abraham, saying, 'In you shall all *the nations* be blessed.'"

---

[14]Andrew Kim Seng Tan, "The Rhetoric of Abraham's Faith." (PhD diss., University of Cape Town, 2016), 268.

Gathercole objects when he says, "The *content* of the doctrine of justification by faith should be distinguished from its *scope*."[15] However, he overstates his point. We note that Romans 4:9-19 focuses on *who* can be Abraham's heir (compare Galatians 3:7-14). Therefore, it's better to say that "scope" *is* the "content" of justification by faith.[16]

Getting Paul's priority correct is important. By overemphasizing "how," we easily overlook the Jew-Gentile question and so fail to address issues related to group identity, including ethnocentrism, nationalism, and prejudice. By settling for moral-istic views of justification, the law loses its distinctive Jewishness. If we merely focus on "how," we might never follow Paul's example of addressing problems concerning collective identity, loyalty, and tradition.

Why do some people overemphasize the "how" of justification and miss the "who"? In Western culture, one's identity is largely shaped by how one differs from others. One's actions essentially define identity. However, Easterners tend more quickly to recognize that honor and identity are only partially determined by personal achieve-ments or failures. A person is also ascribed honor and so gains social status via rela-tionships, gender, ethnicity, and position.

Paul uses Israel's ancestors to testify against his Jewish contemporaries. This is a powerful argument in traditional honor-shame cultures. He cites David in Romans 4 (compare Romans 3:4) and uses Abraham to support his argument for justification by faith. These men are two of the most venerated figures in Israel's history. Far from overthrowing the law (Romans 3:31), Paul shows how faith achieves the purpose of God's covenant—that all nations would be blessed in Abraham.

Tragically, Paul's Jewish opponents rejected the promise that Abraham believed. In Romans 4:17-18, Paul clarifies the content of Abraham's faith (quoting Genesis 17:5, then Genesis 15:5). His opponents refused to believe Gentiles can be justified as Gen-tiles. Unlike Abraham, they effectively become like the Gentiles of Romans 1, who don't "give glory to God . . . who gives life to the dead and calls into existence the things that do not exist" (Romans 4:17, 20; compare 1:21-23).

ROMANS 4 IN CONTEXT

Does this reading of Romans 4 fit the larger context of Romans? Indeed, it does. Romans 9 reinforces the conclusions of Romans 4. After recalling Israel's privileges, Paul says,

---

[15]Simon Gathercole, "Justified by Faith, Justified by his Blood: The Evidence of Rom 3:21–4:25" in *Justification and Variegated Nomism*, Vol. 2, ed. D.A. Carson, T. O'Brien, M. A. Seifrid (Tübingen: Mohr Siebeck, 2004), 156. Emphasis original.

[16]Compare Peter Leithart, *Delivered from the Elements of the World: Atonement, Justification, Mission* (Downers Grove, IL: IVP Academic, 2016), 198-99.

But it is not as though the word of God has failed. For not all who are descended from Israel belong to Israel, and not all are children of Abraham because they are his offspring, but "Through Isaac shall your offspring be named." This means that it is not the children of the flesh who are the children of God, but the children of the promise are counted as offspring. (Romans 9:6-8)

Just as Paul does not "overthrow the law" (Romans 3:30), so also God's word does not fail. Paul contrasts "children of the flesh" with "children of the promise." As in chapter 4, where faith leads Paul to explicitly discuss God's "promise" (Romans 4:13, 14, 16, 20), Paul again raises the topic in 9:4, 8-9. "Flesh" marks those who are Jews merely by heritage (Romans 9:9-13). Paul unmistakably distinguishes two groups. In the language of Romans 2:28-29, children of the flesh are "outward" Jews whereas the children of promise are Jews "inwardly . . . of the heart, by the Spirit, not by the letter."

A key expression in Romans 4 first appears in Romans 2. Paul eleven times uses *logizomai* ("to reckon, count, impute") in Romans 4. By understanding how faith is "reckoned" as righteousness, we better grasp how faith functions for Paul. His usage in Romans 2:26 is insightful. He asks, "will not his uncircumcision *be regarded as* [*logizomai*] circumcision?" Uncircumcision is reckoned as circumcision (2:26) just as faith "counts" as righteousness (Romans 4:5). Unmistakably, *logizomai* in 2:26 carries implications for a person's identity. Verses 26-27 are supported by verses 28-29, where Paul clarifies who is a Jew inwardly, not merely physically.

Romans 2:25-29

For circumcision indeed is of value if you obey the law, but if you break the law, your circumcision becomes uncircumcision.
26 So, if a man who is uncircumcised keeps the precepts of the law, will not his uncircumcision be regarded as circumcision?
27 Then he who is physically uncircumcised but keeps the law will condemn you who have the written code and circumcision but break the law.
28 For no one is a Jew who is merely one outwardly, nor is circumcision outward and physical.
29 But a Jew is one inwardly, and circumcision is a matter of the heart, by the Spirit, not by the letter. His praise is not from man but from God.

Compare 2:25, where Paul makes a similar remark using a different verb: "your circumcision *becomes* [*gegonen*] uncircumcision." Paul identifies circumcision with *un*circumcision. Practically speaking, he equates the two. In context, those with physical circumcision are equivalent to those with *un*circumcised hearts. "Reckoning" in 2:26 functions similarly: uncircumcision is treated as circumcision.

Obviously, uncircumcision in 2:26 is not a condition explaining *how* a person is reckoned "circumcised." Rather, that he "keeps the law" even while uncircumcised shows he is circumcised in heart (2:26, 27, 29). This observation leads us to the next section.

WHY DOES FAITH JUSTIFY?

The above discussion has implications for understanding the meaning of *dikaioō* ("to justify").[17] For some interpreters, *dikaioō* in Romans 4 *changes* a person's status. God's declaration creates or causes a new state of being. For others, justification *proves* a person already belongs to God's people.

The significance of God's *dikaioō* declaration largely depends on the function of faith in the context. Where faith is a *condition* for justification, *dikaioō* implies a change of status or identity. If *dikaioō* has this meaning, we would expect Paul to discuss *how* people become Abraham's offspring. Alternatively, when faith is a *proof* characteristic of God's people, *dikaioō* connotes authentication or demonstration. Therefore, if *dikaioō* signifies that a person already belongs to Abraham's family, we would expect Paul to stress *who* is declared righteous before God.

As we've seen, in Romans 4, Paul primarily explains *who* can be justified. His overall point in the chapter is that *Gentiles* can be justified. To support this conclusion, he explains *how* a person is justified. Thus, faith serves as *proof* that a person is justified. Justification, as a declaration, proves the conditions for membership in God's people are satisfied. The decisive condition is Christ's life, death, and resurrection (compare Romans 3:25; 4:25). In this sense, justification itself does not create the change needed for salvation. This does not imply faith is unnecessary; faith is the proof that one is declared righteous precisely because it's a subjective condition for salvation. Paul ironically claims that faith, evidence that is "hidden" (compare Romans 2:16, 29), confirms one is righteous. The following chart summarizes the relationship between the two questions ("how?," "who?"), *dikaioō* ("justify"), and the function of faith.

---

[17]The meaning of *dikaioō* is much debated. Summaries of the *dikai-* root include John Reumann, "Righteousness," in *Anchor Yale Bible Dictionary*, ed. David Noel Freedman (New York: Doubleday, 1992), 5:724-73; Elizabeth Achtemeier, "Righteousness," in *Interpreter's Dictionary of the Bible*, ed. George A. Buttrick (Nashville: Abingdon, 1962), 4:80-99; and N. T. Wright, "Righteousness," in *New Dictionary of Theology*, ed. Sinclair B. Ferguson and J. I. Packer (Downers Grove, IL: InterVarsity Press, 2000), 590-92. For examples where God's justifying work demonstrates the true people of God, see 2 Chronicles 6:23; Isaiah 54:10-17; Jeremiah 51:9-10; and compare Revelation 3:8-9. Unambiguous instances where *dikaioō* indicates proving include Matthew 11:19; Luke 7:29, 35.

Table 3. Relationship between two questions

"Justify"	Implied Question	Faith
Change	*How* is one justified?	Condition
Prove	*Who* can be justified?	Proof

Paul's use of *logizomai* in Romans bolsters the above interpretation. While Romans 8:36 and 14:14 are noteworthy, Romans 9:8 is particularly important. Paul concludes, "This means that it is not the children of the flesh who are the children of God, but the children of the promise *are counted as* offspring." Paul again identifies those who "count" as Abraham's offspring.

Significantly, Romans 6:11 says, "So you also must *consider* [*logizomai*] yourselves dead to sin and alive to God in Christ Jesus." Paul does not describe a change one brings on oneself. Paul wants readers to believe *what is already true*. This is a reckoning of identity, whether one is a slave to sin or to righteousness.[18] As in Romans 4, *logizomai* links to justification, which Paul mentions in Romans 6:7, saying, "For the one who died *has been justified* [*dedikaiōtai*] from sin" (my translation). In short, the reckoning of identity in 6:11 illuminates the nuance of justification in 6:7.

JUSTIFICATION AS RESURRECTED HONOR

Romans 4:24-25 brings together what I've said thus far about justification. Paul says, "It will be counted to us who believe in him who raised from the dead Jesus our Lord, who was delivered up for our trespasses and *raised for our justification*." Michael Bird interprets 4:25 in view of 1 Timothy 3:16, where Christ is *"justified* by the Spirit" (my translation).[19] In Paul's sequence of thought, Christ's justification alludes to his resurrection. The resurrection vindicates Christ as God's anointed king (compare Romans 1:3-4). The resurrection shows *who* Jesus is—Christ our Lord.

Believers are justified because of Christ's resurrection. It proves God will vindicate his people via their resurrection. By faith, they are unified with Christ in his death and resurrection (compare Romans 6:1-7). Their faith in the risen Christ proves they too will be raised by God. Christ's resurrection in effect declares his followers are not captive to sin.

Thus, justification restores the believer's honor. It prevents and removes shame (compare Romans 5:5; 10:11). Believers now serve the risen King of kings. They are no longer slaves to sin, compelled to do things that bring shame (Romans 6:21).

---

[18]As we'll see, "sin" in Romans 5–6 is a personified slave master, not mere wrongdoing.
[19]Compare Bird, *The Saving Righteousness of God: Studies on Paul, Justification, and the New Perspective* (Waynesboro, GA: Paternoster, 2007), 53-56.

The resurrection is the manifestation of our justification because it displays Christ's victory and kingship. Likewise, faith demonstrates we are God's people because of what Christ accomplished.

WHAT THEN SHALL WE SAY?

Reading Romans 4 with Eastern eyes makes us more sensitive to Paul's ideas about collective identity. We all belong to various groups, such as families, schools, businesses, countries, tribes, clubs, and teams. Individuals find identity through countless interactions and relationships.

If we underemphasize these dynamics, Romans 4 becomes about how individuals are justified before God without respect to social identity. Individuals do make personal decisions in response to the gospel, but *personal* decisions are not necessarily *private* decisions. Even Abraham's personal decision to follow God's call required he leave his country, kindred, and father's house (Genesis 12:1).

For many first-century Jews, Paul's doctrine of justification seemed like a rejection of Israel's ancestors and their God. God chose Israel from among all nations. By denying the necessity of circumcision, a person in effect would be cut off from God's people. One can almost hear Paul's opponents saying, "Apart from Israel, justification is impossible." What sense does it make to imagine salvation in terms of an individual's relationship with God distinct from belonging to God's people? From an Eastern perspective, such thinking verges on abstraction.

In Romans 4, Paul shows how Christ redefines God's people. Fundamentally, the world doesn't consist of Jews and Gentiles but instead those who give allegiance to Christ and those who do not. The basis for collective identity has shifted. All whom God declares righteous are counted as Abraham's family.

Therefore, justification by faith calls people to change their *allegiance*. In any group, we express allegiance and thus identity in various ways. Some are subtle; others, like circumcision, are overt. Faith redirects our fundamental loyalty to Christ, which entails identifying with the King's citizens above any other group. Faith justifies a person in that it declares her a member of God's people. A "transfer" occurs. When a person follows Christ, she is saved *from* one group and *into* another.

What happens when we "individualize" justification such that it primarily concerns how "I" am made right with God? We subtly foster conditions that divide Christ's people. People imagine their personal relationship with God is private and so doesn't require an essential change in social identity. The church is little more than a bag of marbles, a collection of individuals. It becomes a volunteer organization—good and helpful, but optional. Basic loyalties to bloodline, social class, nationality, and so on are not fundamentally challenged.

Justification concerns social identity just as much it is does salvation. If believers' fundamental group identity centers on anything other than those who have faith in Christ's resurrection, they effectively divide his kingdom.[20] For this reason, the gospel is at stake.

THE RELATIONSHIP BETWEEN
THE GOSPEL AND JUSTIFICATION

People often equate the gospel and justification by faith.[21] They claim the gospel is a message about *how* individuals get saved. However, this section explains why they are not equivalent. Justification by faith is an *implication* of the gospel. I trace out Paul's logic below, highlighting six interconnected ideas that reemphasize the importance of honor-shame themes.

1. Jesus is King over the world. Paul's gospel declares this core message: Jesus is the King, the promised Christ from David's line, God's royal son (Romans 1:1-4; 2 Samuel 7:13-14). Through Christ, God rules the earth. Romans 10:9 concisely proclaims, "Jesus is Lord." In Romans 2–4, Paul begins to unpack the implications of this gospel.

2. Christ is not only the king of Jews; he is the king of Gentiles. Since Jesus has authority over the world, including life and death, he is not merely the king of one nation. The Christ of Israel is king over all nations. This is the same logic used in Romans 3:29-30, where Paul defends justification by faith by appealing to monotheism.[22] Because there is one God, he is God of Jews *and* Gentiles. The line of thought applies to the one true king, whom God resurrected.

3. Both Jews and Gentiles are included among his people. Christ's identity determines the identity of everyone in the world. In effect, this comment echoes the chorus of Romans 4. God made a "promise to Abraham and his offspring that he would be heir of *the world*" (Romans 4:13). Therefore, Paul concludes, both Jew and Gentile belong to Abraham's family.

4. Gentiles do not have to become Jews. Before God, Gentiles need not be ashamed because they lack the heritage, tradition, or whatever distinction they think gives Jews special privilege. God is not partial to either Jews or highly respected

---

[20]I expound on this idea below and in chapter 12.

[21]For example, Millard Erickson, *Christian Theology*, 2nd ed. (Grand Rapids: Baker, 2002), 1073; John Murray, *Redemption: Accomplished and Applied* (Grand Rapids: Eerdmans, 1980), 130.

[22]For similar logic, compare Galatians 3:16; 1 Timothy 2:5; Ephesians 2:18; 4:5-6. The two lines of reasoning (Christ as King of kings; God as one) are not only parallel. They converge when we recognize the royal implications of monotheism (see especially Isaiah 40–66). Because there is one God, there is only one King. To rephrase Romans 3:29-30: "Or is Christ the king of Jews only? Is he not the king of Gentiles also? Yes, of Gentiles also, since Christ is the one true king."

Gentile Greeks. Just as Jews are not righteous before God based on group identity, so Gentiles are neither excluded nor put to shame because of social distinctions.

5. Gentiles do not have to do works of the Mosaic law. *Who* we are determines what we do. Likewise, *who* we want to be shapes *how* we attempt to gain that identity. Socially, circumcision marked Israel's collective identity. Those who obeyed the Mosaic law were regarded as Jews in a national-ethnic sense.

This view of the law is the key to Paul's logic. "Circumcision" concerns more than moral rule keeping. When Paul's opponents say Gentiles must be circumcised, they in effect claim God *and thus his kingly* reign over Israel but not the nations. Why does Paul reject justification by works of the law? Circumcision symbolically severs Christ's kingdom into factions.

At this point, we should highlight a significant but easily missed observation. The opposite of Paul's doctrine of justification is not salvation by "good works" *in some general moral sense*. Otherwise, there is no need to press the distinction between Jews and Gentiles. Theoretically, Gentiles could just as well do "good works" without being Jewish and certainly without being circumcised. On that note, it's hard to imagine why circumcision would be a point of contention at all if Jewish identity were not the fundamental issue at stake. There is nothing inherently moral, good or bad, about cutting one's foreskin.

6. Gentiles are justified and ultimately saved by faith. If God's promises come via the law, "faith is null and the promise is void" (Romans 4:14). Not only does "the law bring wrath" (Romans 4:15), it limits membership among God's people to Israel. God's promise would be threatened. God's own honor is at stake.

If the law cannot bring God's blessing to the nations, what can we conclude? In Romans 4:16, Paul answers, "That is why it depends on faith, in order that the promise may rest on grace and be guaranteed to all his offspring." Faith alone honors the righteousness of God, who keeps his promise (Romans 4:20-21). Thus, we see how justification by works dishonors God.

Justification by works limits Christ's honor. He becomes one nation's king, whom a rival kingdom shamed on a cross. By contrast, justification by faith turns our attention to the glory of the resurrection. Paul uses these precise terms to describe the justifying faith of Abraham (Romans 4:17-19).[23]

Paul shows the subtlety of the Jews' confusion. For them, circumcision validates their claim to be God's people. Even Paul notes that Abraham received "the sign of circumcision as a seal of [his] righteousness" (Romans 4:11). Yet readers of Genesis 15 see that God justifies Abraham prior to receiving circumcision. Though circumcision

---

[23]The writer of Hebrews (11:12, 19) reinforces Paul's interpretation in Romans 4.

marks a person's identity in a secondary sense, it was not the fundamental proof of Abraham's justification. *Faith* in the gospel proves who are God's people.

THE GOSPEL DEFINES IDENTITY

Because the gospel demands allegiance to Christ, it necessarily entails belonging to his kingdom people. It fundamentally changes *who* we are. More than rescuing us from death, this gospel makes us disciples. The Jew-Gentile division might seem distant and irrelevant today, but the gospel still shapes how we look at our historical circumstances and the relationship between subgroups in society.

Our fundamental identity is not determined by bloodline, birthplace, name, nor nationality. In the West and non-West, for example, I've encountered prejudice against adoption. In many cultures, shame surrounds the subject to the point that children never learn they are adopted. Others spend a fortune on fertility treatments because they want "their own kids" and don't want to "settle" for adoption. Paul's words highlight the effect of a common but subtle perspective that applies to adoption and also extends to other areas, like gender and skin color. When we think about identity, how often do we default to biology rather than Scripture? The former is an accident of birth; the latter shows us the new humanity in Christ.

The church is not immune to the temptation to discriminate. Sometimes among churches in Wenzhou, nicknamed "China's Jerusalem" due to its high Christian population, "Mandarin services" (*putonghua juhui*) are seen as "outsiders' services" (*waidiren juhui*). One local church leader sees Mandarin services in the Wenzhou church as a euphemism for separate migrant services: "Since we Wenzhounese also speak Mandarin, why are there still Mandarin services? Because we look down on them. So we leave them alone and don't care if they live or die." He considers this division in the church to be a product of the larger Wenzhou culture, which stresses local pride. However, this element of local culture also reflects a general sense of urban supremacy.[24]

In Wenzhou, migrants face consistent discrimination, even among Christians. An "implicit but deliberate rule" exists whereby those from outside Wenzhou are given limited opportunities to minister in the church.[25] What differentiates insiders from outsiders? Language. In the Wenzhou church, speaking the local dialect validates social status.

In practice, what criteria determine identity in our communities? Culture? Biology? Skills? God's kingdom transcends the narrow relational circles afforded by birth and circumstance. As citizens in his kingdom, our fundamental allegiance no

---

[24]Nanlai Cao, *Constructing China's Jerusalem* (Stanford, CA: Stanford University Press, 2001), 156.
[25]Cao, *Constructing*, 128-30, 155.

longer belongs with those from our culture and family tree. Consequently, Christ's followers suffer a degree of separation in those relationships not defined by Christ. The pain of this experience can cut their hearts more profoundly than mere physical circumcision.

A distorted sense of identity can tempt people to use "works" to gain approval, but their effort is not oriented toward God. Some idolize children or friends. Others hate the label "single." In China, unmarried women over thirty years old are called "leftovers." Men spend their lives trying to honor the family name and win their parents' acceptance. These individuals seek *social* distinction, not salvation. For some people, the main obstacle to salvation is inherently social. Why? *Who* people are within their community prevents them from being *who* they could be within God's kingdom family.

The previous paragraphs illustrate that reading the Bible with Eastern eyes does not imply Easterners are impervious to correction. Yet reading with Eastern eyes can better attune us to certain problems like mistaken collective identity.

A MIDDLE WAY?

Does justification *primarily* concern how individuals are saved, or does Paul teach justification *mainly* to build church unity? Scholars struggle to reconcile the dual emphases. Paul's earlier writings lay greater stress on the law's social function and church unity between Jews and Gentiles.[26] Over time, though, Paul gave greater attention to matters of salvation. In this sense, the above two perspectives "are both right, just not at the same time."[27] Romans acts as a sort of midpoint where the social and soteriological planes merge.

How do we discern Paul's emphasis when he seems to address both salvation and social dynamics in the church? How do we interpret his letters without prematurely giving priority to one theme over another? Our study of Romans 4 offers a way forward.

Interpretation depends on the role we assume when reading Romans. If readers take an outsider's perspective (that is, Gentiles), they will naturally emphasize "how" to be justified. By assuming an insider's perspective (that is, Jews), conversion is not one's primary concern. Paul's Jewish opponents did not use the law to join God's people. They argued that the law demonstrates their identity as God's people.

Does justification emphasize ascribed and achieved honor? Honor concerns social status; it is one's claim of worth. Inasmuch as justification is "the recognition by God of the worth of a person," debates about justification should account for the fact that people seek both ascribed and achieved honor. Accordingly, law keeping does not

---

[26] Anderson, *Paul's New Perspective.*
[27] Anderson, *Paul's New Perspective*, 379.

necessarily refer to individuals' efforts to achieve salvation, since the law also marks one's identification with God's people. Otherwise stated, boasting in the law (Romans 2:23), like boasting in the hope of the glory of God (Romans 5:3), need not indicate achieved honor.

Whatever role we assume, affirming one viewpoint does not deny the truth of the other. If Paul highlights *who* can be justified, this does not deny truths about *how* people are justified. How many theological debates persist because people oversimplify data and forge false dichotomies? This is precisely what can result if we read Romans from only one cultural vantage point. By also reading Scripture with Eastern eyes, we regain a more balanced perspective and can perhaps find a middle way.

7

FAITH *in the* FILIAL
CHRIST (ROMANS 5–6)

When Joey Tan began following Christ, his mother responded in typical fashion:

How could you betray your family and your ancestors? You are a Chinese! How could you convert to a foreign religion? Don't you know that Christians do not worship their ancestors? What will happen to me after I die? Aren't you going to give me any food after I die? How could you do this to me!? I raised you for over twenty years as a single mum, and is this how you are going to repay me? Betray and forsake me?[1]

His family called him "unfilial" by dishonoring his family. Filial piety is the virtue of children who honor their parents. A Chinese idiom says, "Of all virtues, filial piety is first" (*bai shan jing wei xian*). For many East Asians, children must show filial piety to all family ancestors, not only their immediate parents. When someone follows Christ, he implicitly scorns the ways of his family.

To understand the importance of filial piety in Chinese culture, consider *The Twenty-Four Paragons of Filial Piety*, a highly influential set of stories that present idealized depictions of children honoring their parents.[2] In one story, Yu Qianlou's father has a mysterious disease. Since no one can diagnose the problem, Yu tastes his father's stool to discern the severity of the disease. In another story, a poor family cannot afford mosquito netting. The eight-year old Wu Meng devises a plan to keep mosquitos away from his parents. Each night, Wu removes his shirt so mosquitoes drink his blood instead of waking his sleeping parents.

The consequences of not showing filial piety are significant even today. In 2013, Beijing enacted a law allowing parents to sue unfilial children. In Shanghai, failing to visit elderly parents could lead to a decreased credit score. Unfortunately, parents sometimes use filial piety as a tool to manipulate children.[3]

---

[1]Hann-Tzuu Tan, *The Chinese Way: Contextualizing the Gospel for the Chinese* (self-published, 2012), Kindle loc. 140-43.

[2]In Chinese, *er shi si xiao*, also known as *The Twenty-Four Filial Exemplars*. For an English translation, see http://www.ruf.rice.edu/~asia/24ParagonsFilialPiety.html.

[3]Berlin Fang, "Parents Must Let Kids Leave the Nest," *China Daily*, June 27, 2012, www.chinadaily.com.cn /opinion/2012-06/27/content_15524988.htm.

Ancient Israel held a similar perspective. Just as children should honor their parents (Exodus 20:12; Deuteronomy 5:16), so all people were expected to keep the ways of their elders and ancestors. According to Deuteronomy 21:18-21, a rebellious son could be stoned to death. When Naboth refused Ahab's lucrative offer to buy his land, he said, "The LORD forbid that I should give you the inheritance of my fathers" (1 Kings 21:3). Naboth guarded his ancestral land as though it were a divine obligation. Ancient Jews linked filial honor, land, and worship of God. As a result, ancient Jews were able to

> harness the natural energies of filial piety and loyalty to kin and land, and to identify them with loyalty to Yahweh and the preservation of Israel's relationship to him. . . . Hence, a man's responsibility to his family and its land took on the form of a reflex of his primary responsibility to God himself. To fulfil the first was to go a long way towards fulfilling the second.[4]

When Israel was disobedient, the LORD rebuked them, "A son honors his father, and a servant his master. If then I am a father, where is my honor?" (Malachi 1:6).

We see a similar picture in the New Testament and throughout the Second Temple period. In 1 Maccabees 2:50-52, Mattathias's last words to his sons appeal to Israel's ancestors and honor/glory:

> Now, my children, show zeal for the law, and give your lives for the covenant of our ancestors. Remember the deeds of the ancestors, which they did in their generations; and you will receive great *honor* (*doxa*) and an everlasting name. Was not Abraham found faithful when tested, and it was reckoned to him as righteousness?

In the New Testament, Jewish leaders repeatedly invoke ancestral authority and debate who truly follows Abraham and Moses (Matthew 3:9; John 8:33, 39, 53; 9:28). In Acts 6:11-14, the Jews' offense stems from Stephen's apparent disregard for Moses.

> We have heard [Stephen] speak blasphemous words *against Moses and God* . . . This man never ceases to speak words against *this holy place and the law*, for we have heard him say that this Jesus of Nazareth will destroy this place and will change *the customs that Moses* delivered to us.

Paul before his Damascus experience saw reverence for ancestors as a badge of honor. He reminds the Galatians, "I was advancing in Judaism beyond many of my own age among my people, so extremely zealous was I for the traditions of my fathers" (Galatians 1:14). Elsewhere, he boasts,

---

[4]Christopher J. H. Wright, "The Israelite Household and the Decalogue: The Social Background and Significance of Some Commandments," *Tyndale Bulletin* 30 (1979): 119.

If anyone else thinks he has reason for confidence in the flesh, I have more: circumcised on the eighth day, of the people of Israel, of the tribe of Benjamin, a Hebrew of Hebrews; as to the law, a Pharisee; as to zeal, a persecutor of the church; as to righteousness under the law, blameless. (Philippians 3:4-6)

FAITHFULNESS AND FILIAL PIETY

This background gives perspective on why Paul's message offended his Jewish opponents. He not only seems to them to cast aside the law; he even appears to place Abraham among the "ungodly" (Romans 4:5). To avoid potential misunderstanding, Paul reiterates his own identification with Israel in Romans 11:1: "I myself am an Israelite, a descendant of Abraham, a member of the tribe of Benjamin." Paul rejects neither his ancestors nor his people. Rather, because of their ignorance (Romans 10:3), he labors "to make my fellow Jews jealous, and thus save some of them" (Romans 11:14).

On the other hand, he contrasts the Jews' unfaithfulness (Romans 3:3) with Abraham's faithfulness (Romans 4:20).[5] The Greek *pistis* encapsulates both the idea of faith (as belief) and faithfulness, and one should not press a sharp distinction between "belief/faith" and "faithfulness." Paul clearly speaks of Israel's unfaithfulness, not mere unbelief, when he sets God's truth and faithfulness (*pistis*) over against Israel's *apistia* in 3:4, vividly described in Romans 2:17-24; 3:10-18.

Romans 4 relieves some of the tension built since Romans 3:3. Since Romans 3:20, a natural question emerges. How will God justify the nations, establishing righteousness in the world? Since all people—including Israel—are unfaithful, how will God be faithful to bless all nations through Abraham's offspring? From Romans 3:22 through Romans 4, faith remains the solution. But how and why?

For ancient Jews, faith(fulness) is expressed in practical ways. Abraham typifies such faith, especially through offering Isaac in Genesis 22.[6] Abraham not only undergoes the covenant ceremony in Genesis 15:9-17, he with his household willingly "received the sign of circumcision as a seal of the righteousness that he had by faith" (Romans 4:11; compare Genesis 17:10-14). The faith(fulness) of Abraham directly contrasts with the unrighteous in Romans 1.[7] Whereas the latter dishonor the Creator God, Abraham glorifies God by trusting the promises of him "who gives life to the dead and calls into existence the things that do not exist" (compare Romans 4:17-21).

---

[5]Implicitly, he also contrasts himself and their unfaithfulness (11:20, 23).

[6]Abraham's faithfulness is epitomized in his offering of Isaac. James 2:21-23 explicitly connects Genesis 15 and 22. Compare Hebrews 11:8-17. Among extrabiblical examples, see 1 Maccabees 2:52; 2 Maccabees 1:2; Sirach 44:20.

[7]Edward Adams, "Abraham's Faith and Gentile Disobedience: Textual Links Between Romans 1 and 4," *Journal for the Study of the New Testament* 65 (1997): 47-66.

Naturally, the faith(fulness) of father Abraham should mark his offspring (Romans 4:11-12, 16, 24).[8] Therefore, none can claim to be Abraham's offspring based on birth or national identity (Romans 9:6-8). In this case, Jews do not honor their ancestor simply by receiving circumcision and keeping the law. What then does it mean to walk in faith(fulness) as Abraham's offspring?

Throughout the letter, Paul presents Jesus Christ as the paragon of filial piety. Paul characterizes the relationship between God and Jesus as Father and Son. Even when familial language is missing, Paul does not veer far from this imagery. Paul explicitly and repeatedly depicts Jesus as God's Son (Romans 1:3-4, 7, 9; 5:10; 8:3, 29, 32). He scatters references to God as Jesus' Father throughout the letter. Often, Jesus' sonship is linked to that of his followers (Romans 1:7; 6:4; 8:15; 15:6). As we'll see below, Paul's filial descriptions of Christ enable him to weave together multiple threads of his argument.

Paul portrays Christ as "the firstborn among many brothers" (Romans 8:29), recalling God's collective designation for Israel in Exodus 4:22. Similar language peppers the Old Testament (Jeremiah 31:9; Hosea 11:1; compare Deuteronomy 32:6; Malachi 1:6). This observation takes on special significance in view of the broader context of Romans 5–8, which is framed by Israel's exodus story.

In Romans 5–6, "sin" and "righteousness" represent Pharaoh and the Lord, respectively. In Romans 6, slaves are set free after they pass through water (that is, the Red Sea and baptism). Romans 7 reflects Israel's receiving the law at Sinai. Just as Israel inherits Canaan, so Romans 8 narrates how God's people find freedom in the new creation that God ultimately brings about in the coming age. In short, Christ is the collective embodiment of Israel, Abraham's offspring.

Christ is the personification of Israel, God's Son, because he is the anointed offspring of David.[9] The psalmist says of David, "I will make him the firstborn, the highest of the kings of the earth" (Psalm 89:27; compare 2:2, 7). Concerning David's offspring, God promises, "He shall build a house for my name, and I will establish the throne of his kingdom forever. I will be to him a father, and he shall be to me a son" (2 Samuel 7:13-14; see 1 Chronicles 17:13). Therefore, we should not underestimate the importance of Paul's introduction to Romans. He is "set apart for the gospel of God, . . . *concerning his Son*, who was *descended from David* according to the flesh and was declared to be the *Son of God* in power according to the Spirit of holiness by his resurrection from the dead, Jesus Christ our Lord"

---

[8]To borrow Jesus' line, "If you were Abraham's children, you would be doing the works Abraham did" (John 8:39).

[9]The name "David" routinely symbolizes his offspring who reign after him. Compare Ezekiel 34:23-24; 37:24-25; Hosea 3:5.

(Romans 1:1-4).[10] As God's son, Christ must be faithful; otherwise his reign will not endure.[11]

Does Paul discuss Christ's faithfulness in Romans? Many scholars argue that phrases like *pisteōs Iēsou Christou* (3:22, 26) are best translated "the faithfulness of Jesus Christ" rather than "faith in Jesus Christ."[12] The double mention of Jesus' faithfulness prepares us for Romans 4, where Paul uses the same construction (*pisteōs Abraam*) to describe Abraham's faithfulness (Romans 4:16). Paul certainly does not refer to "faith in Abraham." The Abraham discussion is sandwiched between Romans 3:22, 26 and 4:25ff, where Paul highlights how God through Christ brings righteousness and produces offspring from all nations. Accordingly, the mention of "Abraham's faith" in the immediate context informs our reading of Romans 3:22, 26. Through faith, Abraham becomes the father of countless offspring. Similarly, Paul in Romans 5–8 explains how Christ's faithfulness brings justification (Romans 6:7) thus making children of God from all nations (Romans 8).

Someone might protest that "faith" language is largely limited to Romans 3–4, claiming we should not link "faithfulness" with Christ's work in Romans 5–8.[13] In response, recall how Paul frames the letter. Romans 5–8 functions as a larger unit of thought flowing directly from Romans 4, which culminates in Christ's ministry (Romans 4:25). This explains why Romans 4 and 8 both emphasize the theme of "offspring." Romans 8 rounds out the discussion from Romans 4. Romans 5–8 particularly focuses on how Christ redeems "offspring," a pivotal motif in Romans 4 and 8. The major motifs of Romans 4–8 are seen in 3:21-26, which serves as a miniature outline for what follows in Romans 4–8. In short, the themes of Romans 3:21-26 that are dispersed throughout Romans 4–8 include faith(fulness), justification, and redemption. Fittingly, "faithfulness" and "righteousness" are interchanged in Romans 3:4-5.

---

[10]Lest we forget, he later quotes Isaiah 11:1, 10, "The *root of Jesse* will come, even he who arises to *rule* the Gentiles; in him will the Gentiles hope" (Romans 15:12).

[11]This is not unlike the ancient Chinese notion of *tianzi* ("Son of Heaven"), the emperor who governed under the "Heavenly Mandate." If he should prove himself unworthy by not securing righteousness, the emperor loses his heavenly mandate and thus his right to rule.

[12]For a balanced presentation of both sides of the debate, see Michael Bird and Preston Sprinkle, eds., *The Faith of Jesus Christ* (Peabody, MA: Hendrickson, 2009). A brief scholarly overview can be found in Matthew Easter, "The *Pistis Christou* Debate: Main Arguments and Responses in Summary," *Currents in Biblical Research* 9, no. 1 (2010): 33-47.

[13]Compare Joel White, "N. T. Wright's Narrative Approach," in *God and the Faithfulness of Paul: A Critical Examination of the Pauline Theology of N. T. Wright*, ed. Christoph Heilig, J. Thomas Hewitt, and Michael Bird (Tübingen: Mohr Siebeck, 2016), 201.

FAITH IN THE FILIAL SON

Although ancient Jews saw themselves as offspring "in Abraham," they did not honor their ancestor Abraham. Their filial piety, like Christ's, should consist in sharing in Abraham's faithfulness. Thus, Abraham's true offspring are found "in Christ."[14] Explanations of "union with Christ" imagery invariably highlight the significance of collective identity.[15] As Easterners well know, family is the most common and fundamental of all collective relationships.

As "firstborn," Jesus embodies his family honor. In Christ, God's children are ultimately glorified (Romans 8:30), being conformed to Christ's "image" (Romans 8:29). Paul's language not only echoes the Adam story; it also shows Christ reversing the idolatry and honor problem in Romans 1:23, 3:23.[16] Unlike Adam, Jesus is a filial (that is, faithful) son. In Romans 3:24-26, Christ's sacrifice demonstrates God's righteousness. Christ's achievements in Romans 5–6 continue the righteousness theme of Romans 2–4. Because of Christ's faithfulness, "many were made righteous" and so "reign in life" (Romans 5:17-19). Those formerly "in sin" are now "baptized into Christ . . . have been united with him . . . shall certainly be united with him in a resurrection like his" (Romans 6:1-2, 5).

What does being "in Christ" mean? In the LXX, similar phrasing conveys allegiance to King David. In a war of words, "the men of Israel answered the men of Judah, 'We have ten shares *in the king* [*en tō basilei*], and *in David* [*en tō Dauid*] also we have more than you. Why then did you despise us? Were we not the first to speak of bringing back our king?'" (2 Samuel 19:43; compare 2 Samuel 20:1; 1 Kings 12:16; 2 Chronicles 10:16). Paul uses similar imagery elsewhere. The phrase *en nomō* describes people who are "under the law" (compare Romans 2:12; 3:19; 7:2, 4, 23). Those "in sin" are "slaves of sin."[17] "Sin" is a personified king that reigns over people, who receive the wage of death.[18]

In a context echoing the exodus, Paul in Romans 6:7 says that whoever has died (with Christ) is "justified" (*dedikaiōtai*) from sin. He echoes Isaiah 40–55, which

---

[14]For example, Romans 3:24; 6:4-8, 11, 23. For a detailed examination of "union with Christ" in Romans, see Wendel Sun, *A New People in Christ: Adam, Israel, and Union with Christ* (Eugene, OR: Pickwick, 2018).

[15]Theologians variously interpret Paul's imagery. Unfortunately, people use a family of complicated theological terms to describe the significance of our union with Christ, including "federal headship," "participation," "corporate solidarity," and "incorporation."

[16]Various scholars see allusions to Adam in Romans 1:23; 3:23. For a recent discussion, see Haley Goranson Jacob, *Conformed to the Image of His Son: Reconsidering Paul's Theology of Glory in Romans* (Downers Grove, IL: IVP Academic, 2018), 85-98.

[17]For *tē hamartia*, see Romans 6:1, 2, 6, 10, 11, 13. For "slaves to sin," see Romans 6:16-17; compare 6:19, 22.

[18]Romans 6:9, 12, 14, 23; compare 5:21. In contrast, those "in Christ" are "slaves of righteousness/God" (Romans 6:19-23). Paul imitates the Old Testament writers who personify death and Sheol, from whom God redeems his people. See Psalm 49:15; Hosea 13:14 (quoted in 1 Corinthians 15:55); compare Isaiah 28:15, 18.

conjoins justification and exodus language.[19] One could say Israel was "justified from Pharaoh."[20] Those justified from "sin" are no longer enslaved "in sin." Because of justification, "slaves of righteousness" are "obedient from the heart" and set free from "the things of which you are now ashamed" (Romans 6:17, 21).

In Romans, "in Christ" can signify one's authority and source of identity. Those "in Christ" are slaves of righteousness just as someone "in sin" is a slave of sin. Likewise, people in/under the law give allegiance to the law and *de facto* are defined by it. "In Christ" and "in the Lord" identify fellow coworkers and loved ones in Romans 16.[21]

Paul's language reflects Isaiah 45:23-25 (quoting Isaiah 45:23 in Romans 14:11). Isaiah writes,

> By myself I have sworn; from my mouth has gone out in *righteousness* a word that shall not return: "To me every knee shall bow, every tongue shall swear allegiance. Only *in the* LORD, it shall be said of me, are *righteousness* and strength; all who were incensed against him shall come to him and *be ashamed*.[22] *In the* LORD [*and in God*, LXX] all the *offspring* of Israel *shall be justified* and *shall be gloried* (or *boast*)."[23] (my translation, adapted from ESV)

The italicized phrases resonate with many core themes in Romans. The Lord in righteousness promises all will confess allegiance to him.[24] What is this confession? God is righteous. Why? The offspring of Israel are justified in him. Therefore, they will be glorified and not put to shame. Their allegiance marks them as "in the Lord."

In summary, what is true of Christ becomes true for those "in him." Therefore, *"Justification is all about being declared to be a member of God's people*; and this people

---

[19]Especially Isaiah 52–53. Scholars recognize both Isaiah's influence on Romans and Isaiah's presentation of Israel's return from exile as a second exodus. See the intertwining of redemption and exodus imagery in Isaiah 43; 62:12–63:16. For justification language, see Isaiah 46:13; 50:8; 51:5-8. Compare Sun, *A New People in Christ*, 185-87; Rikki Watts, "Echoes from the Past: Israel's Ancient Traditions and the Destiny of the Nations in Isaiah 40–55," *Journal for the Study of the Old Testament* 28, no. 4 (2004): 481-508.

[20]Peter Leithart, *Delivered from the Elements of the World: Atonement, Justification, Mission* (Downers Grove, IL: IVP Academic, 2016), 347n28; Tom Holland, *Romans: The Divine Marriage* (Eugene, OR: Pickwick, 2011), 91.

[21]For example, Romans 16:3, 7, 8, 9, 10, 12, 13.

[22]Both *bwsh* (MT) and *aischynō* (LXX) can mean "put to shame."

[23]The final verb can be translated both ways. The Hebrew *hll* typically conveys "exult" or "boast." In the LXX, *endoxazomai* expresses the passive voice, for example, Exodus 14:4, 17; 33:16; Haggai 1:8; Isaiah 49:3; Ezekiel 28:22; 38:23. In favor of the latter is the immediate contrast "be put to shame" in Isaiah 45:24. The syntax of Isaiah 45:24-25 in the LXX also supports a passive reading. "Strength" is replaced with "glory" in 45:24, providing the parallel verbs in the last clause of 45:25. Both translations fit the context of Romans. Paul later says God's people "boast in the hope of the glory of God" (Romans 5:3) and will be glorified (for example, Romans 8:17, 30).

[24]Isaiah 45:22 uses the phrase "all the ends of the earth." Paul simply says "all the nations."

is defined in relation to the Messiah himself."[25] Christ is the collective embodiment of Abraham's offspring. He glorifies the Father and so is ascribed honor by his resurrection. Thus, Christ's followers give filial honor to the Father. They do not primarily seek achieved honor. Rather, they seek ascribed honor from the Son.

---

[25]Wright, *Paul and the Faithfulness of God*, 856 (italics original). Also, compare Wright, *Paul and the Faithfulness of God*, 828-29.

8

THE HOPE *of* GLORY THROUGH
SHAME (ROMANS 5–8)

Middle schoolers understand honor and shame. Students rise and fall in the social hierarchy through shaming and being shamed. I am no exception. In seventh grade, I hatched a plan to impress my peers. I'd start a trend by spiking the hair on *one side* of my head.

The boys in my first class gave the following reviews within six seconds:

"Look at his hair!" (laughter)

"It looks like his head is on fire." (more laughter)

"Yah, like a flame."

From this exchange came my nickname for that year: "FLAMER!!"

Adults are no different. They use money, social media, clothing, education, titles, plastic surgery, and wit to seek recognition. The hope for glory never dies. The desire for honor is basic to being human.

In Romans, Paul urges his readers to seek glory that does not burn up in flames. Accordingly, he writes Romans 5–8 to illustrate how Christ radically transforms a Christian's worldview. Whereas the law brought about Israel's exile, Christ became the hope of glory for the entire world. For concision, this chapter primarily looks at Romans 5:1-11, which introduces the ideas of Romans 5–8.

THE RESURRECTION OF HOPE

Romans 5:1-5

Therefore, since we have been justified by faith, we have peace with God through our Lord Jesus Christ. ² Through him we have also obtained access by faith into this grace in which we stand, and we rejoice in hope of the glory of God.
³ Not only that, but we rejoice in our sufferings, knowing that suffering produces endurance, ⁴ and endurance produces character, and character produces hope,
⁵ and hope does not put us to shame, because God's love has been poured into our hearts through the Holy Spirit who has been given to us.

Paul's logic is explicit: *since* we are justified, our view of honor-shame is transformed. Because we *in Christ* are God's people, "we boast in hope of the glory of God." But what does he mean by "boasting" (*kauchaomai*)?

Paul uses boasting to express an honor-shame perspective. The practice carries connotations both negative (Romans 2:17, 23; 3:27; 4:2) and positive (Romans 5:2, 3, 11). Generally, "boasting" refers to one's reason for confidence and rejoicing. English translations of Romans 5:2, 3, 11 often use "rejoice," which masks that the verb also appears in Romans 2:17, 23, where it's often translated "boast." "Boast" and "rejoice" both convey similar ideas, as when someone exults, delights, or celebrates something. Modern English speakers might even say one who *boasts* in fact *rejoices* in some quality or achievement. Particularly in Romans, Paul closely connects boasting with faith. Boasting reflects and, in some sense, determines someone's identity. A person's boast is the reason he has "face" within his community.

Similarly, observe how boasting shapes the Galatian controversy over justification. Paul writes,

> For even those who are circumcised do not themselves keep the law, but they desire to have you circumcised that *they may boast in* your flesh. But far be it from me *to boast* except in the cross of our Lord Jesus Christ, by which the world has been crucified to me, and I to the world. (Galatians 6:13-14)

Negative and positive boasting distinguish two groups. The former boasts in the flesh; the latter in the cross. In view of Galatians 2–3, the dispute concerns identity such that Paul accuses Peter of forcing "the Gentiles to live like Jews" (Galatians 2:14).

The Judaizers use honor manipulatively. Paul says, "They make much of you, but for no good purpose. They want to shut you out, that you may make much of them" (Galatians 4:17). He then adds, "It is those who want to make a good showing in the flesh who would force you to be circumcised, and only in order that they may not be persecuted for the cross of Christ" (Galatians 6:12). In the Galatian church, works of the law became a means of getting "face," signifying social inclusion and status.[1]

Why speak of boasting so differently in Romans 2 and 5? The implicit contrast highlights the unique boast of Christ's followers. Christ's resurrection demonstrates Christ's faithfulness even in death. Therefore, his followers rejoice in the hope of God's glory. Paul does not fixate on avoiding suffering; moreover, he even rejoices in

---

[1]Compare Philippians 3:2-6, where Jews by tradition are contrasted with those who "boast" in Christ, who has "surpassing worth." Compare 1 Thessalonians 2:19-20; Philippians 1:26; Hebrews 3:3, 6. In the LXX and extrabiblical literature, writers likewise equate "boasting" and "glory." See, for example, Psalm 97:6; 149:5; Jeremiah 13:11; 1 Chronicles 16:27; Sirach 11:4; 44:7; 48:4.

sufferings. For him, salvation is not relief from personal pain; rather, it is God's glory manifested among all nations.

We are saved *for glory*, not merely *from punishment*. Stressing the former has implications. What we hope in determines our willingness to pay the cost of discipleship. Paul's focus on the glory of God, not of people, enables him to rejoice even at the cost of following Christ, reflecting the glory of Christ's character. Disciples who boast in suffering aren't concerned about seeking honor from peers. Those with worldly perspectives cannot rejoice when shamed by people they want to please. They will not accept the suffering that produces Christlike endurance and character.

Some evangelistic presentations stress personal peace and otherworldly salvation rather than resurrection. They don't motivate steadfast suffering since they appeal most strongly to self-preservation, explaining salvation essentially as relief from suffering. We cannot boast in suffering when our fundamental hope is personal escape from pain.

In summary, we rejoice in worldly shame for the sake of divine glory because we are justified by Christ's resurrection (Romans 4:25). True glory and honor are found in Christ, not in the absence of pain. Salvation manifests in character, not mere comfort. The goal of Christian suffering is godly character and a purified hope. When believers have this perspective of honor and shame, lives are transformed in practical ways.

THE GLORY OF ISAIAH'S SUFFERING SERVANT

As Paul transitions to Romans 5, his subtle allusions to the servant figure in Isaiah frame the presentation that follows. The Lord's "servant" in Isaiah suffers but finally is vindicated with glory.[2] Interpreters widely acknowledged his reference to Isaiah 53 in Romans 4:25 ("handed over"). To my knowledge, only Sivonen highlights the echo of Isaiah 45:22-23 in Romans 5:1-2. He says of Isaiah 45, "In this eschatological passage, the *offspring* of Israel shall be *justified* and *glorified* in God because of the Servant: 'By the Lord shall they be justified [δικαιωθήσονται], and all the offspring of the sons of Israel shall be glorified [ἐνδοξασθήσονται] in God' (Isaiah 45:25 LXX NETS)."[3] In context, God is "righteous" (v. 21) and says "I am swearing an oath according to myself: Unless righteousness shall go forth from my mouth, my words shall not turn back, because every knee shall bend to me, and every tongue shall swear by God, saying, 'Righteousness and glory will come with him, and all who separate them will be shamed'" (vv. 24-25, LXX).

---

[2]See Isaiah 38-55, especially 42:1-4; 49:1-6; 50:4-9; 52:13–53:12.
[3]Mikko Sivonen, "The *Doxa* Motif in Paul." (PhD diss., University of Helsinki, 2018), 134. My emphasis. Paul directly quotes Isaiah 45:23 LXX in Romans 14:11. Others suggest Isaiah 32:17 LXX also lies in the backdrop of Romans 5:1.

Paul's appeal to the "servant" in this context is strategic. Isaiah provides a backdrop for understanding Paul's ironic juxtaposition of suffering and glory. Like Isaiah, Paul presents a paradoxical vision for how God displays his glory and righteousness through his people. Even Paul's use of *doulos* (slave/servant) appears to come from Isaiah. Except for Romans 6, Paul does not refer to all Christians as *douloi*. Yet, it is a common term for God's servant(s) in Isaiah. Thus, Sivonen's summary offers a preview of Paul's argument and ties together several themes in the coming chapters:

> Paul wanted his audience, Jews and Gentiles alike, to identify with the fallen Adam and with Israel, i.e. those who do not display the *doxa* of God due to idolatry. Paul then identifies Christ both as the intrinsic *doxa* of God, who represents God *and* the derivative *doxa* of God, namely the second Adam, the royal king, and the eschatological Servant. Thus, the Christ-event, his death, crucifixion and resurrection, inaugurates the vindication of *doxa* of God and the eschatological transformation of Adam (i.e. humanity), Israel, nations, and the entire creation. This change is not merely a return to humanity's original image and glory, but a metamorphosis into Christ's greater glory.[4]

WHY PAUL HOPES IN GOD'S GLORY

What is the hope of the "glory of God [which] does not put us to shame"? Paul refers to glory *from* God given at believers' resurrection. Adam lost this glory in death (Romans 3:23, 5:12). Because "all sinned," people give up the glory of "the *immortal* God" (Romans 1:23).[5] In salvation, people regain the glory and immortality of God (Romans 2:7; 8:20-21). As Sprinkle puts it, "Glorification, then, is a necessary qualification for membership in the future heavenly world."[6]

Paul looks forward to the incomparable "glory that is to be revealed to us," saying "the creation waits with eager longing for the revealing of the sons of God" (Romans 8:18-19). However, John Duncan gives an important qualification:

> The emphasis is not so much on the public uncovering of the previously veiled identity or status of the "children of God" as on the decisive eschatological manifestation of the divine glory that triumphs over Sin and Death through the appearance of glorified believers in their resurrected bodies alongside Christ at the παρουσία. Here, again,

---

[4]Sivonen, "The *Doxa* Motif in Paul," iv.

[5]Blackwell states, "If Adam's experience is in the background here, it is not *Adam's* glory that humans lack, but rather *God's* glory. Accordingly, the future experience of glory is not a return to Adam's glory but a participation in God's glory through Christ." Benjamin C. Blackwell, "Immortal Glory and the Problem of Death in Romans 3.23," *Journal for the Study of the New Testament* 32, no. 3 (2010): 291.

[6]Preston Sprinkle, "The Afterlife in Romans: Understanding Paul's Glory Motif in Light of the Apocalypse of Moses and 2 Baruch," in *LebendigeHoffnung–ewiger Tod?!: Jenseitsvorstellungen im Hellenismus, Judentum und Christentum* (ed. Manfred Lang and Michael Labhan; Arbeiten zur Bibel und ihrer Geschichte 24; Leipzig: EvangelischeVerlagsanstalt: 2007), 210.

believers are the conduit for the revelation of divine glory rather than the objects of revelation as such, and the rest of creation waits in breathless anticipation for this apocalyptic event.[7]

Christ's resurrection frees them from the shame of slavery to death (Romans 6:4; 8:11, 23). This hope is Paul's boast since it is the basis for glory and honor.

God's glory in Romans 5 is the glory given to people in Romans 8. Connecting the two, Haley Goranson Jacob writes that

> believers will *reign in life* through the one man, Jesus Christ. It is a point often over-looked. In Jesus, God will restore humanity to their originally created vocation; humanity will again have the honor associated with dominion; they will again share in the glory of God of Romans 5:2. . . . What replaces the reign of death is not life but those who receive God's abundant grace.[8]

Romans 8 develops 5:1-11. In both passages, one needs *patience* as we *hope* for *glory*. Paul appeals to the Spirit and justification. Believers are "children" or "heirs" of Abraham/God. Paul reminds readers of their love for God and his love for them to strengthen them through suffering and potential doubt. He points to the coming salvation because of Christ's death and resurrection.

We boast in what we glorify. Paul's boast "in the glory of God" in Romans 5:2 is rephrased simply as boasting "in God" in Romans 5:11. Similarly, Paul's opponents boast "in God" (Romans 2:17) and "in the law" (Romans 2:23). These restatements illustrate an important idea: a person's boast is one reason or source of honor.[9]

Whereas Paul seeks God's praise, his opponents use the law to seek human approval (Romans 2:29). Their boast depends on making comparisons that divide people into insiders and outsiders based on convention. They differ little from Greeks, who used comparison for the sake of self-praise.[10] By contrast, Christ creates a new standard of honor. Therefore, Paul seeks glory even while making deprecating comments about himself and other believers (using the words "weak," "ungodly," "sinners," and "enemies of God").

Our subjective glory entwines with our objective status before God or community. Thus, the subjective boasting of Romans 2 and 5 indicates whether one obtains the

---

[7]John Duncan, "The Hope of Creation: The Significance of ἐφ' ἐλπίδι (Rom 8.20c) in Context," *New Testament Studies* 61 (2015): 414-15.

[8]Haley Goranson Jacob, *Conformed to the Image of His Son: Reconsidering Paul's Theology of Glory in Romans* (Downers Grove, IL: IVP Academic, 2018), 117.

[9]Compare 1 Thessalonians 2:19-20; 2 Corinthians 8:23-24. Also, see Psalm 149:3-5 (LXX), where people's boasting in glory cannot be distinguishable from their rejoicing in their King. For extrabiblical examples, see Sirach 44:7; 48:4.

[10]Christopher Forbes, "Comparison, Self-Praise and Irony: Paul's Boasting and the Conventions of Hellenistic Rhetoric," *New Testament Studies* 32 (1986): 2-10.

objective glory of Romans 8. Only those who boast in God (not self or others) inherit the glory of God. And since believers hope for an objective glory, they do not boast in individual or sectarian distinctions. They seek to please God rather than peers.

Someone who boasts in social status does not grasp true glory. Paul's opponents narrowly measure worth by the glory and praise that comes from society. They cannot make sense of Paul's boasting about suffering with Christ. They do not perceive the incomparable worth of the glory to be revealed. Thus, "those who are in the flesh cannot please God" (Romans 8:8).

Paul desires the full manifestation of God's glory, not simply eternal life or resurrection. This includes our "adoption as sons," entailing the "redemption of our bodies" (Romans 8:23). God's children will no longer be separated by social barriers (Romans 2–4; 8; 12–14). Everyone will boast in Christ and receive God's commendation.

Christ's followers through resurrection seek vindication from the shame and suffering of death. The Holy Spirit enables them to honor one another in love (Romans 12:10-11; 13:7-8). They are free from the old self of Romans 6–7. Paul ultimately longs for the nations to "glorify God for his mercy" (Romans 15:9). In all these things, subjective and objective dimensions of glory are inextricably linked.

Romans 9:21-26

Has the potter no right over the clay, to make out of the same lump one vessel for honorable use and another for dishonorable use? [22] What if God, desiring to show his wrath and to make known his power, has endured with much patience vessels of wrath prepared for destruction, [23] in order to make known the riches of his glory for vessels of mercy, which he has prepared beforehand for glory— [24] even us whom he has called, not from the Jews only but also from the Gentiles?

[25] As indeed he says in Hosea, "Those who were not my people I will call 'my people,' and her who was not beloved I will call 'beloved.'" [26] "And in the very place where it was said to them, 'You are not my people,' there they will be called 'sons of the living God.'"

RICH IN THE FATHER'S GLORY

Romans 9:23-24 confirms the above reading of Romans 5. Given the prior context, the phrase "riches of his glory" in verse 23 refers to God's glory given to believers. Jacob observes, "The two terms, πλοῦτος ['riches'] and δόξα ['glory'], are brought together throughout the LXX (e.g., 1 Kings 3:13; Eccles 6:2; Psalm 3:4),"[11] such that 1 Chronicles 29:11-12 illustrates the background of Paul's words:

---

[11]Jacob, *Conformed to the Image*, 109.

Yours, O LORD, is the greatness and the power and the glory and the victory and the
majesty, for all that is in the heavens and in the earth is yours. Yours is the kingdom, O
LORD, and you are exalted as head above all. [12] Both *riches and honor* come from you,
and you rule over all. In your hand are power and might, and in your hand it is to make
great and to give strength to all.

This background accords with Jacob's earlier explanation of glory as "a person's honor
or status associated with his character, power, or wealth."[12]

Believers are "vessels of mercy" prepared "for glory." Paul's transition in verse 24
reflects his earlier pattern of thought. Glory is not rooted in group identity. God's
family is composed of all nations. God's calling does not depend on social standards
of worth (compare Romans 9:6-13). He gives grace as he wills (Romans 9:21). Thus, it
is by grace that God honors anyone.

Paul's reference to God's glory is less direct in Romans 6:4 than elsewhere. The
phrase "by [*dia*] the glory of the Father" puzzles commentators. The Father's glory
seemingly acts as an instrument or means that raises Christ from the dead. How does
glory relate to resurrection?

Romans 6:3-9

Do you not know that all of us who have been baptized into Christ Jesus were
baptized into his death? [4] We were buried therefore with him by baptism into
death, in order that, just as Christ was raised from the dead by the glory of the
Father, we too might walk in newness of life.

[5] For if we have been united with him in a death like his, we shall certainly be
united with him in a resurrection like his. [6] We know that our old self was crucified
with him in order that the body of sin might be brought to nothing, so that we
would no longer be enslaved to sin. [7] For one who has died has been set free from
sin. [8] Now if we have died with Christ, we believe that we will also live with him.
[9] We know that Christ, being raised from the dead, will never die again; death no
longer has dominion over him.

"The glory of the Father" reflects the meaning of "glory of God" in Romans 1:23;
3:23; 5:2; and 9:23.[13] That is, it is *glory from God*, which is given by the Spirit.[14] I'll

---

[12]Jacob, *Conformed to the Image*, 37.

[13]Others claim "the glory of the Father" refers to God's power (1 Corinthians 6:4; 15:43; 2 Corinthians 13:4;
Philippians 3:21; Ephesians 1:19-20). Similarly, the Spirit raises Christ. Recall Romans 1:4, where Christ is
"declared to be the *Son of God* in *power* according to the *Spirit* of holiness by *his resurrection from the dead*"
(compare Romans 8:11; Acts 10:38; 1 Tim 3:16). From this perspective, "the glory of the Father" would not be
equivalent to the "glory of God" as I've discussed thus far.

[14]Compare Donald Berry, *Glory in Romans and the Unified Purpose of God in Redemptive History* (Eugene, OR:
Pickwick, 2016), 90-95. He explains "glory" in 6:4, "It is the divine life and all that characterizes it—his very
character and nature—imparted by the Spirit to believers," 92-93.

summarize three lines of evidence. First, Romans 6:4 expresses the logic of 5:2. Both passages insert "glory" (of the father/God) between Christ's and our future resurrection. Having received the Spirit and because of Christ's resurrection, believers have hope of resurrected glory.

Second, "by the glory of the Father" foreshadows Romans 8. Both chapters link resurrection with glory and sonship. The same Spirit that resurrects our bodies enables us to cry, "Abba! Father!" (Romans 8:11, 15). God is only called "Father" in Romans 6:4; 8:15; and 15:6.

Third, Romans 7:6 says we "died to that which held us captive, so that we serve *in the new way of the Spirit* and not in the old way of the written code." The verse develops Romans 6:4, where Paul speaks of "walking in the newness of life." Thus, 6:4 describes the glory acquired through resurrection.

---

1 Corinthians 15:38-44

"But God gives it a body as he has chosen, and to each kind of seed its own body. [39] For not all flesh is the same, but there is one kind for humans, another for animals, another for birds, and another for fish. [40] There are heavenly bodies and earthly bodies, but the glory of the heavenly is of one kind, and the glory of the earthly is of another. [41] There is one glory of the sun, and another glory of the moon, and another glory of the stars; for star differs from star in glory.

[42] So is it with the resurrection of the dead. What is sown is perishable; what is raised is imperishable. [43] It is sown in dishonor; it is raised in glory. It is sown in weakness; it is raised in power. [44] It is sown a natural body; it is raised a spiritual body. If there is a natural body, there is also a spiritual body.

First Corinthians, like Romans, directly links resurrection, glory, and power. In 1 Corinthians 15:43, the body is raised in "glory" and "power." Paul contrasts the sowing of one body with the raising of another:[15]

It is sown in *dishonor* [*atimia*];
it is raised in *glory* [*doxa*].
It is sown in weakness;
it is raised in power.

The contrast of glory/power with dishonor/weakness shows 15:43 does not emphasize the instrument used to raise the body. Dishonor and weakness are not ways of sowing the perishable body. "Sowing" represents death, the quintessential

---

[15]It does not matter that Paul uses *en* (instead of *dia* as in Romans 6:4). Both prepositions can express how (that is, the means or manner) something happens. In fact, even within Romans, 6:4 uses *dia* with "glory," whereas 1:4 uses *en* with "power" (*dynamei*), yet both speak about how Christ was raised.

expression of dishonor and weakness. The "natural body" is "perishable," lacking inherent glory. Dishonor and weakness describe the condition of those like Adam, the "man of dust." "Dishonor" is emblematic of the sinful condition (Romans 1:24, 26-27; 2:23; 6:21). It is both sin's cause and consequence. Death inherently implies people experience a state of dishonor and weakness. If one regards dishonor and weakness as a type of (pre)condition for death, then we might say they are a means or passageway to death. In 15:43, glory and power are not instruments for raising the imperishable body. Paul simply contrasts different "kinds" of glory that suit certain types of bodies.

The "glory of the Father" in Romans 6:4 refers to the state into or with which Christ is raised.[16] The "by" (*dia*) primarily indicates the attending circumstance of the resurrection.[17] His resurrection manifests God's glory. He is raised with or into a state of glory. Given Romans 6:6; 7:6; and 13:14, Romans 6:4 essentially means Christ puts on the Father's glory.[18] The Father's child has an inherent right to such glory.

The "glory of the Father" is for the sake of our resurrection. By this glory, "we too might walk in newness of life." Paul seems to mean a believer's transformed life (Romans 7:6; 8:4-13). Notice how Romans 6:5 supports 6:4, "For if we have been united with him in a death like his, *we shall certainly be united with him in a resur-rection like his*" (compare Romans 6:8). Paul immediately refers to physical resurrection. Both ideas are woven into Romans 6:3-13. Because we will be physically resurrected, death no longer reigns; therefore, Paul says, "reckon yourselves dead to sin" such that "the life he lives he lives for God" (6:9-11). Accordingly, glory accom-panies Christ's resurrection *and* ours.[19]

Romans 6 begins to elaborate more fully on the significance of God's glory in Romans 5–8. The glory of God's children holistically refers to their "reigning" with Christ (compare Romans 5:17). Jacob says, "To be glorified is to experience a

---

[16]By analogy, consider the sentence: "It was *by wearing the wedding dress* that she realized how much she loved her future husband." The action "wearing the wedding dress" is the circumstance with which she comes to the realization. Although a "means," wearing the dress is not an instrument she intentionally uses to ac-complish some goal (for example, as when a carpenter uses a hammer to build a house). In the same way, "by the glory of the Father" does not indicate that God used his glory as an instrument or tool to raise Christ. Yet, the Father's glorification of Christ is the process through which Christ is resurrected to reign.

[17]While *dia* with a genitive does not typically indicate attendant circumstance, it is unusually frequent in Romans, as in Romans 2:27; 4:11; 8:25; 14:20. In such instances and when Paul combines *dia* and *doxa* (as in 2 Corinthians 3:11; 6:8), *dia* conveys "with" or "having."

[18]"Putting on" imagery is most explicit in Ephesians 4:22, 24; Colossians 2:11-12; 3:9-10. However, these verses also resonate with Romans 6:6; 7:6; and 13:14. Their contexts are strikingly similar and mention the resur-rection (as in Romans 6). Accordingly, "the glory of the Father" could parallel the "new self."

[19]Outside of Paul's letters, John 12:16; Acts 3:13; and 1 Peter 1:21 state that God glorified Christ at his resurrection.

transformation of status—to be exalted to a new status, one of honor associated with a representative reign over creation, crowned with glory and honor as Adam was meant to be and as the Messiah now is."[20] Romans 6:4-8 most clearly expresses what Jacob calls humanity's "vocational participation." That is, believers, through union with Christ, "fulfill their vocation as redeemed humans, representing God to his creation and interceding on behalf of creation to God."[21]

WHY PAUL HOPES IN GOD'S GLORY

The very nature of salvation gives reasons why "hope does not put us to shame" (Romans 5:5). In this section, we'll first look at some "subjective" blessings of salvation. "Subjective" describes those blessings *within* people, like a new heart. Paul radically overturns conventional views about what is praiseworthy and shameful, and thus what determines collective identity. Christ's followers are enabled to honor God with their lives. They are no longer slaves to shameful desires and behaviors.

Second, we'll consider reasons why salvation is "objective" and future-oriented (Romans 5:9, 10; 10:9). These aspects of salvation inform the present Christian life, which is full of suffering and reproach. This is the path of salvation for God's people. Like Christ, believers too find glory through shame.

Subjectively, Paul says "hope does not put us to shame, because God's love has been poured into our hearts through the Holy Spirit who has been given to us" (Romans 5:5).[22] The Greek phrase for "God's love" has one of two possible meanings: God's love for us or our love for God. The context suggests the latter, since speaking of "God's love for us" being *in* our hearts makes little sense. Love for others only exists *within the heart* of the person who possesses the love. Paul's verb choice, "pour" (*ekcheō*), confirms this. Joel 2:28-29 LXX twice uses this verb:

> And it shall come to pass afterward, that *I will pour out my Spirit* on all flesh; your sons and your daughters shall prophesy, your old men shall dream dreams, and your young men shall see visions. Even on the male and female servants in those days *I will pour out my Spirit*. (Compare Ezekiel 39:29; Zechariah 12:10; Acts 2:17-18)

Love for God is the effect of God pouring out his Spirit.

When Paul mentions the Spirit in Romans, he emphasizes that the Spirit's ministry includes *changing hearts* (Romans 2:29; 7:6; 8:4-16).[23] In this, Paul recalls the new

---

[20]Jacob, *Conformed to the Image*, 121.

[21]Jacob, *Conformed to the Image*, 122.

[22]Compare Romans 6:17; perhaps 8:6-8.

[23]Robert Jewett and Roy D. Kotansky, *Romans: A Commentary*, ed. Eldon J. Epp (Minneapolis: Fortress, 2007), 356, notes parallel language in Galatians 4:6, "sent the Spirit of His Son into our hearts." Compare 2 Corinthians 1:22; 4:6.

covenant (Jeremiah 31:31; 32:40; Ezekiel 36:16-27) as he often highlights the fruit of the new covenant (Romans 2:15; 6:17; 7:6).[24]

When the Spirit changes hearts, he transforms people's fundamental sense of honor and worth. Accordingly, Paul celebrates those whose "circumcision is a matter of the heart, by the Spirit, not by the letter," and so their "praise is not from man but from God" (Romans 2:29). They do not "boast in the law" (Romans 2:23). Such transformation yields hope since we see the new covenant bearing fruit in our lives for God's glory.

A changed heart brings a changed identity. This has practical ramifications for God's people. They have a new allegiance. God's children please him (Romans 8:7-14). They have a new hope: being glorified with Christ (Romans 8:18), an incomparable glory to be revealed (Romans 8:19), "the freedom of the glory of the children of God" (Romans 8:21). Being unified with Christ, sin is no longer their master (Romans 6:5-11). Believers are free to obey from the heart (Romans 6:17). They are not enslaved to "the things of which you are now ashamed" (Romans 6:21). Reminiscent of Romans 5:2-5, Paul naturally concludes that "those who love God" expect glorification (Romans 8:28, 30).

Objectively, Paul's hope is rooted in Christ's death and resurrection (Romans 5:6-11). After explaining how grace secures the hope of glory, he presents Christ's death to magnify our unworthiness to receive God's grace. Paul describes humanity's shameful condition with increasing intensity. Without Christ, we are "weak," "sinners," and even "enemies" of God. Against this backdrop, Paul spotlights how "God shows his love for us" to demonstrate the incongruity of grace. That is, God's grace in Christ is given "without regard for the worth of the recipient."[25]

Once again, Paul's "outsider" language is noteworthy. Paul is willing to use shame-inducing, outsider designations. He describes believers prior to following Christ, calling them "weak," "sinners," and "enemies" of God. Not only Paul, but all Christ followers are reckoned as "slaves/servants" (Romans 1:1; 6:15-22). We can summarize Paul's perspective using East Asian language: God's people are willing to "lose face" in order to give God "face."

Romans 5:6-11

For while we were still weak, at the right time Christ died for the ungodly. [7] For one will scarcely die for a righteous person—though perhaps for a good person one would dare even to die— [8] but God shows his love for us in that while we were

---

[24]This reading is not surprising. The Spirit is reason for confidence in Ephesians 1:14, where the Holy Spirit "is the *guarantee of our inheritance* until we acquire possession of it, to the praise of his glory."
[25]John Barclay, *Paul and the Gift* (Grand Rapids: Eerdmans, 2015), 73.

still sinners, Christ died for us.[9] Since, therefore, we have now been justified by his blood, much more shall we be saved by him from the wrath of God.[10] For if while we were enemies we were reconciled to God by the death of his Son, much more, now that we are reconciled, shall we be saved by his life.[11] More than that, we also rejoice in God through our Lord Jesus Christ, through whom we have now received reconciliation.

People in honor-shame cultures carefully maintain good relationships, especially with authorities. When relationships are broken, reconciliation is difficult. All parties lose face in a broken relationship, either for causing the breach or being unable to maintain relational harmony.[26] Accordingly, the gravity of human shame is unmistakable: we need salvation from God's wrath (Romans 5:9).

As a result, the fact that "we were reconciled to God by the death of his Son" is striking. Three times, Paul reemphasizes reconciliation, not to mention how God achieves it. In traditional honor-shame cultures, the most important relationships stem from bloodline. Since sons carry the family name, fathers typically treasure sons above other relationships. To lose one's son threatens the family's honor. Yet God shockingly initiates reconciliation by giving his son to restore relationship with his enemies. Paul's words cannot but foster a healthy sense of shame for how people have dishonored God.

We should not underemphasize the necessary link between a changed heart and reconciliation by only seeing reconciliation in legal terms. It is unthinkable that reconciliation can occur without transforming people's hearts such that they seek God's face. Without love for God, they do not glorify him. Instead, they continue to honor creation and tradition above the Creator.

How people seek God matters. Paul reorients the claim of Jews who seemingly "boast in God" but in fact dishonor him (Romans 2:17, 23). The honor God seeks from people is neither superficial nor tied to cultural traditions. The Spirit changes hearts so that "we also boast in God *through* our Lord Jesus Christ" (Romans 5:11). Paradoxically, it is only by Christ's shameful death that we honor God. Paul explicitly states his reason for boasting is *in Christ* (Romans 15:17).

SUFFERING DOES NOT PUT US TO SHAME

Because hope does not put us to shame, Paul boasts in suffering. How is this possible since suffering entails some degree of shame? Paul refers to shame that inevitably

---

[26]Concerning reconciliation in honor-shame contexts, see Jackson W., *Saving God's Face: A Chinese Contextualization of Salvation Through Honor and Shame* (Pasadena, CA: William Carey International University Press, 2013), 168-70.

comes when people hope in a wrong person or cause. In war, for example, the consequences are severe for placing hope in the wrong king. From this perspective, one's
perceived social value or status partly depends on what one hopes in.

The prophets reminded Israel that idolaters are put to shame because they follow
lifeless objects of wood or stone.[27] They chastised those who trusted in idols to save
them from defeat or exile. Ultimately, people share the status of their functional
saviors like money, jobs, or relationships. These "saviors" promise glory and honor.
However, they not only disappoint; they destroy people through a guise of hope. Being
"put to shame" alludes to punishment or pending suffering, not merely psychology.[28]
In short, those without faith will be ashamed because they will be put to shame.

By contrast, justification yields a paradoxical hope for the Christian. The same hope
that enables people to suffer for divine glory is also the hope that leads to worldly
shame. Belonging to Christ brings tremendous social shame and dishonor (2 Corinthians 6:8; 1 Thessalonians 2:2). Nevertheless, Paul endures dishonor because such
"momentary affliction is preparing for us an eternal weight of glory beyond all comparison" (2 Corinthians 4:17; compare Romans 8:17-18). Paul is not ashamed of the
gospel because he knows his hope will be vindicated.

Paul's hope is practical. He does not merely hope despite suffering. He suffers *because* of hope in the glory of God. Christ's followers ultimately attain their hope
through his suffering. Paul highlights this pattern in Romans 4:24-25: "[Righteousness]
will be counted to us who believe in him who raised from the dead Jesus our Lord,
who was delivered up for our trespasses and raised for our justification." Christ's death
and resurrection typify how God's people are saved. Like him, his people are honored
through shame.

The phrase "honored through shame" entails two ideas:

1. God uses shame for glory

2. God (and we) regard shame as glory

The second idea depends on the first. God in Christ uses what the world regards as
"shameful" for glory's sake. Christ's crucifixion is the quintessential example (compare
1 Corinthians 1:26-31). God transforms his people's honor-shame perspective. Humility becomes a virtue. Service and suffering for Christ's name bring everlasting glory
(Romans 8:17-18).

God's people are saved *through shame.* Israel's history illustrates this point. Israel's
exodus frames the story of Christ saving humanity from slavery through shame to the

---

[27]For example, Psalm 97:7; Isaiah 44:9; 45:16; Jeremiah 51:17; Hosea 10:6.
[28]The next chapter discusses what it means (not) to "be put to shame." In Romans, Paul doesn't linger on
punishment, though he gives clear warning in Romans 2:8-9 (compare 1:18ff; 3:5b; 5:9).

freedom of glory.[29] In the exodus, we see the beginning of a pattern that marks Israel's history.

Israel was honored through shame. They first suffer the shame of slavery before enjoying the glory of redemption. Israel later rebels against the Lord and is cast into exile. But God would bring them through exile to the hope of God's glory (compare Isaiah 58:8; 60:19; 62:2; Habakkuk 2:14; Haggai 2:7, 9). This narrative thread underlies Romans 5–8, which demonstrates a key idea: *Christ was honored through shame; therefore, God's people will be honored through shame.*

JUSTIFIED THROUGH SHAME

Using this Old Testament framework, we see why God's people in Romans 6–8 embody the pattern found in Romans 4:25. Just as Christ is glorified through shame for our justification, so we are glorified through shame because of our justification. Paul says, "For one who has died has been *justified* [*dedikaiōtai*] from sin" (6:7, my translation). This reference to justification recalls "our justification" in 4:25. Romans 6:4-7 explains how Christ "was raised for our justification."

Justification is a type of "new exodus." Paul, like the prophets, evokes the exodus to show how God ultimately "justifies" his people from exile.[30] At that time, a Davidic king will manifest the Lord's righteousness. Isaiah uses justification language to describe Israel being redeemed from exile (for example, Isaiah 50:8; 53:11).[31]

Accordingly, Romans 6–8 explains our justification. By resurrecting his son (Romans 6:4), God "justifies" Christ as he did Israel, whom he calls "my firstborn son" (Exodus 4:22; compare Jeremiah 31:9; Hosea 11:1). God vindicates Christ from the shameful injustice inflicted by sin. In the resurrection, God glorifies Christ. Likewise, Christ's resurrection "justifies" God's people. All who are "in Christ" are redeemed from the shame of slavery to sin. However, they still wait for the "redemption of our bodies," the promised hope of glory (Romans 8:23-25).

The parallel between Christ's resurrection, justification, and a glorified body is significant. Christ's resurrection is his justification (compare 1 Timothy 3:16; Romans 1:4). Based on Romans 4:25, *his* resurrection *also is* our resurrection because

---

[29]Compare N. T. Wright, "New Exodus, New Inheritance: The Narrative Substructure of Romans 3–8," in *Romans and the People of God: Essays in Honor of Gordon D. Fee on the Occasion of His 65th Birthday*, ed. Sven K. Soderlund and N. T. Wright (Grand Rapids: Eerdmans, 1999), 26-35; Frank Thielman, "The Story of Israel and the Theology of Romans 5–8," in *Pauline Theology Volume IV: Looking Back, Pressing On*, ed. E. Elizabeth Johnson and David M. Hay (Atlanta: Scholars Press, 1997), 169-95; Sylvia Keesmat, *Paul and His Story: (Re)Interpreting the Exodus Tradition* (Sheffield: Sheffield University Press, 1999), 54-153.

[30]N. T. Wright, "Letter to the Romans," in *The New Interpreter's Bible* (Nashville: Abingdon, 2002), 510, mentions: Isaiah 11:11; 35:3-10; 51:9-11; 52:4-6; Jeremiah 16:14-15; 23:7-8; Ezekiel 20:33-38; Hosea 2:14-23.

[31]Tom Holland, *Romans: The Divine Marriage* (Eugene, OR: Pickwick, 2011), 91.

we are "in Christ" (Romans 6). Elsewhere, "resurrection" is tantamount to glorification (Romans 6:4; 1 Corinthians 15:43; Acts 3:13; John 21:19; 1 Peter 1:21, which also
mentions "hope"; Philippians 3:21).

Where do Christ's followers fit within this narrative? As God's children, they are
led by his Spirit just as when Israel sojourned through the wilderness (Romans 8:14).[32]
God's Spirit dwells among his people just as the glory cloud filled the tabernacle.[33]
Wright summarizes, "*What the one God of Israel had done in the Exodus narrative, and
had promised to do himself at the eschaton, Paul sees being accomplished by the spirit.*"[34]
This perspective is akin to 2 Corinthians 5:1-5, where Paul presents believers as wan-
dering Israelites, groaning in tents yet given the Spirit as a guarantee of life. The "tent"
(*skēnos*) in 2 Corinthians 5:1, 4 echoes related Old Testament terms that refer to the
"tabernacle" (*skēnē*) and "booths" (*skēnopēgia*).

Therefore, Paul echoes the prophets' plea to the exiles to persevere through hardship.[35] His readers ought not to be like the exiles who are content in Babylon. Like
Israel in the wilderness and then in exile, readers are encouraged by this message:
those who remain faithful will not be put to shame.

Christ's followers are sojourners, exiles, outsiders, and foreigners. They lack the
social honor afforded those whom the world regards as "insiders." Having renounced
the kingship of their former master, sin, they are viewed with scorn and distrust. They
seek the glory of another king. Therefore, disgrace and reproach are a normal part of
life for such traitorous vagabonds.

From this perspective, we grasp why Christ's followers are honored *through* shame.
Suffering is a necessary means of expressing loyalty to Christ. Those belonging to
Christ will be vindicated. Therefore, Paul reminds them of this hope in Romans 5:2-5.
Because of hope, Christ's followers willingly suffer the world's reproach. Romans
8:35-37 clarifies the type of suffering mentioned in 5:2-5:

> Who shall separate us from the love of Christ? Shall tribulation, or distress, or perse-
> cution, or famine, or nakedness, or danger, or sword? As it is written, "For your sake we
> are being killed all the day long; we are regarded as sheep to be slaughtered." No, in all
> these things we are more than conquerors through him who loved us.

---

[32]For the Spirit's relationship to the "new exodus," see N. T. Wright, *Paul and the Faithfulness of God*, vol. 1
(Minneapolis: Fortress, 2013), 717-27.

[33]Compare Exodus 25:8; 29:45; 33:19; 40:33-35; Leviticus 26:11. Similar exodus imagery applies to the exiles in
Isaiah 4:5-6.

[34]Wright, *Paul and the Faithfulness of God*, 721.

[35]The prophets used "new exodus" language to describe the restoration of God's people from exile. Wright
characterizes Paul's message in this way: "Adam's race, like Israel itself, has been in exile; Jesus has drawn
that exile on to himself. [Referring to Rom 5–8], Paul is telling the Jewish story as the true-Adam story."
See N. T. Wright, "Romans and the Theology of Paul," in *Pauline Perspectives: Essays on Paul, 1978–2013*
(Minneapolis: Fortress, 2013), 108.

Paul does not talk about ordinary human pain and weakness. The suffering of Romans 5:3-4 is distinctly Christian in that God's people suffer *for* Christ's sake.

Christian suffering has a purpose. God's children are "fellow heirs with Christ, provided *we suffer with him in order that we may also be glorified with him.* For I consider that the sufferings of this present time are not worth comparing with the glory that is to be revealed to us" (Romans 8:17-18). In hard times, God's people simply want to know, "Is it worth it? Will I be vindicated from my shame and suffering?" To persevere, they need to know the coming glory.

Christ's followers are also "honored through shame" in another sense. People typically associate weakness with dishonor and shame, not honor and glory.[36] Those seeking their own glory deny or hide signs of weakness. Consequently, they are unable to boast in the hope of the glory of God. Such hope requires humility to acknowledge weakness.

This is precisely the concession we find in Romans. Paul cries out, "Wretched man that I am! Who will deliver me from this body of death?" (Romans 7:24). Romans 8:19-25 mentions an implicit condition to Christians' hope of glory. The believers' groans testify that confessing their shameful state precedes the glory that comes when they are free from corruption.

REDIRECT THE PURSUIT OF PRAISE

How should this "hope of the glory of God" influence our lives? First, Romans should transform our view of what is worthy of honor or shame. This fresh perspective ought to shape our entire life. What or who do we see as honorable and praiseworthy? On what do we base our reputations? Whose approval do we seek?

Paul does not say *hope in general* will not put us to shame. He specifically refers to the hope of the glory of God. The glory of God that believers inherit entails a new identity with practical connotations. Interpreting Romans 8, N. T. Wright says, "the glory of God's children' refers to the glorious rule or 'reign' of God's children, as in 5:17. . . . What Paul is speaking of is precisely the freedom that will come to the whole cosmos when God's children are 'glorified,' that is, 'reigning.'"[37]

God's people can seek glory because they already have glory. Believers now *"share in the exalted status with Christ in his rule over creation, having received the crown of glory originally given to Adam in their coglorification with Christ, the new Adam."*[38] The hope that believers have should inspire action, not passivity.

---

[36]Compare 1 Corinthians 1:27; 4:10; 15:43; 2 Corinthians 11:21.

[37]Wright, *Paul and the Faithfulness of God*, 488.

[38]Jacob, *Conformed to the Image*, 84.

This new identity redirects the believer's search for glory. Everyone desires some type of honor, glory, or acceptance. No one wants shame or rejection. Professional athletes and actors enjoy one kind of glory; humanitarians enjoy another. The type of "face" we seek determines life's most important decisions, whether about relationships, jobs, or spending habits. The chase for face can transform trivial matters into issues of consequence. What people wear, how they speak, where they eat, and with whom they converse are common ways people express a desire to please others and win approval.

Idolatry is rooted *not* in the *search* for honor but in the *source* of one's glory. Worldly honor is circumstantial and superficial. Within all human cultures, people seek "face" but their hopes are fleeting. Ancient Romans and Greeks boasted in culture, wealth, and social position. Yet both civilizations perished. Idols do not satisfy the deep desire for *lasting* honor.

Paul exhorts readers to pursue praise from God. By honoring God, we become honorable. Our identity and sense of worth largely depend on what (or whom) we most glorify. By linking glory to the resurrection, Paul urges us to consider the long-term implications of seeking glory in one thing versus another. Do we seek the face of the immortal God? What is our hope of glory?

RETHINK GLORY AND HONOR

Honor and glory are important theological categories, not merely social categories. Paul explains sin and salvation via honor and shame. Salvation depends on our seeking honor and glory (Romans 2:7). They are God's reward for the righteous.

Honor-shame language describes objective realities. Dishonoring God is another way of not giving him glory. Yet God is glorious even if humans do not praise him. God's inherent worth does not change if rebellious sinners refuse to glorify him. Likewise, honor from the Father endures forever. Recognizing this point relativizes the worth of social glory.

Speaking about honor-glory from a theological perspective doesn't deny the important contributions of non-theologians in the area of honor-shame. Theologians glean much insight from anthropologists, psychologists, and others.[39] More work needs to be done to integrate research from across cultures and academic disciplines.[40]

---

[39]For example, David deSilva, *The Hope of Glory: Honor Discourse and New Testament Interpretation* (Collegeville, MN: Liturgical Press, 1999). Curt Thompson integrates shame, theology, and psychology in *The Soul of Shame: Retelling the Stories We Believe About Ourselves* (Downers Grove, IL: InterVarsity Press, 2015).
[40]For an initial proposal, see Jackson W., "Have Theologians No Sense of Shame?" *Themelios* 43, no. 2 (2018): 205-19.

WE BECOME WHAT WE GLORIFY

What we boast in reveals what we deem praiseworthy. Therefore, boasting signals our fundamental sense of identity. Whereas Greeks boasted in wisdom, others boast in education, wealth, or position.

Boasting is often expressed symbolically. Flags and monuments mark national pride. Clothing, ceremonies, degrees, and various behaviors reflect our identity and implicit value system. More subtle examples include how do we spend our time or what subjects most interest us. We locate badges of honor in how many children we have, our marriage status, maintaining a clean home, sexuality, even busyness. Because we boast or rejoice in things we value, our "boast" shows our desired sense of identity. Practically, what do we and others want to be known for? Who do they most admire?

Paul urges the Roman Christians to reassess their reasons for boasting. Boasting is not inherently bad, though *why* we boast is important. Our reasons for boasting can divide people into countless social groups based on important but secondary criteria.

Paul wants readers to boast in Christ. Those giving allegiance to Christ boast in him. Other social markers no longer determine one's fundamental identity. Paul distinguishes two groups—those who boast in Christ and those who do not. Christ unites people across the social spectrum.

RECONSIDER CONTEXTUALIZATION AND RESURRECTION

Paul's honor-shame language equips the church to meaningfully communicate the message of salvation. What are a culture's most relevant terms, stories, and idioms? How do we talk about social status and worth? To contextualize the biblical message, we need to discern ways people gain honor and avoid shame.

Christ's resurrection grounds Paul's hope of glory. Glorification is inextricably tied to a future, bodily resurrection. This is important for evangelism. Christ's resurrection overcomes the worst kinds of shame, namely sin and death. Because the resurrection marks Christ's royal victory, it clarifies what is central to gospel preaching: Jesus is king. He commands our allegiance. Our identity is determined by our relationship to him.

Christ's resurrection also highlights the importance of the physical world. The significance of this fact cannot be underestimated given the practical orientation of honor-shame contexts. The gospel transforms our present lives. The resurrection reinforces a holistic worldview whereby God enters our world and does not remain distant in a "spiritual" realm.

FROM PERSPECTIVE TO PRACTICE

An honor-shame perspective expands traditional Western views of salvation. While there is no contradiction between honor-shame and law-oriented explanations of salvation, different emphases come into focus when reading Scripture with Eastern eyes.

To gain an honor-shame perspective of salvation, some readers might need to reorient how they think about "being saved." Salvation concerns both what we're saved *from* and what we're saved *for*. Many people think almost exclusively in terms of the former. We are saved from wrath, punishment, condemnation, and hell. Though a glorious truth, it is a partial truth. Romans 5–8 also tells us what we are saved for. Jacob concludes her study of Romans in this way:

> What is the goal of salvation? For too long, scholars and laymen alike have myopically viewed justification and salvation as ends in themselves, whether for the benefit of the individual or of the incorporative body of Christ. The goal of salvation is believers' conformity to the Son of God—their participation in his rule over creation as God's eschatological family and as renewed humanity—but only and always with the purpose of extending God's hand of mercy, love, and care to his wider creation. This was humanity's job in the beginning; it will be believers' responsibility and honor in the future; it is God's purpose in calling his people in the present.[41]

Perhaps this myopic view of salvation is a natural consequence of stressing legal metaphors at the expense of honor-shame themes. If we take more seriously the law's covenantal nature, we'll avoid much of this problem. People commonly speak of the Mosaic law as mere "law," like that in modern courtrooms. Courtroom judges assess guilt or innocence, thus what someone will eventually do if they are set free is beyond the judge's purview. When reading Romans through a narrower legal (not regal) lens, we overwhelmingly tend to focus on what we are saved from rather than what we are saved for.

A fundamental effect of the gospel is *worldview transformation*.[42] To transform people's worldviews, the gospel message should challenge conventional notions of honor and shame. The goal of gospel preaching is not merely to convince people they are sinners and Christ can save them after they die. Such presentations sound more abstract than practical. A change in doctrine does not necessarily lead to worldview transformation. Without a transformed worldview, people might become mere religious "converts," not disciples. Many so-called converts do not have true faith because Christ has not fundamentally reoriented their worldview, particularly their basic honor-shame perspective.

---

[41]Jacob, *Conformed to the Image*, 263.
[42]An exceptional exposition on this topic is Peter Leithart, *Delivered from the Elements of the World: Atonement, Justification, Mission* (Downers Grove, IL: IVP Academic, 2016), especially 216-81.

God's people are saved *from shame* and *for glory*. Before Christ's coming, they were slaves to sin, whose wage is death. They lived "in Adam" in ways that bring shame. Even when God gives his good law, it exposes their powerlessness. On the other hand, those who are "in Christ" do not suffer the disgrace that comes with divine condemnation. Because of Christ's death and resurrection, God's people are freed from sin and death. They have fundamentally new identities. The "old self" has died, and their "new self" is a "slave of God" (Romans 6:22). In practice, this means they "become obedient *from the heart*" and so walk according to the Spirit (Romans 6:17). Their transformed lives demonstrate they are "led by the Spirit of God [and so] are sons of God" (Romans 8:14).

In short, those who follow Christ gain a new family and the power to live in ways that honor God their Father. In this age, the Spirit transforms their honor-shame perspective. In the coming age, God's children will inherit the glory they lacked due to sin.

With an honor-shame lens, we discern how various aspects of salvation form an integrated whole. Paul does not limit himself to a narrow set of legal metaphors nor does he give a systematic soteriology. His thinking is more practical than abstract. It focuses on identity, not merely destiny. An honor-shame perspective reminds us that salvation is more than a spiritual transaction. It brings transformation. Because of Christ, his people will not be put to shame. God's creation will reflect the Creator's glory.

9

SHAMED *from* BIRTH?
(ROMANS 7)

R omans 7 has found a home in popular Christian teaching, especially when talking about the "sinful nature."[1] Accordingly, Romans 7 shapes how many people understand humility. Andrew Murray says in his book *Humility*, "This is the true self-denial to which our Savior calls us: the acknowledgment that self has nothing good in it, except as an empty vessel which God must fill."[2] Another writer claims, "To be truly humble means that you know there is nothing good in you, in your nature."[3] Christian worship group Hillsong sings these lyrics: "You are good. You are good. When there's nothing good in me."[4]

Does Paul teach there is "nothing good" in us? John MacArthur's interpretation of Romans 7 reflects the view of many, saying that Paul is "speaking about a believer. This person desires to obey God's law and hates sin (7:15, 19, 21). He is humble, recognizing that nothing good dwells in his humanness (7:18)."[5] Another writer agrees: "As a believer, I know there is nothing good in me, for I have a fallen nature."[6] This perspective extends well into Christian history. For example, in his *Institutes* John Calvin quotes with approval John Chrysostom, who said "that every man is not only naturally a sinner, but is wholly sin."[7]

How are listeners likely to respond to these comments about our nature? With guilt or shame? Humility or humiliation? Although Romans 7 lacks explicit honor-shame language, its influence on Christian psychology and evangelism is unmistakable. Many Western Christians generally agree that humans are born evil and so have a "sin nature."

---

[1]"Sinful nature" is the NIV's translation of *sarx*, the Greek word for "flesh," in Romans 7:18, 25.

[2]Andrew Murray, *Humility: The Beauty of Holiness* (Brisbane: Ichthus Publications, 2014), 15.

[3]Tom Steward, *True Mind: How Truth Can Change What You Believe and How You Live* (Bloomington, IN: Westbow, 2001), 138.

[4]Hillsong, "Forever Reign," written by Jason Ingram and Ruben Morgan. Sony/ATV Music Publishing.

[5]John MacArthur, *The MacArthur Daily Bible: Read the Bible in One Year, with Notes from John MacArthur* (Nashville: Thomas Nelson, 2003), 791.

[6]Jack Watts and Robert S. McGee, *Recovering from Religious Abuse: 11 Steps to Spiritual Freedom* (New York: Simon and Schuster, 2012), 212.

[7]John Calvin, *Institutes of the Christian Religion*, ed. Anthony Uyi, trans. Henry Beveridge (Woodstock, Ontario: Devoted Publishing, 2016), 117.

This popular Western teaching contradicts the assumptions of countless East Asians, and many foreign missionaries regard the apparent tension as an obstacle to East Asians following Christ. Confucian cultures typically claim humans are born good; they do not accept people are evil from birth. However, the two views share an interesting commonality: People holding these perspectives tend to use similar arguments to prove their point. Citing texts like Romans 3:10, Western Christians say, "Everyone does bad," and conclude all people are born sinful. Similarly, East Asians assert, "Everyone does good," then claim human nature is good.[8]

Debates about Romans 7 look similar. Interpreters use the same passage to make contradictory claims about human nature. Some say Paul paints a desperate picture of humanity, unable to do what is good because of a sin nature. Others highlight Paul's many optimistic statements about the man who "delights in the law of God" (Romans 7:22).

What then does Romans 7 contribute to our understanding of human nature and the Christian life? Some scholars suggest traditional views reflect the "introspective conscience" of Western theologians like Augustine and Luther more than Paul.[9] Accordingly, interpreters mistake Paul's message by overemphasizing an individual's struggle with guilt feelings. This reading effectively sets aside Paul's collectivistic categories in favor of individualism. Paul's singular focus becomes the individual, not law and sin.

In this chapter I hope to offer a nuanced reading of Romans 7, arguing that Paul does not prioritize the individual and guilt. In fact, doing so can breed shame that is harmful. When read with Eastern eyes, Romans 7 offers a more optimistic view of humanity than is often assumed. If this is true, Paul's perspective mitigates the apparent gap between Western and Eastern views of human nature. Furthermore, this reading preserves a focus on collective identity that is consistent with Paul's broader argument. Finally, we'll consider how this interpretation applies to various theological, cultural, and psychological issues.

HOW DOES THE LAW SHAPE OUR IDENTITY?

Romans 7 fuels speculation about various subjects, including theology, psychology, and anthropology. Readers particularly struggle to discern the meaning of the "I" on whom Paul focuses in 7:7-25. If "I" refers to Paul himself, does he describe the period before or after his becoming a Christian? Some think Paul uses the "I" to speak of a

---

[8]Of course, these are highly simplified summaries. Both groups acknowledge that no one is entirely good or bad, whether by being perfect or doing every evil possible.
[9]Krister Stendahl, "Paul and the Introspective Conscience of the West," *Harvard Theological Review* 56, no. 3 (1963): 199-215.

larger group of people, like Israel, who found themselves powerless to obey God's commands.[10] These options are not mutually exclusive, since Paul could use himself to typify all Jews who lived under the law.

What is clear, however, is that Romans 7 draws inferences from previous chapters. The transition "or" in 7:1 indicates that Paul continues to discuss the interrelationship between the law, sin, life, and death from Romans 6. Accordingly, interpretations of Romans 7 should reflect continuity with Romans 6 and 8. Just as honor-shame shapes the surrounding context, so also we should expect Romans 7 to yield insights related to honor-shame.

At first glance, Romans 7 says little about honor-shame. So far, Paul has largely focused attention on collective identity. However, his extensive use of the first person in Romans 7 raises the question whether Paul now speaks about individuals. He has emphasized the law's covenantal nature and implications concerning ethnic identity, yet Paul now seems to lay stress on the ethical force of the law. To find an answer, we should consider not only what Paul says but what he *does*. The passage serves a distinct function in the flow of Romans 5–8. Once we identify Paul's purpose in the chapter, we then can explore its potential implications.

When reading Romans 7 through an honor-shame lens, an important question emerges: How does the law shape our understanding of identity? We must trace Paul's argument to find an answer. After defending the law's goodness, his next step jolts readers. With surprising vigor, Paul vindicates the "I" and condemns sin, the personified slave master from Romans 5–6. With little qualification, Paul lays blame forcefully on sin, *not* the "I" who commits sinful actions (Romans 7:17-20). Eventually, Paul even says God condemns sin, not the sinner. Accordingly, we will consider Paul's argument and its implications for how we see ourselves and others.

NOT "I" BUT "WE"

When Paul uses "I" in Romans 7:7-25, he does not speak autobiographically. In fact, Romans 7:9 *cannot* refer to Paul. He could never say, "I was once alive *apart from the law* but when the commandment came, sin came alive and I died."[11] Before following Christ, Paul did not have the anxiety of the "I" in Romans 7. He describes himself in Philippians 3:6, "as to righteousness under the law, blameless." Any Jew who recited Psalm 119 in worship would likewise claim to delight in God's law.

---

[10]Wright, "Letter to the Romans," in *The New Interpreter's Bible* (Nashville: Abingdon, 2002), 549-68.
[11]Brett David Burrowes, "From Letter to Spirit: The Transformation of Torah in Paul's Symbolic World as Reflected in His Letter to the Romans" (PhD diss., Durham University, 2004), 106.

What's more, ancient Jewish and Greco-Roman writers commonly used "I" for rhetorical effect.[12] In fact, Quintilian, a contemporary of Paul, gives reason to think Paul might have used this device to convey a perspective *other than* his own.[13]

Romans 7:4-12

Likewise, my brothers, you also have died to the law through the body of Christ, so that you may belong to another, to him who has been raised from the dead, in order that we may bear fruit for God.[5] For while we were living in the flesh, our sinful passions, aroused by the law, were at work in our members to bear fruit for death.[6] But now we are released from the law, having died to that which held us captive, so that we serve in the new way of the Spirit and not in the old way of the written code.

[7] What then shall we say? That the law is sin? By no means! Yet if it had not been for the law, I would not have known sin. For I would not have known what it is to covet if the law had not said, "You shall not covet."[8] But sin, seizing an opportunity through the commandment, produced in me all kinds of covetousness. For apart from the law, sin lies dead.[9] I was once alive apart from the law, but when the commandment came, sin came alive and I died.[10] The very commandment that promised life proved to be death to me.[11] For sin, seizing an opportunity through the commandment, deceived me and through it killed me.[12] So the law is holy, and the commandment is holy and righteous and good.

Readers should distinguish Romans 7:4-6 from Romans 7:7-25. The "you" and "we" in 7:4-6 are those who "were living in the flesh . . . *but now* . . . are released from the law."[14] Paul includes himself in 7:4-6, whereas Romans 7:9 cannot refer to him, either before or after knowing Christ. Accordingly, we cannot assume "I" in 7:7-25 includes the "we" of 7:4-6.

If we assume otherwise, only one type of person satisfies all the criteria of the "I" in Romans 7—a Gentile convert to Judaism who then becomes a Christian. Only this person could previously live "apart from the law," then be "released from the law" (Romans 7:6, 9) yet still attempt to serve the law with delight (Romans 7:22, 25). Paul depicts the "I" positively as a slave to God's law (within his mind; 7:25). If so, this explains the conflicted Gentile conscience of Romans 2:15.

---

[12]See Stanley Stowers, *Rereading Romans: Justice, Jews, and Gentiles* (New Haven, CT: Yale University Press, 1994), 264-72; Richard Longenecker, *The Epistle to the Romans* (Grand Rapids: Eerdmans, 2016), 653-60.

[13]In *Institutio oratoria* 9.2.30, he says, "This figure [of speech] gives both variety and animation to eloquence, in a wonderful degree. By means of it, we display the thoughts of our opponents, as they themselves would do in a soliloquy."

[14]Burrowes, "From Letter to Spirit," 106. Romans 7:5-6 seems to preview the division between Romans 7:7-25 and Romans 8:1-11, which likely depicts the "old self" and the "new self" from Romans 7:1-4. See Michael Bird, *Romans* (Grand Rapids: Zondervan, 2016), 224.

The problem with this view is that we must then argue "in the flesh" (Romans 7:5, 18, 25) describes the Christian experience despite Romans 6 and 8 and the contrast drawn with those living in/according to "the Spirit" (Romans 8:4, 5, 9, 12, 13). This argument is possible (compare 1 Corinthians 3:1; 2 Corinthians 1:17; 10:2; Galatians 5:13) but unlikely because it allows an abnormal way of speaking to trump the immediate context of Romans 5–8.

The "I" does not fit common theological categories. Paul depicts the response of those trying to obey God's commands apart from the Spirit's power. However, his description of "I" in Romans 7:7-25 doesn't sufficiently describe believers, unbelievers, or any of Paul's contemporaries. Whatever our interpretation, we can't be dogmatic because the broader context turns our attention away from the "I." Paul draws from a collectivistic perspective to characterize the "I."

When readers concentrate on the "I," they easily miss how often Paul talks about "we" in context. In Romans 7:4-7, 14, "we" bear fruit for God, previously in the flesh but now released from the law, which "we" know is spiritual. Romans 6 and 8 are chock full of "we" statements. In Romans 7, Paul does not forsake his broader discussion about collective identity. If anything, he continues his argument to ensure his readers reckon themselves "in Christ" and do not define themselves by natural or "fleshly" cultural categories.

Six observations suggest "I" refers collectively to Israel during the exodus rather than an individual. First, the passage comes in a context where Paul uses Israel's story as a framework for talking about the collective identity of God's people. The intensive focus on the law within Romans 5–8 recalls Israel's arrival at Sinai after leaving Egypt.

Second, the chapter contains explicit and implicit allusions to the Pentateuch. Romans 7:7 cites the commandment "Do not covet" (Exodus 20:17; Deuteronomy 5:21). Also, many scholars detect repeated echoes to Adam in Romans 7:7-11.[15]

Third, the dual allusions to Adam and Israel reflect Paul's prior comment, "for sin indeed was in the world before the law was given, but sin is not counted where there is no law. Yet death reigned from Adam to Moses, even over those whose sinning was not like the transgression of Adam, who was a type of the one who was to come" (Romans 5:13-14). In both texts, Paul highlights the transgression of Adam and those under the law. That is, they both disobeyed specific commands from God. Those who lived "from Adam to Moses" did not receive direct commands from God; they "sin" but do not commit "transgression" (hence different nouns in 5:14). Paul effectively restates Romans 5:13, 20 in 7:7, 13. This observation suggests Romans 7 builds on

---

[15]For example, Bird, *Romans*, 240.

Romans 5 and reflects the unique experience of Israel, who, "once alive apart from the law," died when the commandment came (Romans 7:9).

Given Paul's distinction in Romans 5:13-14, the "I" does not represent all humanity. Paul's argument about one's response to the law does not apply to people living from Adam to Moses (and arguably countless Gentiles after Moses). They did not directly receive commands from God.[16]

Fourth, only Israel as a nation fits the description of Romans 7. As a collective group, Israel experienced the circumstances and conflict Paul depicts. They were once alive apart from the law yet died with its arrival. They confessed the law is holy, righteous, and a delight. Although they "agree with the law, that it is good," Israel was later enslaved in exile because of sin (compare Romans 7:14; Isaiah 50:1; 52:3).

Fifth, Galatians 4 presents Israel in a way similar to Romans 7. Paul says everyone under the law is "enslaved" (Galatians 4:1, 3, 7, 9, 24-25). In context, Paul explains the law's purpose and clarifies who are Abraham's offspring. Akin to Romans 7–8, he also contrasts a child "according to the flesh" with one "according to the Spirit," using the analogy between Hagar and Sarah (Galatians 4:21-31).

Sixth, Paul says, "I am of the flesh, sold under sin" (Romans 7:14). The last phrase echoes Isaiah 50:1 and, more broadly, Isaiah 49:24–50:2.[17] Given Isaiah's context, "I" is a figure that represents Israel in exile because of sin. The prophet frequently uses Israel's exodus to foretell her coming restoration.[18] Goodrich adds, "It is, then, Yahweh's ability to restore Israel that becomes the focus of the exchange in Isa 49:24–50:3."[19] Similarly, Paul stresses the fact that "I," being a slave, lacks the ability to carry out what he wants.

WHY TALK THIS WAY?

Why does Paul use "I" to refer indirectly to Israel? How does the extended monologue of Romans 7:7-25 relate to the "you" and "we" of Romans 7:4-6? Paul is mindful not to give wrong impressions about fellow Jews. By speaking in the first person, he lumps himself with Israel, needing Christ's redemption like all who come from Adam. He does this to guard against potential misunderstandings that could emerge if he spoke about Israel directly. For example, it might appear he distances himself from Israel as though he and other readers do not suffer the same inability when in the flesh.

---

[16]John Goodrich, "Sold Under Sin: Echoes of Exile in Romans 7:14-25," *New Testament Studies* 59, no. 4 (2013): 489; compare 491.

[17]Compare Isaiah 52:3. Goodrich offers layers of evidence in "Sold Under Sin," 476-95.

[18]Rikki E. Watts, "Consolation or Confrontation? Isaiah 40–55 and the Delay of the New Exodus," *Tyndale Bulletin* 41, no. 1 (1990): 31-59.

[19]Goodrich, "Sold Under Sin," 485.

However, he does not magnify Israel's sin beyond that of anyone else. In this way, Paul prevents anti-Jewish sentiments from taking root among Roman Christians.

Additionally, Paul's appeal to ancient Israel serves as a warning to Roman Christians. They ought not to put themselves under the law's authority.[20] Otherwise, they become like Adam and Israel, who died in exile.[21] Paul reinforces a theme that spans the letter, though intensified, since Romans 5. All people—Jews and Gentiles—are in Adam. This common identity is more fundamental than one's culture. In Romans 8, Paul highlights the corresponding positive point about the collective identity of those in Christ.

Paul's indirect appeal to Israel is significant. First, it means Paul simply does not discuss a specific individual in 7:7-25. Neither does he talk about a certain group among his contemporaries. Therefore, debates about the identity of "I" and human nature have little or no relevance to Paul's original point. Also, Romans 7 does not explain whether people are born "good" or "evil." It is true that Paul does emphasize human weakness or inability under the law, but we should distinguish between being weak and being evil. Even biblical writers call the law "weak," not evil (compare Romans 8:3; Hebrews 7:18; Galatians 4:9).

In summary, Paul's main point concerns neither human nature nor an individual. Instead, Paul's most explicit statements direct attention elsewhere, namely to sin and the law. He first vindicates the law and then exposes the culpability of sin.

PAUL VINDICATES THE LAW AND "ME"

Romans 7 expands the discussion from Romans 3, where Paul affirms God's righteousness and upholds the law (Romans 3:3-5, 31). In fact, he leaves verbal bread crumbs along the way. For example, Romans 7:7, 13 simply repeat similar claims about the law in Romans 3:20; 4:15; 5:13, 20. In each case, Paul explains the law's purpose. Ultimately, he defends the law's goodness.

Why is this defense necessary? First, Paul addresses an apparent contradiction. As he later quotes, "the person who does the commandments shall live by them" (Romans 10:5; compare Romans 7:10; Leviticus 18:5). Yet Paul seems to imply the opposite in Romans 6:14-15; 7:4-12. Second, if the law is sin or brings death, people would certainly question God's righteousness. Therefore, he defends the law's goodness in order to uphold God's honor.

---

[20]Romans 14 likely applies this point.

[21]If N. T. Wright is correct that the "curse" of Galatians 3:13 alludes to Israel's exile (compare Deuteronomy 28–29), we have another similarity between Romans 7 and Galatians 3–4. See N. T. Wright, *The Climax of the Covenant: Christ and the Law in Pauline Theology* (Minneapolis: Fortress, 1992), 137-56.

> **Romans 7:13-20**
>
> Did that which is good, then, bring death to me? By no means! It was sin, producing death in me through what is good, in order that sin might be shown to be sin, and through the commandment might become sinful beyond measure. [14] For we know that the law is spiritual, but I am of the flesh, sold under sin. [15] For I do not understand my own actions. For I do not do what I want, but I do the very thing I hate. [16] Now if I do what I do not want, I agree with the law, that it is good. [17] So now it is no longer I who do it, but sin that dwells within me. [18] For I know that nothing good dwells in me, that is, in my flesh. For I have the desire to do what is right, but not the ability to carry it out. [19] For I do not do the good I want, but the evil I do not want is what I keep on doing. [20] Now if I do what I do not want, it is no longer I who do it, but sin that dwells within me.

In Romans 7:7-12, Paul mentions the law, sin, and "I." The law and sin are set in opposition. Whereas the law promises life, sin seizes the opportunity to use God's command to deceive and kill "me." This observation leads to the conclusion, "So the law is holy, and the commandment is holy and righteous and good."[22]

Paul shifts his attention in Romans 7:13-25, contrasting "sin" and "I." In Romans 7:17, 20, Paul exonerates "me" and blames sin by saying "it is no longer I who do it, but sin that dwells within me." Paul's sharp distinction seems to excuse sinners from their actions. If Paul didn't repeat himself twice, one might treat it like an obscure passing comment. To complicate the picture, Paul in Romans 8:1-3 says God condemns sin yet never says he condemns sinners.

On balance, Paul paints a generous picture of the "I," who clearly does wrong. Paul says, "I am of the flesh, sold under sin," "I do not do what I want," "I do the very thing I hate," "but the evil I do not want is what I keep on doing." He adds, "I do not understand my actions," and "I agree with the law, that it is good." Furthermore, "I" emphasizes he "hates" his evil actions and wants to do good. Verses 21-25 are even more lucid. Paul says "I delight in the law of God, in my inner being.... So then, I myself serve the law of God with my mind." In contrast to his inner mind, he vilifies "my members," his "body of death," and "my flesh."

> **Romans 7:21-25**
>
> So I find it to be a law that when I want to do right, evil lies close at hand. [22] For I delight in the law of God, in my inner being, [23] but I see in my members another law waging war against the law of my mind and making me captive to the law of sin that dwells in my members. [24] Wretched man that I am! Who will deliver me from this body of death? [25] Thanks be to God through Jesus Christ our Lord! So then, I myself serve the law of God with my mind, but with my flesh I serve the law of sin.

---

[22]One could argue that Romans 5:13 implies as much since sin was in the world before Moses received the law.

VICTIM OR PERPETRATOR?

What gets lost amid the shuffle of proof texts supporting one view or another is the fact that "I" presents himself as sin's *victim*, not merely a perpetrator of sin. He is deceived by sin. He has no ability to do the good he desires but is compelled to do what he hates. This slave to sin even confesses his wretched state in 7:24. To be sure, "I" in Romans 7 does wrong by disobeying commands, which results in death (Romans 6:21, 23; 7:4-5, 10-11). Nevertheless, Romans 7:17, 20 are unambiguous. Sin, not "I," is responsible.

Paul in effect puts sin on trial.[23] Having upheld the rightness of the law, he now vindicates the "I," who represents Israel in exile due to sin. Sin enslaves them just as Pharaoh did their ancestors. The prophets foretold a new exodus that would bring God's righteousness. As with Pharaoh, God uses a sacrifice to condemn sin (Romans 8:3). This reflects a purpose of the Passover lamb—to "execute judgments on all the gods of Egypt" (Exodus 12:12; Numbers 33:4). Once sin is put to shame, the Spirit of Glory leads God's children not back to Canaan but into a renewed world (Romans 8:9-30; 4:13). In short, Paul looks forward to the ultimate hope of the "I."

Other signs confirm that Paul seeks to vindicate the "I" of Romans 7. In addition to being a Passover lamb, Christ also is a "sin offering" (Romans 8:3).[24] This sacrifice atones for "unintentional sins," which are committed due to negligence or ignorance.[25] In Romans 10:2-3, Paul describes Israel in similar terms, saying, "I bear them witness that they have a zeal for God, but not according to knowledge. For, being ignorant of the righteousness of God, and seeking to establish their own, they did not submit to God's righteousness." A few paragraphs later, he adds, "I ask, then, has God rejected his people? By no means! For I myself am an Israelite" (Romans 11:1).

Paul changes his tone dramatically after his harsh critiques of the Jews early in the letter. He is increasingly explicit in affirming Israel's election (compare Romans 11:28-29). He repeatedly and fervently identifies himself with Israel (Romans 9:2-3; 11:1, 14; compare 10:1). Therefore, we see why Paul crafts Romans 7 using "I" as he does.

We observe two familiar goals achieved simultaneously. First, Paul mitigates national prejudice and presumption. Second, he defends God's glory from accusation. We already saw Paul affirm the law's goodness. In addition, he anticipates the objection posed in Romans 9–11, where Paul upholds God's truthfulness. When

---

[23]Wright, "Romans," 565-68.

[24]Wright, *Climax*, 220-30.

[25]See Leviticus 4:2, 22, 27; 5:15; Numbers 15:24-29; 35:11, 15; Joshua 20:3, 9. "Unintentional" is a somewhat misleading translation since this sin contrasts "high-handed sins" in Numbers 15:30-31. However, high-handed sins are not defined based on intentionality alone. This is evident from the fact that high-handed sins cannot be forgiven, whereas people can atone for the intentional sins listed in Leviticus 5:1-6; 6:1-7. Perhaps "negligent" sins is a better translation.

defending Israel in Romans 7, he previews his conclusion in Romans 11:2, "God has not rejected his people whom he foreknew." After all, if God were unfaithful toward the elect, what confidence can readers have in the promises of Romans 8:28-30?

> And we know that for those who love God all things work together for good, for those who are called according to his purpose. For those whom he foreknew he also predestined to be conformed to the image of his Son, in order that he might be the firstborn among many brothers. And those whom he predestined he also called, and those whom he called he also justified, and those whom he justified he also glorified.

Everything Paul says in Romans hinges on his defending God's honor and removing the measures of worth that are based on anything other than Christ.

CULTURES OF FLESH

Much can be gleaned from Paul's continued use of a collectivist perspective. His comments about the weakness of "I" and the law help us understand his critique of human culture. God executes his plan to defeat sin within culture, not merely *despite* culture. The Mosaic law is a concrete expression of that plan. It sets apart a people called to reflect God's character. In establishing Israel, the law claims a foothold for God's kingdom in the world. Still, it is insufficient. This is important for grasping Paul's theology of culture.

Although the law is good, Paul calls its commands "elementary principles of the world" (*ta stoicheia tou kosmou*) that "enslave" people (Galatians 4:2-3). It is like a child's "guardian" or "manager." The word *stoicheion* ("elementary principle") has no inherent negative meaning. Rather, "The significance of the 'fundamental elements' for Paul's description of the past is the genitive 'of the world' (*tou kosmou*). It is the world to which Paul will later argue he died (6:14)."[26] Galatians and other New Testament texts demonstrate that the word's root meaning concerns something that is basic or foundational.[27] Hebrews 5:12 uses the word positively: "you need someone to teach you again the *basic principles* [*stoicheion*] of the oracles of God."

"Fundamental elements" are basic aspects of both the physical *and* social world.[28] They are "the foundational character of what is being described," and thus refer to the

---

[26]Richard Adams, "The Israel of God: The Narrative Rhetoric of Paul's Letter to the Galatians" (PhD diss., Emory University, 2012), 332.

[27]Adams ("The Israel of God," 332) notes the positive use of the verb form *stoicheō* in Galatians 5:25; 6:16. We can add Romans 4:12, concerning those "who also *walk* [*stoicheō*] in the footsteps of the faith" (compare Acts 21:24).

[28]G. Delling, "στοιχέω, συστοιχέω, στοιχεῖον," *Theological Dictionary of the New Testament* (Grand Rapids: Eerdmans, 1971), 7:670-87; J. Louis Martyn, *Theological Issues in the Letters of Paul* (Nashville: Abingdon, 1997), 125-40; Martinus de Boer, *Galatians: A Commentary* (Louisville: Westminster John Knox, 2011), 252-60; "στοιχεῖον," in *A Greek-English Lexicon of the New Testament and Other Early Christian Literature*,

structure and order that shape creation and culture.[29] This explains why Paul likens *stoicheia* to human tradition in Colossians 2:8. Observe also Colossians 2:16, 20 where "the elements of the world [*tōn stoicheiōn tou kosmou*]" concern regulations that include "questions of food and drink, or with regard to a festival or a new moon or a Sabbath."

Paul's seemingly conflicted view of the law resembles what we see in Romans 7. In many respects, he uses "fundamental elements" and "flesh" similarly. Living in "the flesh" is not inherently evil, just as being "in culture" is not evil.[30] Christ is the Son of David "according to the flesh" (Romans 1:3). Paul's kinsmen "according to the flesh" (Romans 9:3, 5) are Jews, whom he calls "my flesh" in Romans 11:14.

Flesh, manifested collectively in culture, should not limit one's values and character. Our "flesh" gives outward expression to inward principles and perspective. Likewise, culture is manifested in practices reflecting a community's collective convictions and assumptions. Paul is concerned that we not be defined by *mere* flesh. When the "fundamental elements" of our (sub)culture define us, we live in "the flesh."

The law is weakened by the flesh when the law becomes a mere social boundary marker. God's law functions as a token of cultural identity. It is a *stoicheion*, an "elementary principle" of the world. Various elements of the law perpetuated the separation that plagued the world since Babel. Even within Israel, it created barriers of shame by labeling some "holy" but others "impure" and "sinful."[31]

If even the law is weak, so are the wisdom and ways of every culture and ideology. This warning applies to Jews and Greeks. Paul's readers are challenged to reconsider their sense of collective identity, pride in tradition, and the conventional things that divide one group from another. This perspective further sheds light on why the law cannot bring God's righteousness. As James K. A. Smith states, "A society that forgets it is NOT ultimate is by nature the most prone to injustice."[32]

---

ed. William Arndt, Frederick W. Danker, Walter Bauer, and F. Wilbur Gingrich (Chicago: University of Chicago Press, 2000); Dieter Roth, "What ἐν τῷ κόσμῳ are the στοιχεῖα τοῦ κόσμου?" *HTS Theological Studies* 70, no. 1 (2014), http://dx.doi.org/10.4102/hts.v70i1.2676. The noun describes natural elements in 2 Peter 3:10, 12.

[29]Peter Leithart, *Delivered from the Elements of the World: Atonement, Justification, Mission* (Downers Grove, IL: IVP Academic, 2016), 30. See discussion on 29-42.

[30]In 1 Corinthians 15:35-49, different "flesh" have differing kinds of glory. For a helpful discussion, see Leithart, *Delivered*, 75-90. In essence, he presents "flesh" as the creaturely state of vulnerability and need (that is, finitude) that arouses our desires to exert power, gain praise, and secure protection.

[31]Compare Leithart, *Delivered*, 91-138.

[32]James K. A. Smith, "Revolution*ism* and Our Secular Age," *Comment* (Fall 2016), www.cardus.ca/comment /article/revolutionism-and-our-secular-age/.

"NOTHING GOOD IN ME"?

So, does Romans 7 tell us whether people are born with a good or evil nature? The above discussion has shown that we can hardly answer this question because it is wrongly framed. We can improve the question by clarifying what Paul does and does not say. By so doing, we can build a bridge of understanding between Eastern and Western philosophical traditions.

As we've seen, Paul presents a more optimistic view of humanity than Western teachers often assume. In Romans 7, he emphasizes humanity's inability, not its evil disposition. The "I" delights in God's law and does not desire evil. It is sin, not "I," that bears the blame for wrongdoing.

Precisely how one reconciles mutual culpability between "sin" and "I" is a separate question. The tension in Romans 7 might be compared to addiction, whereby one is culpable for the decisions that led to the addictive behavior. Over time, the addiction has a destructive impact on a person's neurology, making it increasingly difficult for them to change. Essentially, the addict surrenders control and so becomes a slave to addiction. The person becomes as much a victim as a perpetrator of wrongdoing.

Because these distinctions influence how we see ourselves and others, Romans 7 causes undue shame if misunderstood. Recall the quotations that opened the chapter. People too commonly neglect to see or highlight human goodness, which exists by virtue of our being created in God's image.

In practice, this can cause us to treat people as though *they* were "sin" and not its slaves. Consequently, people do not merely think their *actions* are bad (entailing guilt). They see *themselves* as bad (suggesting shame). Such claims about a person's identity devalue their worth as humans. Actions can be changed, but one has little hope when a person's self is deemed worthless.[33]

This change in perspective tempers much popular teaching that shames people. Such approaches come across as cold, not compassionate. Speaking the truth with conviction should not be set in opposition to tenderness with an eye for restoring those who bring harm to themselves and others. The prophets frequently depict the Lord showing tender compassion to those who spurn him (for example, Isaiah 40:1-2; 54:7-8; Hosea 2:14). Paul in Romans shows similar flexibility. Whereas he calls people "enemies," unbelieving Jews are also regarded as "beloved" (Romans 11:28-29).

---

[33]Unfortunately, "wretched" (used in some translations of Romans 7:25) carries connotations that could imply people have wicked dispositions. However, *talaipōros* routinely conveys the anguish of one's suffering or state. In this sense, it is "an antonym of *makarios* [blessed]." See "ταλαίπωρος," in Arndt, Danker, Bauer, and Gingrich, eds., *A Greek-English Lexicon of the New Testament*. That the "I" is a captive needing rescue (Romans 7:23-25) confirms this reading of *talaipōros*. Also, compare Isaiah 33:1 (LXX); Tobit 13:10; 2 Maccabees 4:47; 4 Maccabees 16:7; Josephus, *Antiquities* 1.204.

What about the apparent tension between Christianity and Confucian views of human nature? The above interpretation highlights a surprising degree of affinity between these traditions. The common Christian teaching that people are "born evil" can be reconciled with Confucian claims that people are "born good." Confucian thinkers primarily focus on human potential.[34] Christians affirm a similar idea when saying people have consciences and the ability to do good because we bear God's image. Likewise, Confucians do not deny that people do wrong. In fact, human weakness is assumed as an encumbrance to virtue. This perspective resembles what we find in Romans 7, which stresses human inability.

Confucian writers agree with Paul's message in two respects. First, laws are insufficient to bring about the harmony God desires for the world. For instance, Confucius says,

> If the people are led by laws, and uniformity among them be sought by punishments, they will try to escape punishment and have no sense of shame. If they are led by virtue, and uniformity sought among them through practice of ritual propriety, they will possess a sense of shame and come to you of their own accord.[35]

Second, as in Romans, "the classical [Confucian] texts indicate that their concern was not just to instill a deeper sense of shame but to *change the things for which people feel shame*."[36]

The point of this comparison is not to equate Confucian and Christian teaching. Rather, when seeing through an East Asian lens, we observe more of what Paul says about the human condition in Romans 7. Even in the face of our inability, we are reminded that good can be redeemed within humanity. A more balanced reading of Romans 7 can prevent miscommunication between Christians and non-Christians, especially those from East Asia.

To be sure, Paul's message contradicts certain *applications* of a Confucian view of human nature. For example, "Parents tend to blame their children's misbehavior on the influence of their children's bad neighbors, poor teachers, and bad classmates."[37]

---

[34]*Mencius, Mengzi with Selections from Traditional Commentaries*. Translated by Bryan W. Van Norden (Indianapolis, IN: Hackett Publishing Co, Inc. 2008), 6A2, 6A6, 6A7, 6A15, 7B24. Even Xunzi, who argued human nature was born evil, is often misunderstood. See Hung-Chung Yen, "Human Nature and Learning in Ancient China," in *Education as Cultivation in Chinese Culture*, ed. Shikkuan Hsu and Yuh-Yin Wu (Singapore: Springer, 2015), 31-42.

[35]*Analects* 2:3. Translation comes from Jeffrey Riegel, "Confucius," in *Stanford Encyclopedia of Philosophy*, http://plato.stanford.edu/entries/confucius.

[36]Nathaniel Barrett, "A Confucian Theory of Shame," *Sophia* 54 (2015): 146, italics original. He lists examples from *Analects* 4.9, 4.22, 5.15, 5.25, 8.13, 9.27, 13.20; *Mencius*, 2A7, 4B18, 5B5, 7A6, 7A7. Given Romans 6:22, the nonbeliever is not necessarily ashamed. Rather, shame comes after following Christ.

[37]Mark Strand, "Explaining Sin in a Chinese Context," *Missiology* 28, no. 4 (2000): 431. *Jiao bu xin shi zhi duo* and *yang bu jiao fu zhi guo* similarly blame parents and teachers for a child's failings.

Also, since human inability limits human potential, people should reassess their expectations of themselves and others, knowing that impatient, high-pressure tactics do not guarantee the changes they want.

WHEN "I" INTERPRET THE BIBLE

We have further seen how an individualistic or collectivistic lens influences our interpretation. In recent times, many people hesitate to speak broadly about entire groups to avoid stereotypes. Nevertheless, one's self-perceptions—especially in non-Western contexts—are intricately tied to larger groups regardless of individual distinctions. Countless times I've heard someone say, "We Chinese all . . . ," usually followed by a patently false overgeneralization about Chinese people. A young Chinese man recently told me, "We believe people are born good because that is what Chinese philosophers teach us. We don't have individual thoughts about it." That is what individuals tend to accept in collectivistic cultures. Tradition and culture are powerful authorities.

A perspective that prioritizes "us" and "them" influences our interpretations in subtle ways that a focus on "I" might not. Romans 7 is such an example. A group's history and patterns of behavior will not fit every individual's experience, yet we must not underestimate how easily we are affected by social trends and cultural patterns of thinking.

What happens if we ignore a collectivist perspective due to differences among individuals? We miss potential warnings and encouragements. Twice Paul says ancient texts are written for the sake of his readers (Romans 4:23; 15:4; compare 1 Corinthians 10:11). No sweeping characterization of ancient Israel perfectly fits each member of the nation. One could say Moses, Phineas, Caleb, Joshua, and others had faith and were righteous, yet countless others turned to wickedness and idolatry. Paul quotes Elijah to say God has not rejected his people, though some individuals were unfaithful, since the Lord preserves a remnant (Romans 11:1-5). Despite individual exceptions, Paul's interpretation of the Old Testament tells how God works in a world made up of Jews and Gentiles, not individuals.

This chapter has taken a close-up look at Romans 7. Since we have already considered Romans 8, we now turn to Romans 9–11.

10

THEY WILL NOT BE PUT
to SHAME (ROMANS 9–11)

People have long used shame to enforce social standards of behavior. In preindustrial London, authorities used whipping and maiming to punish offenders and warn against vice.[1] Although public shaming looks different today, the practice remains common. For instance, Chinese officials in 2015 shamed citizens for "uncivilized behavior" while traveling.[2]

This is not merely an Eastern phenomenon. Westerners increasingly suffer immense shame through social media.[3] Arizona posts online the names of "deadbeat dads" who don't pay child support.[4] Children commit suicide because they suffer public shame.[5] The threat of shame is a powerful deterrent. Its persistent use in history testifies to a universal fact: people fear being shamed. Many authorities exploit this fear to manipulate others. So can shame ever be legitimately used for good?

Paul knows his readers fear being shamed. In Romans, he frequently reminds them that Christ's followers will never be put to shame. What does Paul mean?

This chapter examines how the Old Testament shapes Paul's use of honor and shame in Romans. A few key passages include Romans 10:9-13 (compare Isaiah 28; Joel 2); Romans 8:33-34 (compare Isaiah 50); and Romans 9:19-24 (compare Exodus 9; Isaiah 41, 45). These texts clarify Paul's meaning in saying people "will not be put to shame." As we'll see, being "put to shame" is the objective consequence of sin, not simply a psychological response and fear.

---

[1]Matthew Green, "A Grim and Gruesome History of Public Shaming in London: Part 1," *Londonist*, January 26, 2016, https://londonist.com/2015/12/publicshaming1.

[2]Melissa Locker, "Chinese Publicly Shames Its Own Worst Tourists," *Travel and Leisure*, December 27, 2015, www.travelandleisure.com/articles/china-tourism-blacklist.

[3]Jon Ronson, *So You've Been Publicly Shamed* (New York: Riverhead Books, 2015).

[4]Biz Carson, "Arizona Is Publicly Shaming Deadbeat Dads on Twitter," *Business Insider,* February 12, 2016, www.businessinsider.com/arizona-shames-deadbeat-dads-2016-1.

[5]Nina Golgowski, "Washington Teen Jumps to Death after Being Shamed in Online Video Taken by Dad," *New York Daily News*, June 5, 2015, www.nydailynews.com/news/national/teen-kills-public-shaming-allegedly-dad-article-1.2247168.

"WHOEVER BELIEVES IN HIM WILL NOT BE PUT TO SHAME"

In Romans 9:33 and 10:11, Paul quotes Isaiah 28:16 (LXX). The LXX gives Paul the precise language found in his letter, especially Romans 5–10. We will first review the context of Isaiah 28:16 to see how he uses its themes.

Isaiah 28:1-6, 15-19 (LXX)

Ah, the crown of pride, the hired workers of Ephraim, the flower that has fallen from its glory on the top of the stout mountain—those who are drunk without wine![2] See, the wrath of the Lord is a strong and harsh thing, like hail rushing down where there is no shelter; violently rushing down like a great flood that sweeps a country, it will give rest to the land.[3] With hands and feet the crown of pride will be trampled—the hired workers of Ephraim.

[4] And the flower that has fallen from its *hope of glory* [*tēs elpidos tēs doxēs*] on the topmost of the lofty mountain will be like an early fig; the one who sees it will want to eat it up before he takes it into his hand.[5] In that day the Lord Sabaoth will be *the crown of hope* [*ho stephanos tēs elpidos*], *the weave of glory* [*ho plakeis tēs doxēs*], to the remnant of my people.[6] They will be left for a spirit of judgment—for judgment and strength in forbidding anyone to destroy....

[15] Because you have said, "We have made a covenant with Hades and agreements with death, if a rushing storm passes through, it will not come to us; we have made falsehood *our hope* [*tēn elpida hēmōn*], and in falsehood we will be sheltered";

[16] therefore thus says the Lord, See, I will lay for the foundations of Zion a precious, choice stone, a highly valued cornerstone for its foundations, and *the one who believes in him will not be put to shame* [*ho pisteuōn ep autō ou mē kataischynthē*].

[17] And *I will make justice to be hope* [*thēsō krisin eis elpida*], and my mercy will become weight balances, and as for you who trust vainly in falsehood, I tell you that the tempest will not pass you by,[18] lest it also take away your covenant of death. And *your hope* [*hē elpis hymōn*] regarding Hades will not remain; if a rushing storm comes, you will be trampled down by it.[19] When it passes by, it will take you; early, early in the day it will pass by, and *at night it will be an evil hope* [*en nykti estai elpis ponēra*]; learn to hear.*

Adapted from the New English Translation of the Septuagint

Isaiah 28 largely describes the Lord's coming judgment against Israel's pride (with important exceptions in 28:5-6, 16-17). In Isaiah 28:1, 3, the prophet chastises "the crown of pride," which likely refers to Samaria, its priests, and prophets (Isaiah 28:7).[6] The rulers presume they will escape death, but this is false hope (Isaiah 28:14-15). Ephraim is like a flower "fallen from its *hope of glory*" (Isaiah 28:1, 4).

---

[6]In Hebrew, Isaiah 28:1, 3, 7 condemn the "drunkards" (*shikkore*) of Ephraim.

What is this hope of glory? The writer combines images from Isaiah 28:1-4 to say the Lord "will be the crown of hope, the weave of glory" (Isaiah 28:5-6). Verse 16 elaborates, "See, I will lay for the foundations of Zion a precious, choice stone, a highly valued cornerstone for its foundations, and the one who believes in him will not be put to shame." Isaiah looks forward to God's saving intervention. The imagery of laying a foundation suggests the Lord will make his people secure.

The Greek phrase behind "the one who believes" can be understood in two ways. It could refer to "the one who is faithful" to the Lord. Or, it might mean "the one who trusts" the Lord by believing the promises made in context (for example, Isaiah 28:16-17). In fact, the text doesn't allow us to separate the two options. The passage presents the Lord as a king who sets things right for his people (28:5, 16-17). Accordingly, the one who is faithful to the king does so by believing his promises.

The LXX inserts "hope" three times in Isaiah 28:17-19, picking up from Isaiah 28:4-5. Verse 17 explains how the Lord becomes "the crown of hope, the weave of glory" to his people. The Lord fulfills their hope for salvation by establishing justice and mercy. Although some have "false hope" of escaping death (via a "covenant with death"), the Lord brings their hope to ruin (28:18-19; compare 28:4, 15).

God's people have a hope of glory in two senses. First, the Lord is their hope and glory (28:5). Second, the prophet foretells the people's coming deliverance (28:16-17). These are two ways of saying the same thing. The Lord is their hope of glory precisely because he fulfills their hope that justice and mercy will overcome the wickedness surrounding them.[7]

What is meant by Paul's phrase "will not be put to shame"? Given its original context in Isaiah 28:17-19, it does not primarily refer to a psychological state, whether disappointment or embarrassment. It describes an objective state. The one who believes "will not be put to shame" because of what the Lord accomplishes in 28:17. Not being "put to shame" indicates one does not suffer the condemnation of 28:18-19.

Drawing from Isaiah 28, Paul urges readers to persevere by believing the Lord's promises. As their true King, he is their true hope of glory (compare Romans 5:2, 11). Other hopes are false, leading to the shame of condemnation. "They will not be put to shame" is another way of saying they are justified and will be saved.

Romans 10:9-13

If you confess with your mouth that Jesus is Lord and believe in your heart that God raised him from the dead, you will be saved. [10] For with the heart one believes

---

[7]Similarly, Paul boasts in *the hope of the glory of God*, then simply says he boasts *in God* (Romans 5:2, 11). Like Isaiah, Paul boasts in God because he is the surest hope of gaining the glory Paul seeks (compare Romans 2:7, 10).

and is justified, and with the mouth one confesses and is saved. [11] For the Scripture says, "Everyone who believes in him will not be put to shame." [12] For there is no distinction between Jew and Greek; for the same Lord is Lord of all, bestowing his riches on all who call on him. [13] For "everyone who calls on the name of the Lord will be saved."

Paul quotes Isaiah 28:16 in Romans 10:11 to support his claim in the previous verse. Paul uses Isaiah's phrase "in him" to refer to Christ. Romans 10:9-10 highlight the result of believing in him. When Paul says believers "will not be put to shame," he describes one who is justified and thus will be saved (compare Romans 5:1, 9-10).

Robert Olson captures what is going on in Paul's use of Isaiah in Romans 9:30–10:16:

> The themes of "escaping shame" and "gospel" again come together, both drawn directly from Isaiah. For Paul (Rom 9:30-33), one who believed on Christ would "not be put to shame" (Rom 9:33; 10:11/Isa 28:16), a phrase used in Isaiah with eschatological and forensic connotations, so that in this context of Romans it becomes the scriptural support and conceptual parallel of attaining righteousness by faith as expressed in Rom 9:30.[8]

For those who are not put to shame, the Lord "bestows his riches" since "the same Lord is Lord of all" (Romans 10:12). This hope of salvation is assured (Romans 10:13; compare Joel 2:32). Hope in other "gods" or "lords" leads to shame. Again, Paul does not use shame language to refer to a mere psychological state. He instead describes the condition where people stumble over "the stumbling stone," the "rock of offense" (Romans 9:32-33).

SAVED FROM SHAME

From what are those who call on the name of the Lord saved? The answer in Joel 2:26-27 is often overlooked. There God twice states that "my people shall never again be put to shame." God's people will be saved *from shame*.

Joel 2:23-27, 32

Be glad, O children of Zion, and rejoice in the LORD your God, for he has given the early rain for your vindication; he has poured down for you abundant rain, the early and the latter rain, as before. [24] The threshing floors shall be full of grain; the vats shall overflow with wine and oil. [25] I will restore to you the years that the swarming locust has eaten, the hopper, the destroyer, and the cutter, my great army, which I sent among you. [26] You shall eat in plenty and be satisfied, and praise the name of the LORD your God, who has dealt wondrously with you. And my people *shall never*

---

[8]Robert C. Olson, *The Gospel as the Revelation of God's Righteousness: Paul's Use of Isaiah in Romans 1:1–3:26* (Tübingen: Mohr Siebeck, 2016), 85-86.

146 READING ROMANS WITH EASTERN EYES

> *again be put to shame.* [27] You shall know that I am in the midst of Israel, and that I am the LORD your God and there is none else. And my people *shall never again be put to shame.* . . .
>
> [32] And it shall come to pass that everyone who calls on the name of the LORD shall be saved. For in Mount Zion and in Jerusalem there shall be those who escape, as the LORD has said, and among the survivors shall be those whom the LORD calls.

What is this shame? In Joel 2:17, Joel cries out, "Spare your people, O LORD, and make not your heritage a *reproach*, a *byword* among the nations. Why should they say among the peoples, 'Where is their God?'" People are saved from the "reproach" of the nations. This is more than hurt feelings. God's people were exposed and vulnerable. Their food is destroyed. The "shame" in Joel 2 includes the suffering of Joel 1:1–2:11.

What is at stake is God's honor, not merely Israel's. The nations question the Lord's power and faithfulness by asking "Where is their God?" The Lord's reputation could be dishonored. God's glory is vested in the honor of his people. Accordingly, he says, "Behold, I am sending to you grain, wine, and oil, and you will be satisfied; and I will no more make you a *reproach* among the nations" (Joel 2:19). How does God vindicate his name and remove the reproach from his people?

According to Joel 2:23, the people will again have food when the Lord "has given the early rain for your *justification*."[9] Although this justification language seems out of place to modern readers, other Old Testament writers use similar imagery to indicate the salvation or flourishing brought about by the Lord (Isaiah 45:8, 24-25; 54:17; Jeremiah 51:10; Micah 7:9; compare Psalm 71:1-3). When God justifies or bestows righteousness, his people enjoy honor, not shame (Isaiah 45:24-25). By granting rain in Joel 2, the Lord rescues the people from famine and so removes their reproach. Furthermore, the Lord promises that "my people shall never again be put to shame."

Being saved and not being put to shame are "functionally equivalent."[10] We've seen this in Joel 2 and in Romans (5:5, 9-10; 10:11-13). In addition, this conclusion is confirmed repeatedly throughout the Bible and in other ancient texts.[11]

JUSTIFIED FROM SHAME

Consider how honor and shame shape Romans 8:33-34. Paul writes, "Who shall bring any charge against God's elect? It is God who justifies. Who is to condemn? Christ Jesus is the one who died—more than that, who was raised—who is at the right hand

---

[9] My translation. Instead of "justification," the ESV renders the Hebrew *tsedaqah* as "vindication."
[10] N. T. Wright, "Letter to the Romans," in *The New Interpreter's Bible* (Nashville: Abingdon, 2002), 517, 665. Although Wright's comment concerns Romans 5:5 and 10:11-13, this pattern is found throughout the Bible.
[11] For example, Psalm 22:5; 31:1-2, 17-18; Isaiah 45:16-17; 49:24-25; Zephaniah 3:17-20; Zechariah 10:5-6; Daniel 12:1-2; Luke 9:24-26; Mark 8:35-38; Phil 1:19-20; among extrabiblical texts, Sirach 2:10-11.

of God, who indeed is interceding for us." Paul draws from Isaiah 50:8-9, which says, "He who vindicates me is near. Who will contend with me? Let us stand up together. Who is my adversary? Let him come near to me. Behold, the Lord GOD helps me; who will declare me guilty? Behold, all of them will wear out like a garment; the moth will eat them up." Both "justifies" (Romans 8:33) and "vindicates" (Isaiah 50:8 LXX) translate *dikaioō*. Both writers ask who will "condemn" or "contend" against them.

Isaiah intertwines justification with honor-shame. The servant in Isaiah 50 states, "I gave my back to those who strike, and my cheeks to those who pull out the beard; I hid not my face *from disgrace and spitting*. But the Lord God helps me; therefore *I have not been disgraced*; therefore I have set my face like a flint, and I know that *I shall not be put to shame*" (Isaiah 50:6-7). In context, shame and disgrace refer to more than a subjective psychological state. Olson summarizes a key observation from Isaiah 40–55 (LXX):

> αἰσχύνομαι and its cognates, generally reflecting the masoretic בוש and its cognates, are used to describe and contrast the shame that is the result of misplaced trust (Isa 42:17; 44:9–11; 45:16, 24; 47:3; so also, e.g., Isa 1:27–29; 20:4–5; 26:9–12; 30:3–5) with the total absence of shame, or vindication, that is the result of placing one's trust in the Lord and his promise and provision of salvation (Isa 41:8–12; 49:23; 45:16–17, 24–25; 50:7–9; 54:4; so also, e.g., Isa 7:9: 28:16;). The term is used in the context of the revelation of God's righteousness, both in judgment and salvation, and so acquires forensic overtones in keeping with the "courtroom motif" prevalent in this section of Isaiah (see esp. Isa 50:7–9).[12]

The servant of Isaiah 50 is not only concerned with whether God declares him guilty or innocent. While no doubt important, this is only one aspect of the truth. God's servant allows himself to suffer humiliation.[13] Nevertheless, he remains confident he will not be put to shame. He knows the Lord will justify (or vindicate) him.

Isaiah 49 not only is the background for Isaiah 50; it also links various strands in Paul's thought. Isaiah 49:22-23 offers a wealth of insight:

> Thus says the LORD GOD: "Behold, I will lift up my hand to the nations, and raise my signal to the peoples; and they shall bring your sons in their arms, and your daughters shall be carried on their shoulders. Kings shall be your foster fathers, and their queens your nursing mothers. With their faces to the ground they shall bow down to you, and lick the dust of your feet. Then you will know that I am the LORD; those who wait for me shall not be put to shame."

---

[12]Olson, *The Gospel as the Revelation of God's Righteousness*, 86-87.
[13]Gospel writers echo Isaiah 50:6 when describing Jesus' suffering in Matthew 26:67; 27:26; Mark 15:19; Luke 22:63.

In the LXX, verse 23 uses the same language found in Romans 5:4-5, where Paul says *endurance* produces hope that *does not put to shame*. The noun form of *hypomenō* ("wait for") in Isaiah 49:23 is translated as "endurance" in Romans 5:4 (ESV).

The combination of terms is not coincidental. Psalm 69 is on Paul's mind when writing Romans. This is evident by the fact he explicitly quotes the psalm in Romans 11:9-10; 15:3. Examining the psalm more closely, we can confirm how Paul connects multiple themes from Psalm 69. The psalmist says,

> Let not *those who hope in you be put to shame* through me, O LORD GOD of hosts; let not those who seek you be brought to *dishonor* through me, O God of Israel. For it is *for your sake that I have borne reproach, that dishonor has covered my face*. I have become a stranger to my brothers, an alien to my mother's sons. For zeal for your house has consumed me, and the reproaches of those who reproach you have fallen on me. (Psalm 69:6-9)

Although the verb *hypomenō* here is translated as "hope in," its noun form conveys "endurance" in Romans 5:4 (ESV). Again, "endurance" is linked with not being "put to shame" in the context of suffering or persecution. Also, Psalm 69:9 reiterates a point taken from Joel 2:17—the honor of God and his people are inextricably bound together.[14]

Why do these Old Testament writers have this hope? Why does the servant of Isaiah 50:8 believe God will justify him? Isaiah 49:22 provides details. The Lord promises, "I will lift up my hand to the nations, and raise my signal to the peoples." The prophet reiterates a key theme of the entire book in which God raises a "signal" or "standard" for the nations. This imagery depicts a flag that people could see from afar and directs those disoriented by conflict or war (Isaiah 5:26; 11:10, 12; 13:2; 18:3; 30:17; 31:9; 62:10). This signal indicates God saves his people by defeating their oppressors (Isaiah 49:22-26). Anticipating Isaiah 50:8, God assures, "I will contend with those who contend with you" (Isaiah 49:25). For this reason, the servant proclaims, "I know that I shall not be put to shame. He who justifies me is near" (Isaiah 50:7-8).

Paul draws from Isaiah 11, where the writer twice proclaims the Lord will raise a "signal" to stand among the nations (11:10, 12). This glorious "signal" will come from Jesse (11:1, 10) and bring about the restoration of God's people. Paul quotes Isaiah 11:10 (LXX) in Romans 15:12, saying, "The root of Jesse will come, even he who arises *to rule* the Gentiles; in him will the Gentiles hope." The phrase "who arises *to rule* the Gentiles" (LXX) expresses the Hebrew version, which says, "who shall stand *as a signal* for the peoples." The "signal" or "standard" in whom Isaiah has hope is for Paul the one who arises to rule, and thus is Paul's hope.

---

[14]We hear unmistakable echoes of Isaiah 50 and Psalm 69 in Romans 5:2-5. Each context makes the same point: those who wait with endurance on the Lord will not be put to shame (compare Psalm 25:3).

These observations from Isaiah 49–51 show how honor-shame influences Paul's message. Paul knows that "God is the one who justifies" (Romans 8:33; Isaiah 50:8) because Christ has risen as king over the nations. He is the "standard" of hope (Romans 15:12; Isaiah 49:22). In Romans 15:12, "arise" is a wordplay reminding readers of Christ's resurrection.[15] "Hope" recalls the resurrection throughout Romans (4:25–5:5; 8:23-25; 15:12; compare 4:17-21 with Hebrews 11:19). Paul's hope for justification is explicitly grounded in the resurrection of Christ, the root of Jesse (Romans 8:33-34). In short, Paul uses this Old Testament backdrop to tell readers they will not be put to shame because the risen Christ is the royal "standard" who justifies his people. This is why Paul has hope.

God honors Isaiah's servant figure, who is shamed by those around him. Isaiah writes,

> And [GOD] said to me, "You are my servant, Israel, in whom *I will be glorified*." . . . And now the LORD says, he who formed me from the womb to be his servant, to bring Jacob back to him; and that Israel might be gathered to him—for *I am honored* [glorified][16] in the eyes of the LORD. . . . "I will make you as a light for the nations, that my salvation may reach to the end of the earth." Thus says the LORD, the Redeemer of Israel and his Holy One, *to one deeply despised, abhorred by the nation.* (Isaiah 49:3, 5-7)

The Lord glorifies the servant, vindicating him from dishonor, because the servant glorifies the Lord.

Therefore, Isaiah appeals to those who "pursue righteousness" (Isaiah 51:1; compare Romans 9:30-31), urging them to "look to Abraham your father" (Isaiah 52:2; compare Romans 4). Justification is contingent on God keeping promises to Abraham (Isaiah 50:8-9; 51:2), fulfilling his creation purposes (Isaiah 51:3). The influence of Isaiah 51:5 on Paul is apparent when reading the LXX. The Lord says, "My righteousness approaches quickly, and even my salvation will go forth as a light, and nations will *hope in* [*elpizō*] my strength. Islands will *wait for* [*hypomenō*] me and will *hope in* [*elpizō*] my strength" (compare Romans 1:16-17; 5:4-5; 13:11; 15:12).

Fittingly, Isaiah's exhortation (like Paul's) concerns the honor-shame perspective of the righteous. Isaiah says those "who know righteousness" are people "whose heart is my law" (Isaiah 51:7). Thus, he adds, "fear not the *reproach of man*, nor be dismayed at their *revilings*."

---

[15]Wright, "Romans," 748. In *Romans 9–16* (Dallas: Word, 1998), 850, James D. G. Dunn points out that *anistēmi* refers to the resurrection in other texts like Acts 17:3; 1 Thessalonians 4:14, 16; Ephesians 5:14. This dual meaning ("rise" and "resurrect") is evident in Acts 3:22, 26; 7:37. In Romans 1:3-5, Christ is the "son of David" and "son of God," as declared by the resurrection. Paul's apostleship is "for the sake of [Christ's] name among all nations."

[16]Hebrew: *kbd*; the LXX has *doxasthēsomai* here.

In summary, this study of Isaiah clarifies how Paul connects honor and shame with other themes in Romans. These include justification, salvation, hope, suffering, kingship, God's righteousness, and his promises concerning the nations. The servant glorifies God even while suffering shame and reproach from enemies. Therefore, the Lord glorifies the servant.

The righteous are not put to shame because they hope in the Lord, who justifies his people. Their hope of glory arises with their justification. Because God's law is in their hearts, they need not fear human reproach. Why do the righteous willingly endure public shame? Because they, like the servant, can say, "I am honored in the eyes of the Lord."

VESSELS OF HONOR AND DISHONOR

The Old Testament background of Romans 9:19-24 also illustrates how Paul uses honor-shame language.

Romans 9:14-24

What shall we say then? Is there injustice on God's part? By no means! [15] For he says to Moses, "I will have mercy on whom I have mercy, and I will have compassion on whom I have compassion." [16] So then it depends not on human will or exertion, but on God, who has mercy. [17] For the Scripture says to Pharaoh, "For this very purpose I have raised you up, that I might show my power in you, and that my name might be proclaimed in all the earth." [18] So then he has mercy on whomever he wills, and he hardens whomever he wills.

[19] You will say to me then, "Why does he still find fault? For who can resist his will?" [20] But who are you, O man, to answer back to God? Will what is molded say to its molder, "Why have you made me like this?" [21] Has the potter no right over the clay, to make out of the same lump one vessel for honorable use and another for dishonorable use? [22] What if God, desiring to show his wrath and to make known his power, has endured with much patience vessels of wrath prepared for destruction, [23] in order to make known the riches of his glory for vessels of mercy, which he has prepared beforehand for glory— [24] even us whom he has called, not from the Jews only but also from the Gentiles?

In Romans 9, Paul upholds God's freedom in election such that even Gentiles can find righteousness. God's word to Abraham has not failed, since election is not based on worth (Romans 9:6-13). Thus, Paul defends God's righteousness (Romans 9:14). God uses Pharaoh, whose hardened heart results in Israel's salvation. Why? Verse 17 answers, "For this very purpose I have raised you up, that I might show my power in you, and that my name might be proclaimed in all the earth" (quoting Exodus 9:16).

Paul's potter-clay analogy in Romans 9:20-21 comes directly from Old Testament passages that are chock full of honor-shame connotations.[17] To illustrate how the Old Testament applies this imagery, we will study Isaiah 41 and 45, which resemble Paul's usage in Romans.

ISAIAH 41: GOD TRAMPLES ON CLAY

In Isaiah 41, God promises Abraham's offspring, "And you shall rejoice in the LORD; in the Holy One of Israel you shall glory" (Isaiah 41:16). Later, the "King of Jacob" challenges the idols to prove they are gods (Isaiah 41:21-27). God's unique glory as Creator is at stake. He plans to "trample on rulers as on mortar, as the potter treads clay" (Isaiah 41:25).

Isaiah 41:21-27

Set forth your case, says the LORD; bring your proofs, says the King of Jacob.[22] Let them bring them, and tell us what is to happen. Tell us the former things, what they are, that we may consider them, that we may know their outcome; or declare to us the things to come.[23] Tell us what is to come hereafter, that we may know that you are gods; do good, or do harm, that we may be dismayed and terrified. [24] Behold, you are nothing, and your work is less than nothing; an abomination is he who chooses you.

[25] I stirred up one from the north, and he has come, from the rising of the sun, and he shall call upon my name; he shall trample on rulers as on mortar, as the potter treads clay.[26] Who declared it from the beginning, that we might know, and beforehand, that we might say, "He is right"? There was none who declared it, none who proclaimed, none who heard your words.[27] I was the first to say to Zion, "Behold, here they are!" and I give to Jerusalem a herald of good news.

God reveals how he will rescue Israel. He asks, "Who declared it from the beginning, that we might know, and beforehand, that we might say, 'He is righteous'?" (41:26).[18] In 41:27, the message of God's righteousness is called the "gospel," precisely as Paul says in Romans 1:16-17!

What is the relationship between the potter-clay analogy and honor-shame? The imagery magnifies the sovereign Creator's glory and exposes the impotence of false gods and those who hope in them. Therefore, Isaiah writes, "Behold, all who are incensed against you *shall be put to shame and disgraced*; those who strive

---

[17]See Isaiah 29:16; 30:14; 41:25; 45:9; 64:8; Jeremiah 18:2-6; and Lamentations 4:2; compare Isaiah 43:1, 7; Job 10:9. In other ancient texts, see Wisdom 15:7; Sirach 36:13.

[18]My translation, adapted from the ESV. "Righteous" is a typical rendering of Hebrew *tsaddiq* and helps readers connect Isaiah 41:26 with other uses of the word (for example, Isaiah 24:16; 45:21; 53:11; 60:21). The LXX uses *alēthē* ("true"), which explains God's righteousness in Romans 3:3-4.

against you *shall be as nothing and shall perish*" (Isaiah 41:11-12, adapted from ESV). The point is reemphasized in Isaiah 42:17, "They are turned back and utterly put to shame, who trust in carved idols, who say to metal images, 'You are our gods.'"[19]

Why does God utterly shame idolaters? The one "who created the heavens" says, "I am the LORD; that is my name; my glory I give to no other, nor my praise to carved idols" (Isaiah 42:5, 8). When God demonstrates his righteousness, people give glory and praise to God among the nations (Isaiah 42:10, 12). God's own justification in Isaiah 41:26 is a public vindication of his identity and honor.

ISAIAH 45: CREATING CONFUSION

Romans 9:19-20 closely paraphrases Isaiah 45:9, which says, "Woe to him who strives with him who formed him, a pot among earthen pots! Does the clay say to him who forms it, 'What are you making?' or 'Your work has no handles'?" The objection in Isaiah concerns God's plan to use Cyrus, a Gentile king, to accomplish his saving purposes for Israel (Isaiah 44:28). Alec Motyer summarizes the implied criticism:

> What can the Lord be thinking of by destroying our hopes? How can he ever bring it off by using a conqueror to liberate? For by using a Gentile conqueror to liberate Israel it was not only the pride of the nation that was threatened but the Lord's promises. Under a Gentile liberator the people would in principle return to the same situation from which they had been deported. The times of the Gentiles would continue in Jerusalem. There would be no sovereign state, no Davidic revival! The Cyrus-plan was the death-knell to all such hopes.[20]

Somehow, God's plan demonstrates "righteousness" (Isaiah 45:19, 24) such that nations say to his people, "Surely God is in you, and there is no other, no god besides him" (Isaiah 45:13-14).

Isaiah 45:16-25

All of them are put to shame and disgrace*; the makers of idols go in disgrace* together. [17] But Israel is saved by the LORD with everlasting salvation; you shall not be put to shame or disgrace* to all eternity.

[18] For thus says the LORD, who created the heavens (he is God!), who formed the earth and made it (he established it; he did not create it empty, he formed it to be inhabited!): "I am the LORD, and there is no other. [19] I did not speak in secret, in a

---

[19]These words intend to give hope amid hardship and apparent uncertainty (Isaiah 41:10; 42:2-4, 7, 16).
[20]J. A. Motyer, *The Prophecy of Isaiah: An Introduction & Commentary* (Downers Grove, IL: InterVarsity Press, 1996), 361.

land of darkness; I did not say to the offspring of Jacob, 'Seek me in vain.' I the LORD speak righteousness*; I declare what is right. [20] Assemble yourselves and come; draw near together, you survivors of the nations! They have no knowledge who carry about their wooden idols, and keep on praying to a god that cannot save.

[21] "Declare and present your case; let them take counsel together! Who told this long ago? Who declared it of old? Was it not I, the LORD? And there is no other god besides me, a righteous God and a Savior; there is none besides me. [22] Turn to me and be saved, all the ends of the earth! For I am God, and there is no other.

[23] "By myself I have sworn; from my mouth has gone out in righteousness a word that shall not return: 'To me every knee shall bow, every tongue shall swear allegiance.'

[24] "Only in the LORD, it shall be said of me, are righteousness and strength; to him shall come and be ashamed all who were incensed against him. [25] In the LORD all the offspring of Israel shall be justified and shall glory."

* Adapted from ESV

Isaiah reiterates the Lord's "forming" power throughout Isaiah 43–45.[21] This imagery honors God, who says, "Before me no god was formed, nor shall there be any after me" (Isaiah 43:10). The Lord addresses "everyone who is called by my name, whom I created for my glory, whom I formed and made" (Isaiah 43:7).

This context forms the backdrop for Isaiah 45:16-17, which says, "All of them are put to shame and disgrace; the makers of idols go in disgrace together. But Israel is saved by the LORD with everlasting salvation; you shall not be put to shame or disgraced to all eternity" (my translation, adapted from ESV). Israel's everlasting salvation juxtaposes the idolaters' eternal shame and disgrace. The contrast demonstrates that shame concerns both salvation and condemnation. Olson highlights shame's forensic connotations in Isaiah:

> Those whose faith is placed outside of God's redemptive promise will find certain shame (Isa 41:11; [42:17;] 44:9, 11; 45:16, 24), whereas those whose faith rests in these redemptive promises will not be put to shame (Isa 45:17; 49:23; 50:7; 54:4), but rather will experience God's eschatological righteousness in the justification granted through the Servant's sacrifice (Isa 45:25; 50:8, 10; 53:11; 54:14, 17).[22]

In this way, "shame" in Isaiah has theological importance. As I have been attempting to make clear, shame is more than a psychological feeling or anthropological construct.

Isaiah 45:18 explains why idolaters are put to shame (note the "for" [*ki*]) by saying that God alone created and formed heaven and earth. How does this explain verses

---

[21]For example, Isaiah 45:7, 11, 18. Compare Isaiah 44:9-10, which contrasts God with idols.

[22]Olson, *The Gospel as the Revelation of God's Righteousness*, 329.

16-17? Verses 20 and 22 clarify that the key issue is sovereignty. Because the Lord is Creator and thus formed all things, only he can save. God not only predicts the future; he is able to achieve his purposes.[23] The potter alone decides the clay's purpose. Idols—creations formed of wood and stone—have no power or purpose. They cannot save.

Because the Lord is Creator, he is the world's supreme king, as all will recognize when the Lord fulfills his word. He determines the future and thus speaks truth about what comes to pass (Isaiah 45:19). A link between God's righteous word and human faith/allegiance becomes apparent when the Lord says, "By myself I have sworn; from my mouth has gone out in righteousness a word that shall not return: 'To me every knee shall bow, every tongue shall swear allegiance'" (Isaiah 45:23; compare Romans 14:11). Since idolaters do not acknowledge the Creator's global reign, they will be put to shame (Isaiah 45:16-17, 20, 24b; compare 26:11; 41:11). Isaiah 41:2, 26 illustrate nicely how the Lord expresses his righteousness. God is declared righteous when he tramples kings, "as a potter treads clay," bringing victory for his people and causing them to "glory" in the Lord (41:16).

As in Romans 9, Isaiah uses potter-clay imagery to magnify God's righteousness.[24] The sovereign Lord even uses Gentile kings to save his people from the shame of slavery (Isaiah 41:2, 25; 45:13).[25] This salvation demonstrates his righteousness (Isaiah 45:8; 13; 19, 23-24a). Isaiah 45:19 says, "I the LORD speak *righteousness* [*tsdq*]."[26] This does not simply mean God speaks what is true and accurate; his speaking brings about righteousness. God *does* what is righteous. This interpretation is confirmed by Isaiah 45:23, where God states, "from my mouth has gone out in righteousness a word that shall not return." God's righteousness is similarly described as "going forth" elsewhere in Isaiah 51:5; 61:11-62:1 (compare Jeremiah 51:10; Malachi 4:2).

What results when God brings forth righteousness? Isaiah 45:25 says, "In the LORD all the offspring of Israel *shall be justified* and *shall glory*." The Hebrew "glory" (*hll*) here likely means "boast" or "exult" and is juxtaposed with being put to shame (Isaiah 41:11, 16). Here, in seed form, we have precedent for the contrast in Romans 5:2-5 between boasting and (not) being put to shame.[27]

---

[23]John Oswalt, *The Book of Isaiah, Chapters 40–66* (Grand Rapids: Eerdmans, 1998), 283.

[24]Compare Isaiah 10:6, 22-23 (cited in Romans 9:27-28); 28:17 with 29:16; 64:5, 8.

[25]In Isaiah 41:2, God stirs up from the east one "whom righteousness calls to its foot" (translation by Oswalt, *Isaiah, 40–66*, 81-83). Some translations use "victory" (ESV) or "victor" (NRSV), yet this is an interpretive gloss more than a translation of the *tsdq* itself. Isaiah 42:10 might echo 41:2, where God addresses his servant, "I will uphold you with my righteous right hand."

[26]My translation.

[27]The LXX uses Paul's *kauchaomai* to translate *hll* in 1 Kings 20:11; Jeremiah 9:23-24.

As Paul does in Romans, Isaiah 45:24-25 contrasts being righteous ("justified") with being shamed. The LXX overtly links righteousness and glory in the two verses. Verse 24 says "*righteousness* [*dikaiosynē*] and *glory* [*doxa*] will come with him." By comparison, in verse 25, God's people are "*justified* [*dikaiōthēsontai*] by the Lord and *will be glorified* [*endoxasthēsontai*] by God."

Throughout Isaiah 41 and 45, we see that the righteousness and glory of God's people depend on his own righteousness. The offspring of Israel are only justified once the Lord demonstrates his righteousness (Isaiah 45:19, 21, 25; 41:26).

HONOR, SHAME, AND THE POTTER'S RIGHTEOUSNESS

Now it is time to summarize the relationship between God's righteousness, potter-clay imagery, and honor-shame in Isaiah. First, Isaiah frequently situates "put to shame" language in contexts that highlight the Lord's *preeminence*. The potter-clay analogy magnifies the point. The Lord as Creator alone has the right to accomplish his creation purposes. Because "there is no other god besides me, a righteous God and a Savior; there is none besides me" (Isaiah 45:21), he is uniquely worthy of praise and glory. Idolaters don't understand true glory and so are put to shame.

Second, God's glory is manifest in *power*. The Creator is sovereign King over the world. He establishes righteousness. He puts kings and idolaters to shame. Righteousness is found "only in the LORD," to whom "every knee shall bow, every tongue shall swear allegiance" (Isaiah 45:23-24). So vast is the Lord's authority that his righteous ones "shall not be put to shame or disgraced to all eternity" (Isaiah 45:17).

Third, the Creator King reigns over *all people*. Since there is one true God, honor and shame do not consist in cultural opinions and distinctions. Humanity's glory ultimately depends on God's righteousness. Honor and shame depend not on the relative shape of clay but on the potter's character. Thus, he is right to put to shame those who hope in idols from every culture.

Fourth, the Lord demonstrates righteousness for the sake of *praise*. He says that "the people whom I *formed* for myself *that they might declare my praise*" are those "whom I *created for my glory*, whom I *formed* and *made*" (Isaiah 43:7, 21). Furthermore, "I am the LORD; that is my name; my glory I give to no other, nor my praise to carved idols" (Isaiah 42:8; compare 48:9).

Honoring creation above the Creator is inherently shameful. Isaiah writes of Assyria, "Shall the axe *boast* over him who hews with it, or the saw *magnify* itself against him who wields it? As if a rod should wield him who lifts it, or as if a staff should lift him who is not wood!" (Isaiah 10:15). Similarly, the clay glorifies itself as though it is worthy of greater honor than the potter. Therefore, it is right(eous) for the Creator to put his creatures to shame by exposing their vainglory. Observe Isaiah's ironic depiction of God's fiery judgment against Assyria:

> Therefore the LORD GOD of hosts will send wasting sickness among his stout warriors, and under his *glory* a burning will be kindled, like the burning of fire. . . . The *glory* of his forest and of his fruitful land the LORD will destroy, both soul and body, and it will be as when a sick man wastes away. (Isaiah 10:16, 18)

Apart from the Creator, creation's glory proves worthless. In short, "They are turned back and utterly put to shame, who trust in carved idols, who say to metal images, 'You are our gods'" (Isaiah 42:17; compare 44:9; 45:16; Jeremiah 10:14; Hosea 4:7, 12).

Fifth, God's righteousness gives his people a new honor-shame *perspective.* The Lord foretells, "And you shall rejoice in the LORD; in the Holy One of Israel you shall glory" (Isaiah 41:16; 45:25). God transforms what was shameful into something honorable. Specifically, he restores his people's honor. Although Israel was considered a "worm," the Lord later calls Israel "my glory" (Isaiah 41:14; 46:13).

Sixth, when Isaiah says people will (not) be put to shame, the context typically concerns God's *promises.* The Lord sharply contrasts himself with so-called gods by claiming he alone brings about his word. Because God is righteous, he fulfills his purposes and those who hope in him are not put to shame.

Creation is not like the Creator. Idols cannot foresee the future or fulfill hopes for salvation. Idolaters do not speak what is right. Isaiah 41:29 says, "They are all a delusion; their works are nothing; their metal images are empty wind." The Lord "shall trample on rulers as on mortar, as the potter treads clay" (Isaiah 41:25), with the result that those who oppose God's people "shall be put to shame and confounded" (Isaiah 41:11).

Finally, Isaiah uses shame language to urge *perseverance.* He not only seeks to motivate God's people to remain faithful amid persecution. He might also want to convince them of the certainty of suffering. To Isaiah's contemporaries, the phrase "they will not be put to shame" likely means "they will not *always* be put to shame." They will not perpetually suffer shame.

This sort of admonition shows the nature of their temptation and struggle. Everyone desires acceptance and honor. Shame leads to social rejection and so is a serious threat to faith. In these circumstances, people must decide to whom they will swear allegiance (Isaiah 45:23).

HOW DOES PAUL APPLY ISAIAH?

How do the above insights help us interpret Paul's letter and identify potential applications for contemporary readers?

Paul demonstrates God's supremacy over all things. Like Isaiah, he focuses on God's word. God doesn't merely foretell the future. He accomplishes his purposes in ways that overturn conventional thinking. Most of Paul's Old Testament citations are in Romans 9–11. This is not coincidental. The plethora of quotations and allusions confirm that God's word has not failed. The section concludes with the exclamation, "Oh, the depth of the riches and wisdom and knowledge of God! . . . To him be glory forever. Amen" (Romans 11:33, 36).

In Romans 9, Paul vindicates God's honor from accusations of unrighteousness (Romans 9:6, 14). God reigns over creation as a potter is sovereign over clay. The Creator is not arbitrary in governing the world. Rather, the potter-clay analogy magnifies God's sovereignty precisely to prove how he demonstrates righteousness. How so?

Paul quotes Exodus 33:19, stating that God is free to show mercy and compassion as he wills (Romans 9:15). Paul's answer only makes sense if we remember that Exodus 33 follows the golden calf debacle in Exodus 32. Michael Bird explains, "God's freedom to bestow his mercy on whomever he so chooses . . . is the only determinative cause of God's people continuing to carry his promises forward. . . . This is to imply that Israel, when left to its own devices, becomes unfaithful and apostate."[28]

Paul affirms God's righteousness in two ways. First, God's freedom allows him to keep his covenant promises to Abraham (Romans 9:6-13) despite Israel's sin. Second, the Creator shows himself King over all nations. In righteousness, he exalts himself over creation so that his "name might be proclaimed in all the earth" (Romans 9:17).

Accordingly, Paul defends God's honor by showing the certainty and scope of God's purposes. In a sense, Romans 9 completes the argument begun in Romans 3:1-6: God is faithful despite Israel's unfaithfulness. Contrary to expectation, he manifests his righteousness by justifying Gentiles, not merely Jews (compare Romans 3:26-30; 9:24-31). God is worthy of honor as covenant keeper and Creator King.

The potter-clay imagery humbles human presumption by relativizing social identity. God's calling is not according to human measures of worth (Romans 9:10-13). We are not wrong to want to be vessels of honor (compare Romans 2:7-10), but our glory depends on the plan of the potter.

God's freedom ensures his impartiality (Romans 2:11). Social norms do not bind him. God does not call people according to ethnicity, nationality, birth order, social position, or even moral successes and failures. He is not the God of Israel only (Romans

---

[28]Michael Bird, *Romans* (Grand Rapids: Zondervan, 2016), 330.

9:6-7). The righteous *should* seek glory and honor without yielding to social relativism (Romans 2:6-11).

Because righteousness consists in glorifying God, unrighteousness leads to shame. This is because the unrighteous confuse the potter with the clay. They exchange the glory of one for the other (Romans 1:21-23; Psalm 106:20; Jeremiah 2:11). They are put to shame in that God gives them up to "dishonorable passions," thus becoming shameful (Romans 1:24-28).

Additionally, Romans 9:21-23 uses honor-shame language to explain the significance of the potter and clay. The clay is not necessarily something dishonorable and shameful.[29] Verse 21 says, "Has the potter no right over the clay, to make out of the same lump one vessel for *honorable* use and another for *dishonorable* use?" (compare 2 Timothy 2:20-21). The potter alone has the right to determine human honor. Neither honor nor dishonor is intrinsic to clay. Vessels of honor are "vessels of mercy, which [God] has prepared beforehand for glory," whether Jews of Gentiles (Romans 9:23-24).

Several practical implications follow from the study in this chapter. I will briefly note a few. Most of the passages highlighted above contain the threat of shame. These warnings will only have their intended effect if people have an inward sense of shame. Shameless individuals will be slow to repent in response to such ominous words. Communities that do not foster a righteous sense of shame among its members will bear the consequences.[30]

These texts also point to a natural desire to avoid shame. How might this disinclination affect our motivations and behaviors? First, it spurs people to reconsider the source of their hope. Do they trust in a person or thing that is trustworthy? Or will they be put to shame when their hope is finally proven futile? Second, the looming threat of shame provides strong motivation to repent from an unwise and wayward lifestyle.

A third and related application is subtle but significant. These verses remind us of strongholds that bind the hearts of many people who are unwilling to turn to the Lord. The fear of shame can grab people's attention and consider the Lord's call; in the same way, the fear of being shamed by one's community might be a stumbling block or obstacle to faith. This insight should make us more sensitive when sharing the gospel and raising up mature disciples.

---

[29]From some Old Testament texts, such imagery seems inherently to concern judgment. However, a closer reading suggests it simply distinguishes two kinds of status. For instance, Isaiah 64:8 says, "But now, O LORD, you are our Father; we are the clay, and you are our potter; we are all the work of your hand."

[30]A more controversial inference requires qualification. The pervasive threat of shame suggests, in principle, it is a legitimate tool for instruction or discipline. However, we've only seen examples where the Lord brought shame upon those who rebel against him. No passage gives indication how people might wisely use shame in a similar way, if it's even possible. Nevertheless, this observation is noteworthy in view of various contemporary debates.

Whether by hook or by crook, the social powers will attempt to cajole believers to compromise their faith. Such leaders are akin to the "crown of pride" from Isaiah 28:1, 3. At times, they will promise a figurative "covenant with death" (Isaiah 28:18), security from whatever danger is feared. For some people, the potential of financial or physical hardship matters little compared to threat of shame and social isolation. How might God's people respond? We find clues in the prophets, Romans, and in other New Testament letters, such as Hebrews and 1 Peter. For instance, Isaiah 45:25 reminds readers that God will vindicate his people and they "shall be glorified in God." Likewise, Christ's followers learn patience from Paul's reminder in Romans 9:22-23 that God has "endured with much patience vessels of wrath prepared for destruction *in order to* make known the riches of his glory for vessels of mercy, which he has prepared beforehand for glory."

In conclusion, Paul's honor-shame language reflects several Old Testament passages. The righteous shall receive honor as they glory in the Lord. The unrighteous are put to shame. Punitive shame entails physical and psychological pain. It includes being excluded from a group, such as when one is alienated from a father or king. Those who inflict such shame treat others as having diminished worth. Accordingly, punitive shame objectively changes one's identity.

11

HONOR ONE ANOTHER
(ROMANS 12–13)

Two millennia after Paul wrote Romans, we're still asking, "Who are God's people?" The average person in China uses "Christian" (*jidutu*) to describe Protestants, as distinct from "Catholics" (*tianzhu jiaotu*).[1] The International Mission Board of the Southern Baptist Convention seems to equate "Christian" and "evangelical" when it says people groups are unreached unless 2 percent of their population is evangelical.[2] Even the term *evangelical* is disputed. The National Association of Evangelicals defines an evangelical using four theological criteria.[3]

By contrast, many news agencies rely on polling organizations who assume "evangelical" only includes white people, although a quarter of evangelicals, sociologically defined, are nonwhite. Many Christians do seem to be unified more by moral and political issues than theology. Despite their vast theological differences, some Roman Catholic and evangelical scholars have pledged to work together for the sake of "Christian mission."[4] In practice, this cooperation has focused on issues like abortion, gay marriage, and religious freedom.

Why do these distinctions matter? The church's reputation and witness are at stake. After the 2016 US presidential election, commentators claimed evangelicals lost credibility by voting overwhelmingly for Donald Trump. In just five years, the percentage of white evangelicals who believed politicians who were immoral in their private lives could "nonetheless behave ethically and fulfill their duties" in public life increased from 30 percent to 72 percent, a number higher than Americans with no religious affiliation.[5]

---

[1] Although a word for "Protestant" (*xinjiaotu*) exists, few people use it or distinguish "Protestant" and "Christian."

[2] Zane Pratt, "Here's What We Mean by Unreached Peoples and Places," November 22, 2016, www.imb.org/2016/11/22/what-do-we-mean-by-unreached-peoples-and-places.

[3] These include biblicism, evangelism, conversion, and the necessity of Christ's death on the cross for redemption. See "What Is an Evangelical?" National Association of Evangelicals, http://nae.net/what-is-an-evangelical (accessed November 22, 2016).

[4] "Evangelicals and Catholics Together: The Christian Mission in the Third Millennium," *First Things*, May 1994, www.firstthings.com/article/1994/05/evangelicals-catholics-together-the-christian-mission-in-the-third-millennium.

[5] Robert Jones, "Donald Trump and the Transformation of White Evangelicals," *Time*, November 19, 2016, time.com/4577752/donald-trump-transformation-white-evangelicals.

Some researchers claim that "evangelical Protestants are more likely to be divorced than Americans who claim no religion."[6] However, others dispute studies that define *evangelical* based on self-identification, not practice.

If those in the church do not distinguish themselves, outsiders will. Romans 1–11 largely focus on historical and theological convictions uniting Christ's followers. Beginning in Romans 12, Paul shifts his attention to how God transforms the church's practice. In this chapter, then, we explore ways honor and shame affect how Christ's followers relate to one another and outsiders.

CHRISTIAN COLLECTIVISM

Romans 12 uses the words "sacrifice" and "body"—two images common in traditional honor-shame cultures—to emphasize holiness and harmony in two ways. First, Paul calls believers to present their bodies as "a living sacrifice, holy and acceptable to God" (Romans 12:1). This language concerns purity, holiness, and sacredness. Why does this imagery have honor-shame implications? In short, it signifies boundaries that demarcate places, people, and things to be treated with special honor. By contrast, shame is linked with what is impure or defiled.

By grace, Paul is called "to be a minister of Christ Jesus to the Gentiles in the priestly service of the gospel of God, so that the offering of the Gentiles may be acceptable, sanctified by the Holy Spirit" (Romans 15:16). He likely draws from Isaiah 66:18-20, where the Lord says,

> For I know their works and their thoughts, and the time is coming to gather all nations and tongues. And they shall come and *shall see my glory*, and I will set a sign among them. And from them I will send survivors to the nations . . . that *have not heard my fame or seen my glory*. And *they shall declare my glory among the nations*. And they shall *bring all your brothers from all the nations as an offering* to the LORD, on horses and in chariots and in litters and on mules and on dromedaries, to my holy mountain Jerusalem, says the LORD, just as the Israelites bring their grain offering in a clean vessel to the house of the LORD.

Paul's priestly task is to declare the Lord's fame and glory among those who do not yet honor him. When the nations glorify the Lord, they become an offering to the Lord. In effect, Paul depicts the world as God's temple, his sacred space. Regardless of place or people, the sovereign God is worthy of unique glory (compare Romans 14:9, 11).

Second, Paul uses the human body as a metaphor for the church's collective identity (Romans 12:3-8). This imagery encourages harmony by helping readers properly

---

[6]Jerry Park, Joshua Tom, and Brita Andercheck, "CCF Civil Rights Symposium," Council on Contemporary Families, February 4, 2014, https://contemporaryfamilies.org/50-years-of-religious-change.

perceive themselves and others. This metaphor suits an honor-shame perspective that emphasizes group unity.[7]

Paul's body metaphor both humbles and honors individuals within the larger community. He says,

> For by the grace given to me I say to everyone among you not to think of himself more highly than he ought to think, but to think with sober judgment, each according to the measure of faith that God has assigned. For as in one body we have many members, and the members do not all have the same function, so we, though many, are one body in Christ, and individually members one of another. (Romans 12:3-5).

Both individualism and collectivism at their extremes have problems. Paul's imagery balances the two and so cuts across cultures. Here he highlights collective identity to ensure his reader does not "think of himself more highly than he ought to think."

Verses 4-5 begin with "for" and support verse 3. Romans 12:3 is noteworthy for two reasons. First, it credits God's grace for individual distinctions. Second, the significance of these differences is found *within* the body of Christ. However, an individualistic mindset that loses sight of the community makes us prone to pride, focusing attention on our differences. By emphasizing personal distinctions apart from one's role in a community, we forsake the humbling benefits that come by recognizing our similarity with others.

These observations prepare us to understand the significance of Paul's exhortations concerning godly character and behavior. They are no random collection of moral commands. Instead, he offers an alternative honor-shame perspective that is inextricably tied to the Romans' collective identity as Christ's church.[8]

LOVING HONOR

What does it mean to be holy, honorable in God's sight? God's people are "saints," holy ones, in two respects.[9] First, they have a distinct identity and vocation. Saints are distinct from the world even while being set apart for its sake (compare 12:1-2). Second, they are called and equipped to reflect God's unique worth. His people should pursue harmony. Their collective unity ultimately proclaims God is not partial to any culture or social group.

---

[7]The body metaphor is found across cultures. See Andreas Musolff, "The Metaphor of the 'Body Politic' Across Language and Cultures," in *Cognitive Explorations into Metaphor and Metonymy*, ed. Polzenhagen, Frank, Zoltán Kövecses, Stefanie Vogelbacher, Sonja Kleinke (New York: Peter Lang, 2014), 85-99.

[8]For more on Paul's redefinition of honor-shame in Romans, compare J. R. Harrison, "The Erasure of Distinction Paul and the Politics of Dishonour." *Tyndale Bulletin* 67, no. 1 (2016): 63–86.

[9]Paul's use of holiness language here is no coincidence. In Romans, he calls believers "saints" eight times, second only to Ephesians (nine). Most instances (six) appear in Romans 12–16. This observation may suggest a strong link for Paul between holiness and belonging to the community of God's people.

Romans 12:9-18

Let love be genuine. Abhor what is evil; hold fast to what is good. [10] Love one another with brotherly affection. Outdo one another in showing honor. [11] Do not be slothful in zeal, be fervent in spirit, serve the Lord. [12] Rejoice in hope, be patient in tribulation, be constant in prayer. [13] Contribute to the needs of the saints and seek to show hospitality.
   [14] Bless those who persecute you; bless and do not curse them. [15] Rejoice with those who rejoice, weep with those who weep. [16] Live in harmony with one another. Do not be haughty, but associate with the lowly. Never be wise in your own sight. [17] Repay no one evil for evil, but give thought to do what is honorable in the sight of all. [18] If possible, so far as it depends on you, live peaceably with all.

Christ's followers are called to "love one another *with brotherly affection.*" Love among Christians is not simply general benevolence irrespective of one's relationship to another. Instead, love between believers reckons as *family* others in the church.

Familial relationships create additional obligations that do not exist in other relationships. In other words, the way we show love to people depends on our relationship with them. Collective identity has practical implications for how we love others. Without this observation, Paul's family imagery loses its significance. For many modern Christians, calling one another "brother" or "sister" is little more than tradition.

Notice *how* God's people show familial love: "Outdo one another in showing honor." Jewett and Kotansky render 12:10, "Take the lead in honoring one another."[10] The exhortation to "outdo one another in showing honor" is possible in light of God's grace, distributed to His people according to His will (12:3–5). Therefore, "the competition is not *for* honour, but *to* honour." Why? "The competitive practices of ancient and modern honour are predicated on the fear that honour is limited and many must miss out. But if grace abounds then we have nothing to fear, for there is more than enough to share."[11] Christ's followers are free to celebrate and so honor others for the grace shown in others' lives. In this way, the Roman Christians should show genuine love.

Honor is essential to love in three ways. First, we convey that others have worth when we honor them. Second, the way believers show honor in Romans 12:10 undermines distrust, shame, and discord that stem from the competition for status and praise. Third, when members of the body show honor in this way, none lack the honor they desire.

---

[10]Robert Jewett and Roy D. Kotansky, *Romans: A Commentary*, ed. Eldon J. Epp (Minneapolis: Fortress, 2007), 761.

[11]Mark B. Stephens and Georgiane Deal. "The God Who Gives Generously: Honour, Praise and the Agony of Celebrity." *Scottish Journal of Theology* 71, no 1 (2018): 66.

Romans 12:16 more directly says, "Have the same mind toward one another."[12] This rendering indicates how harmony is achieved. The commands that follow explain the honor-shame perspective that is critical for mutual love and harmony. The charge not to be proud (that is, "do not be haughty") echoes Romans 12:3 and contrasts "associate with the lowly." The "lowly" refers to people who lack high social status.[13]

Harmony is possible when people cease making themselves the basis for honor. Paul reiterates the same warning elsewhere (Romans 1:22; 11:25; 16:19). A worldly honor-shame perspective assesses other's worth relative to one's own perceived worth. The desire for acceptance and honor drives people to use whatever standard is convenient, including national identity, moral behavior, or education.

Our sense of honor and shame becomes distorted as our thinking narrows to our own group or ourselves. By contrast, Paul expands our field of vision in Romans 12:17-18. Rather than being mindful of themselves, Paul's readers should "give thought to do what is honorable *in the sight of all.*" The emphasis falls on the last phrase, as verse 18 shows: "If possible, so far as it depends on you, live peaceably *with all.*"

Typical honor-shame perspectives are warped in two ways. First, a worldly view of honor is not oriented toward God (Romans 12:1-3, 11). Second, people lack a godly sense of honor and shame when their identity is based on social distinctions rather than Christ (compare Romans 12:5). A Christian perspective of honor and shame divides the world into two groups: the family of "saints" (Romans 12:13) and outsiders. Paul's exhortation here derives from the fact that one God is Lord of all (Romans 3:30; 10:12).[14] Accordingly, worldly measures of honor and shame make no sense because they are partial to one social group (Romans 2:11).

Someone might object that Paul's ethic does not fundamentally differ from others since he simply redefines "insiders." Romans 12:19–13:8 refutes this objection. Christ's followers willingly endure public shame from outsiders (Romans 12:19-21). They show respect to their enemies and those authorities who reject Christ. Why?

The reason stems from Christians' collective identity, which gives them a transformed view about what deserves praise or shame. Barclay states,

> The goal of Paul's mission is the construction of communities which attempt to disregard these old values, and the contests for honour that surround them, even if these communities are imperfectly formed and their goals imperfectly articulated by Paul himself.

---

[12]My translation; in agreement, Jewett and Kotansky, *Romans*, 768. The ESV's translation conveys the result when believers honor one another before themselves in love.

[13]Compare Matthew 11:29; Luke 1:52; 2 Corinthians 7:6; 10:1; James 1:9; 1 Peter 5:5.

[14]Verse 16 essentially restates Romans 11:20, 25, where Paul warns Gentiles against pride, thinking themselves wiser than Jews who rejected Christ. This observation links Romans 12:16-18 with Romans 2–4.

What he wants is not deracination or the obliteration of all previous identities, but a radical disinvestment in such identities as bearers of symbolic worth.[15]

Christ exemplifies true glory, which was manifest through shame. All who measure worth in view of Christ belong to him and one another. Therefore, Barclay adds,

> If what really counts for worth among Pauline believers is what they have been made in Christ, they can use or disregard these other identities as fits the purpose of the good news and the interests of the community. To live, as he puts it "under grace" (Rom 6.14-15) is to be subordinate to a new authority, a new standard of worth that reshuffles and recalibrates all previous systems of value.[16]

The church regards as "insiders" those who worship the one true God as king.

Members of any group seek honor or approval from the head of the group, whether it is a king, father, supervisor, or coach. This means the church's honor ultimately is not decided by worldly authorities, who are subordinate to God. No human authority determines another person's identity, honor, shame, or worth. They cannot give true "face." Thus, Christ's people are free from the pressure to compete for social status. They can obey the command, "love your neighbor as yourself" (Romans 13:9).

Of course, many neighbors are not followers of Christ. At some level, we belong simultaneously to multiple social groups, even if Christ's people fundamentally identify with his church. In Romans 13, Paul considers the church's relationship with "outsiders." How do God's people honor governing authorities?

TAKE DOWN THE CROSS

Imagine living in a country that is somewhat tolerant but not friendly toward Christianity. After your church spends millions of dollars on a new building, the government says it is four times the allowed size. Because your church lacks the required permits, the government has the right to tear down the structure. Similar notices are issued to other churches. Some churches might be spared if they simply remove the large crosses protruding into the skyline from atop their buildings. How should your church respond?

This dilemma faced churches in Wenzhou, China. One local church leader explains,

> We admit that many churches are not completely legal. This is because the provincial government hardly ever grants permits for large churches. Since there is a need for larger churches here in Wenzhou, it's been a common practice for churches to be built larger than is permitted and local governments always cut us some slack.[17]

---

[15]John Barclay, "Pure Grace? Paul's Distinctive Jewish Theology of Gift," *Studia Theologica* 68, no. 1 (2014): 14.
[16]Barclay, "Pure Grace?," 14-15.
[17]Zhang Yu, "Concern Rises in Wenzhou as Christianity Booms in Capitalist Fashion," *Global Times*, April 17, 2014, www.globaltimes.cn/content/855208.shtml.

Nevertheless, Wenzhou Christians in spring 2014 protested government orders to take down the cross from a prominent church building. Negotiations failed. The situation became an international spectacle when thousands of people blocked bulldozers converging on the scene.

Church leaders explained their objections to the government's actions. Some claimed the situation exemplified persecution against Christians. A petition to the provincial government stated, "The government should protect people's right to freedom of religion, as is granted by the Constitution."[18] One believer argued that Christians could not "allow people to remove the crosses from our churches whenever they want. This is brutally trampling our right to believe."[19] Another local woman insisted, "We are not taking the cross down. It is a symbol of our love. A church without a cross is just a warehouse."[20] On a visit to Wenzhou, I asked my students for their thoughts. Many agreed when a student summarized a common sentiment among local pastors, "They think we should not take down the crosses because we must obey Christ, not the government."

Should Wenzhou Christians obey regulations to remove crosses, especially where churches lack appropriate permits? Is this religious persecution against Christians? Or were church leaders instead angling for political rights in the name of Christ? Do Christians compromise the gospel if their building lacks a large cross? Do Wenzhou believers confuse what is essential to the Christian faith with tradition?

The rest of this chapter considers the relationship between Christ's followers and those outside the church, particularly governing authorities. Romans 13 is not a comprehensive political theology, yet what Paul says can equip the church to "pay honor to whom honor is owed," even when it means honoring those in political power.

HONOR, HIERARCHY, AND AUTHORITY

By reading Romans 13 with Eastern eyes, we find answers to many pressing questions. Hierarchy and authority are of prime importance in traditional Eastern cultures. This contrasts with individualistic Western worldviews, which tend to emphasize equality, egalitarianism, and individual rights. Although leaders exist everywhere, authority and hierarchy are critical features of an honor-shame worldview.

---

[18]Yu, "Concern Rises in Wenzhou."

[19]Kate Tracy, "China Lifts High the Cross (Right Off Dozens of Churches)," *Christianity Today*, May 30, 2014, www.christianitytoday.com/gleanings/2014/may/china-lifts-high-cross-right-off-dozens-churches-zhejiang .html.

[20]Mia Li, "Faithful Rush to Protect Church with a Cross Deemed Too Tall," *New York Times*, April 4, 2014, http:// sinosphere.blogs.nytimes.com/2014/04/04/faithful-rush-to-protect-church-with-a-cross-deemed -too-tall.

Ideally, authorities embody and enforce a group's distinctive values. Those who contribute and conform to social expectations win praise and respect. Group loyalty and allegiance to authority are interlaced. This holds true for churches, clubs, and countries. Our status partly depends on how we respond to those in high positions. How do we respond to those with power? What should we do when one group's norms conflict with those of another? People continually decide who they are by choosing which leaders they honor.

The gospel redefines God's people in Christ. By confessing Jesus as Lord, they relativize the claims of Caesar, tradition, and every other authority. Paul's redefinition of God's people has practical social implications for the church.

Romans 13:1-8

Let every person be subject to the governing authorities. For there is no authority except from God, and those that exist have been instituted by God.[2] Therefore whoever resists the authorities resists what God has appointed, and those who resist will incur judgment.[3] For rulers are not a terror to good conduct, but to bad. Would you have no fear of the one who is in authority? Then do what is good, and you will receive his approval,[4] for he is God's servant for your good. But if you do wrong, be afraid, for he does not bear the sword in vain. For he is the servant of God, an avenger who carries out God's wrath on the wrongdoer.

[5] Therefore one must be in subjection, not only to avoid God's wrath but also for the sake of conscience.[6] For because of this you also pay taxes, for the authorities are ministers of God, attending to this very thing.[7] Pay to all what is owed to them: taxes to whom taxes are owed, revenue to whom revenue is owed, respect to whom respect is owed, honor to whom honor is owed.[8] Owe no one anything, except to love each other, for the one who loves another has fulfilled the law.

The sensitive nature of Romans 13 leads Paul to communicate in a less direct manner. This indirectness has fueled debate about Paul's political theology. Did he take a mild stand regarding governing authorities? Was he counter-imperial? If Jesus is Lord, as Paul emphasizes, Caesar must not be. Paul's comments demonstrate he is not counterrevolutionary in any conventional sense. Yet "the Romans did not persecute Christians because they said, 'Jesus is Lord of my heart,' but because they insisted that 'Jesus is Lord' and his kingdom will eclipse that of Caesar."[21]

These questions miss the subtlety and significance of Paul's argument. His comments are akin to a theocratic Trojan horse. Readers should "be subject to the governing authorities" *because* the latter are subordinate to God. They are "from God," being "instituted" or "appointed" by God. Rulers, therefore, are "God's

[21] Michael Bird, *Romans* (Grand Rapids: Zondervan, 2016), 448.

servants" and "ministers of God." Paul six times in six verses highlights God's sovereignty over governing rulers *while simultaneously* exhorting readers to be subject to them.

Paul's words create a quandary. If local authorities applaud Paul's charge to obey governing officials, in so doing they acknowledge they are accountable to God. Either piety or social mores would prevent ancient authorities from claiming to stand above God. In this way, rulers cannot censure Paul, although his words effectively relativize their own power.

In Romans 13:3-4, 7, Paul five times uses some form of *phobos*, that is, fear or respect. With more sensitivity to honor-shame, people have increased awareness to hierarchy and power. People fear those in power. Paul subtly forges a wedge between human and divine authority, yet he does not create a false dilemma, forcing citizens to choose whether to honor God *or* governing authorities.

Ironically, Paul's charge to give "honor to whom honor is owed" is subversive. This is because submission to worldly authorities stems from one's supreme allegiance to God. Absolute obedience is *not* required to honor secondary authorities, whether parents, officials, or tradition. If authorities order people to dishonor God, they are not obliged to obey. Such authorities demand greater honor than is owed them.

Romans 13:7 explains why readers owe honor to governing authorities. The command "pay back" (*apodidōmi*) must be read alongside Romans 13:4, where governing authorities are God's servants "for you."[22] According to the principle of reciprocity, Christians are obligated to pay taxes, respect, revenue, and honor. Of course, many of Paul's contemporaries would be incredulous at such a claim. In this period, dissension about taxes grew, eventually leading to war in 66 CE between Rome and the Jews. Paying taxes is an emblematic way of affirming the legitimacy of government authority. Because of Paul's allegiance to Christ, he can resist social pressures that come amid political struggle.[23]

It is noteworthy that Paul also changes how he refers to "outsiders." He has no desire to provoke tension or raise the suspicions of the governing authorities. Trebilco notes the shift in tone.

> The lack of any "high boundary" terminology in 13:1-7 (such as "outsiders," "unbelievers," "the unrighteous") means that the emphasis is on the ways the Christ-believing community can be part of and belong to the wider society. . . . Not only will being "good

---

[22]Jewett and Kotansky, *Romans*, 801; compare "ἀποδίδωμι," in Arndt, Danker, Bauer, and Gingrich, eds., *A Greek-English Lexicon of the New Testament*.

[23]Compare Tacitus, *Annals* 13.50; Josephus, *Jewish War* 2.409; Dean Pinter, "Josephus and Romans 13:1-14: Providence and Imperial Power," in *Reading Romans in Context: Paul and Second Temple Judaism*, ed. Ben Blackwell, John Goodrich, and Jason Maston (Grand Rapids: Zondervan, 2015), 143-50.

citizens" mean the Christ-believing group will not attract adverse attention from the authorities, or from any casual visitor to the group, but also the way in which Paul makes this call, with its general terminology ("good and bad" [v3], "respect and honour" [v7]) recognisable to all and its lack of high boundary outsider designations, emphasises harmony and good relations in society.[24]

Paul is careful to avoid language that breeds unnecessary division or disrespect. Additionally, Christians owe authorities *ascribed honor.*[25] This honor is due to the authorities' position, which God gives them. Therefore, his people show allegiance to God by honoring the governing authorities, despite the fact that rulers tolerate, endorse, or even administer injustice against God's people (Romans 12:19-21). In humility, believers practically demonstrate hope for God's vindication (12:19).

Paul's readers should relativize, not reject, the governing authorities. This is key to honoring social leaders properly. When citizens of God's kingdom obey his law, they love their neighbor as themselves (Romans 13:9). They persevere to bless, live peaceably with all, and seek social good (Romans 12:13-18). Loving authorities is a far greater good than merely tolerating them. Loyalty to Christ produces love for Caesar.

People constantly choose what to do based on competing identities. One is a Christian and a Roman, a son and soldier, a mother and wife, a pastor and parent, a citizen and employee. Paul doesn't offer pragmatism but rather a broader perspective. Sociopolitical boundaries are insufficient, being too provincial for us to discern what is truly honorable or shameful in God's eyes. Paul directs attention to the authority atop every social hierarchy. He then reminds his readers of the nearness of their coming salvation in Romans 13:11-14:

> *Besides this* you know the time, that the hour has come for you to wake from sleep. For salvation is nearer to us now than when we first believed. The night is far gone; the day is at hand. *So then* let us cast off the works of darkness and put on the armor of light. Let us walk properly as in the daytime, not in orgies and drunkenness, not in sexual immorality and sensuality, not in quarreling and jealousy. But put on the Lord Jesus Christ, and make no provision for the flesh, to gratify its desires.

In short, he supports the command to love and honor governing authorities by linking ethics to eschatology.

Finally, Paul appeals to readers' conscience (Romans 13:5). After all, Christ's followers have new hearts (Romans 2:15, 29; 5:5; 6:17). Paul's exhortation to the Romans

---

[24]Paul R. Trebilco, *Outsider Designations and Boundary Construction in the New Testament: Christian Communities and the Formation of Group Identity* (Cambridge: Cambridge University Press, 2017), 229.

[25]In agreement, Halvor Moxnes, "Honour and Righteousness," *Journal for the Study of the New Testament* 10, no. 32 (1988): 74.

resembles the quotation from Confucius, cited in chapter 9.[26] Those with true virtue have a right sense of honor and shame. Such people do what is right regardless of laws or perceived threats against them.

Although Paul refers to judgment, praise, and wrath in Romans 13:2-5, he does not settle for base motives. Rather, Romans 12:19; 13:5, 8-12 represent Paul's more common, positive approach. He does not appeal to God's wrath in Romans 13:4-5. The Greek simply says "wrath" (orgē), which likely refers to that of the governing authorities. God is the "avenger" who "bears the sword" but gives "his approval" to those who do right.

DOES THE CHURCH HAVE A SOCIAL BENEFIT?

Romans 13:3 presents a problem for modern readers. It seems Paul urges readers to do good works to win the favor of governing authorities. How can Paul guarantee "you will receive his approval" if they "do what is good"? Such assurance appears naive, especially given Romans 12:19-20 and his own experience. A subtle dynamic must be at work in Paul's appeal.

Some scholars suggest Romans 13:3-4 concerns benefaction, a customary practice in Greco-Roman civic life.[27] Wealthy benefactors (or patrons) bestowed gifts for the benefit of clients, who then reciprocated with public honors.[28] Winter explains, "Not only did rulers praise and honour those who undertook good works which benefited the city, but at the same time they promised likewise to publicly honour others who would undertake similar benefactions in the future."[29] Official guarantees were used to motivate generosity by potential benefactors. Ancient sources use the same language found in 13:3-4.[30]

With this background, we infer that Paul "intends to deliver a mild shock in his call to action."[31] The church now plays the role of benefactor, whose benefaction is "humble service."[32] The authorities, including the emperor, assume the role of clients

---

[26]Analects 2:3. Translation comes from Jeffrey Reigel, "Confucius," in Stanford Encyclopedia of Philosophy, http://plato.stanford.edu/entries/confucius.

[27]Bruce Winter, Seek the Welfare of the City: Christians as Benefactors and Citizens (Grand Rapids: Eerdmans, 1994); Philip Towner, "Romans 13:1-7 and Paul's Missiological Perspective: A Call to Political Quietism or Transformation?" in Romans and the People of God: Essays in Honor of Gordon D. Fee on the Occasion of His 65th Birthday, ed. Sven K. Soderlund and N. T. Wright (Grand Rapids: Eerdmans, 1999), 149-69; Bird, Romans, 445.

[28]D. D. Walker, "Benefactor," in Dictionary of New Testament Background, ed. Craig A. Evans and Stanley E. Porter (Downers Grove, IL: InterVarsity Press, 2000), 157-59.

[29]Bruce Winter, "The Public Honoring of Christian Benefactors," Journal for the Study of the New Testament 34 (1988): 87.

[30]For example, tō agathō ergō, epainon, eis to agathon; see Winter, "Public Honoring," 92-93.

[31]Towner, "Romans 13:1-7," 167.

[32]Towner, "Romans 13:1-7," 166-67. He elaborates on such a role reversal in "Can Slaves Be Their Masters' Benefactors? 1 Timothy 6:1-2a in Literary, Cultural and Theological Context," Current Trends in Scripture Translation 182/183 (1997): 39-52.

who return praise ("approval," *epainos*) to their benefactor in 13:3. It's noteworthy that Roman officials rewarded benefactors with "a public ceremony at which the benefactor was proclaimed. The term *epainos* referred to this public declaration."[33] Paul essentially says, "Give benefaction and you will receive the praise due to a patron."

The Roman congregation is perfectly suited for Paul's exhortation. Christianity was well received by the Roman upper class.[34] In Philippians 4:22, Paul writes, "All the saints greet you, especially those of Caesar's household." Many scholars suggest Urbanus, Stachys, "those who belong to the family of Aristobulus," and "those in the Lord who belong to the family of Narcissus" in Romans 16:9-11 are members of the imperial household.[35] Yet Paul's comments are laced with irony. The governing authority is God's "servant." Therefore, a Christian's "praise [*epainos*] is not from man but from God" (Romans 2:29).

Although the text's meaning does not need to be limited to benefaction, we must take this theme seriously. Too few writers consider its implications for the church's social ministry. This neglect is especially poignant when we recognize how often contemporary cultures still use benefaction practices, even if informally, using terms like *reciprocity* and *gift exchange*. Related concepts include *guanxi* in China, *blat* in Russia, and *wasta* in Arab countries.

Paul urges Christians to do works that serve the public good. He does not want his readers simply to be moral citizens with private spirituality. His exhortation has explicit expectations—local officials will praise believers' good works. This implies such works are public and so are noticed. Through public benefaction, believers will "do what is honorable in the sight of all."

Social ministry highlights the nature of the gospel. Because of their allegiance to Christ, Roman Christians should engage in social ministry as an expression of honor and love (Romans 13:7-10). Paul is mindful of Christ's coming salvation. Therefore, he urges the church to show love and honor via social ministry (Romans 13:11-12).

Romans 13 further contributes to "Paul's redefinition of the people of God."[36] Within many groups, collective identity is associated with certain leaders or hierarchical structure. In responding to authorities, whether Christ or civic officials, people reflect

---

[33]Winter, "Public Honoring," 92.

[34]Rodney Stark, "Early Christianity: Opiate of the Privileged?" *Faith & Economics* 54 (2009): 1-18.

[35]Stark, "Early Christianity," 7; A. von Harnack, *The Expansion of Christianity in the First Three Centuries*, vol. 2 (New York: G. P. Putnam's Sons, 1905), 195-97; J. B. Lightfoot, *Philippians* (Whitefish, MT: Kessinger, 2010), 17, 175; Tom Holland, *Romans: The Divine Marriage* (Eugene, OR: Pickwick, 2011), 464-75. If Junia is a Latin name for Joanna (Luke 8:3), she too had wealth. See Richard Bauckham, *Gospel Women: Studies of Named Women in the Gospels* (Grand Rapids: Eerdmans, 2002), 172-80. Additionally, the fact that Paul repeatedly sends third-person greetings through his readers shows his awareness of a larger Roman community, many of whom could have had wealth.

[36]Dunn, *Romans 9–16*, 769.

what they regard as being honorable or shameful. Accordingly, Paul reminds readers they are God's people, not Caesar's. Above all, they "are called to belong to Jesus Christ," not Rome (Romans 1:7). This identification with Christ produces love. For those with a collectivist, honor-shame perspective, the implications are clear: "Love means group attachment and the behavior that such attachment requires."[37]

A NEW PERSPECTIVE ON POWER

Romans 13 gives a clear message that believers should not want to destabilize governments. By obeying local laws and contributing to their community, Christians convey God's desire for social order and peace. But Christ's followers too often confuse political opinions with God's explicit commands. They too quickly resist governing authorities. Thus, Christian believers need humility to consider carefully the differences between personal convictions and biblical commands. On this point, Paul's discussion in Romans 14 gains new relevance when political controversy threatens church unity.

The gospel affects how God's people respond to authority and power. In hierarchical societies, few issues are more sensitive. Paul's basic strategy is to broaden readers' perspective to see the larger sphere of God's authority. He *de*localizes honor-shame by giving it a global orientation. This fundamental shift doesn't make the church apolitical. Rather, it changes believers' basic approach to power.

An honor-shame perspective is inherently political. We make a political statement when choosing whom to honor. From this standpoint, we see the true nature of political power. Viewed through an honor-shame lens, politics is simply about *public influence*. In truth, influence is always public. However, many who read this book with Western eyes will assume a distinction between public and private. Yet only individuals can pretend to ignore the dynamics of power typified in political systems. Private influence doesn't exist, since we all live in a web of countless interconnected social relationships.

Important implications follow from this realization. First, all actions are "political" in some sense. What people regard as private morality is a statement about who has authority in their lives. Christian conduct illustrates what allegiance to Christ looks like (Romans 13:13-14). Believers fulfill the law through love, respecting and honoring social leaders. In this way, the church proves that it doesn't seek to usurp government authority.

The church exerts influence in counterintuitive ways. Convinced of God's sovereignty, his people accept suffering with hope. Christ's followers endure hardship knowing God raises the dead. This perspective enables the church to seek peace without passivity. They don't fear persecution and pressure from governing authorities

---

[37]Bruce J. Malina and John J. Pilch, *Social-Science Commentary on the Letters of Paul* (Minneapolis: Fortress, 2006), 282. Given the context, it is not accidental that Romans 13:8-10 explains "law" in terms of love.

who demand conformity and compromise. In being subject to authorities, the church subverts worldly powers.

Romans 13 helps contemporary readers find wisdom in responding to anyone with social authority. Parents and ancestors in many traditional cultures have tremendous authority. Ancestor veneration is controversial in churches across the world. Some Christians resist ancestor veneration, saying only one God exists or belief in ancestral spirits is superstition. However, this approach could miss the mark and devolve into speculative arguments.[38] Paul begins with a basic premise: because there is one Creator God, he alone reigns over the world. This truth not only undergirds Romans 13 but also reframes the issue of ancestor veneration.

Veneration of ancestors primarily is a question about authority, not the number of gods or spiritual beings. The problem with treating deceased ancestors as though they have power among the living is that one ascribes ancestors with authority that is not properly theirs. Descendants effectively treat deceased relatives as though they had God's authority, as if their power transcends death. Ancestor veneration confuses divine and human authority. Just as social leaders are subject to God and exercise authority within a given sphere, so ancestors are not granted power beyond the sphere of the living. A Christian response to ancestors, governments, and parents should reflect this truth: Christ is "Lord both of the dead and of the living" (Romans 14:9).

This point is far more relevant to Westerners than some might think. G. K. Chesterton describes the influence of ancestors in the West when he says, "Tradition means giving a vote to the most obscure of all classes, our ancestors. It is the democracy of the dead. Tradition refuses to submit to the small and arrogant oligarchy of those who happen to be walking around."[39] His message is a positive one, beckoning people to consider the wisdom of past generations. I quote Chesterton to make a different point. His words eloquently illustrate what tradition entails. "Giving a vote to . . . our ancestors" could work both for our good and to our harm. Whether in democracies or denominations, people in the West also yield to ancestral authority in subtle yet similar ways found in East Asia.

Paul's message also applies to church leaders. Westerners can learn from problems common within Eastern communities. In Eastern cultures, leaders often have authoritarian leadership styles. Pastors with strong hierarchical perspectives are prone to strong, top-down approaches to leadership.[40] Such pastors can become domineering and divisive. When discussing ideas, they quickly resist compromise for fear of

---

[38]By contending that belief in ancestral spirits is superstitious, we can easily go too far by essentially arguing against the existence of other non-divine spiritual beings like angels and demons. Compare Michael Heiser, *The Unseen Realm: Recovering the Supernatural Worldview of the Bible* (Bellingham, WA: Lexham Press, 2015).

[39]G. K. Chesterton, *Orthodoxy* (Walnut, CA: MSAC Philosophy Group, 2008), 37.

[40]See Jackson W., "Authority in a Collectivistic Church: Identifying Crucial Concerns for a Chinese Ecclesiology," *Global Missiology* 1, no. 9 (2011), http://ojs.globalmissiology.org/index.php/english/article/view/679/1689.

losing face. Their personal sense of honor is attached to their position rather than their character.

Such pastors undermine Paul's vision for the church. Their tendency to control others stifles the exercise of diverse gifts in the church. Questions and disagreements are taken as challenges to their authority and even to God. They confuse conformity with unity, producing controversies like in Romans 14. Functionally, church leaders don't subject themselves to Christ when they assume authority beyond proper limits. Paul not only relativizes the status of governing authorities; by extension, he reminds church leaders "there is no authority except from God, and those that exist have been instituted by God."

How can churches become a constructive public influence? One way is for Christians to serve as godly benefactors in society. Churches must not shy away from so-called social ministries, forgetting that Paul delays his missionary journey to Spain to assist struggling believers in Jerusalem. Through their giving, Gentile churches demonstrate how faith in Christ brings practical benefit to the world. The gospel fosters unity across cultures that not even governing authorities can establish.

We can imagine other ways honor and shame might influence our responses to various practical and theological questions. For example, how do we distinguish patriotism and nationalism? Does paying taxes implicitly endorse a government and its decisions? If so, what does it mean for the church to show honor without giving approval? Can we honor governing authorities while publicly protesting their policies? How might Christians protest injustice yet "live peaceably with all"? Is Romans 13:1-7 an example of indirect, peaceful protest? What about political affiliation? In a place like China, can Christian believers also be members of the Communist Party?

Scholars debate whether Paul was anti-imperial, effectively declaring "Jesus is Lord and Caesar is not." If so, Paul is far from explicit about the point. However, he had to know his gospel had political overtones. The gospel undoubtedly implies "Jesus is Lord and Caesar is not," but this statement must be qualified. Romans 13 makes abundantly clear that God endorses the establishment of political powers. Paul does not suggest divine approval of all that rulers do with their power. Believers cannot honor the shameful behavior of authorities. In this sense, honor is relative. We honor everyone but not in every way.

By understanding honor and shame, we can improve how we interpret and apply Paul's message. Such a perspective does not solve every problem. Nevertheless, new insights emerge when we look at old problems with a fresh perspective.

12

THE CHURCH as "HARMONIOUS SOCIETY" (ROMANS 14–16)

In 2006, China announced its highest priority: creating a "harmonious society." The president chose "eight honors and eight disgraces" to be the moral foundation for China's harmonious society.[1]

Table 4. Eight honors and eight disgraces

Honors	Disgraces
Love the country	do it no harm
Serve the people	never betray them
Follow science	discard superstition
Be diligent	not indolent
Be united, help each other	make no gains at other's expense
Be honest and trustworthy	do not sacrifice ethics for profit
Be disciplined and law-abiding	not chaotic and lawless
Live plainly, work hard	do not wallow in luxuries and pleasures

In China, "Harmony is the measure of all things."[2] To achieve harmony, society needs a proper sense of shame.[3] Accordingly, leaders explicitly used honor and shame to frame the campaign.

---

[1] The translated list comes from China's official Xinhua news service. See Xinhua News Service, "CPC Promotes 'Core Value System' to Lay Moral Foundation for Social Harmony," October 18, 2006, www.gov.cn /english/2006-10/18/content_417140.htm.

[2] Ralph Covell, *Confucius, the Buddha, and Christ: A History of the Gospel in Chinese* (Maryknoll, NY: Orbis, 1986), 11.

[3] Recall Confucius' comment quoted in chapter 9: "If the people are led by laws, and uniformity among them be sought by punishments, they will try to escape punishment and have no sense of shame. If they are led

What can we glean from these observations? China's officially atheistic government has never hesitated to enact laws to enforce its will. Yet its leaders know legislation cannot produce a "harmonious society" just as regulations do not guarantee harmonious families. A common perspective of honor and shame creates an enduring sense of group identity.

Kwang-Kuo Hwang describes an alternative approach:

> Morality in [a] Western culture of individualism is right-based as it emphasizes "negative duties" or "duties of omission." An individual should take "respecting other's right[s]" as a fundamental principle for moral judgment. . . . Practicing "positive duty" is a kind of "virtue"; [yet] it is all right for an individual to choose not to practice it.[4]

Instead of mere negative duties ("duties of omission"), Eastern cultures emphasize *positive* duties ("duties of commission").[5] People are mindful of their responsibilities, not simply their rights. This mindset can foster moral lives that are proactive and public rather than passive and private. In cultures that honor individual rights above all other values, toleration is the best one can hope for. But toleration is a far cry from harmony.

These reflections raise questions for the church. Do contemporary Christians have a genuine sense of collective identity? How does a biblical honor-shame perspective strengthen the church to "live in harmony with one another" (Romans 12:16)? Paul helps us address these questions. In Romans 14–16, Paul uses honor and shame to exhort believers to maintain unity amid controversy.

EATING FOR CHRIST'S SAKE

The Roman church was divided. They couldn't agree about what they could eat or which days to celebrate. It wasn't the first time this kind of thing had happened. As we'll see, the controversies in Romans 14 and 1 Corinthians 8 are remarkably similar. Meat was routinely sacrificed to idols. Some people thought eating such meat honored false gods.

The key issue in Romans 14 is loyalty. Paul reemphasizes Christ's universal reign. Accordingly, Romans 14 depicts a gospel problem, not merely one problem among others. When believers dishonor fellow brothers and sisters in Christ, they do not honor the Lord.

---

by virtue, and uniformity sought among them through practice of ritual propriety, they will possess a sense of shame and come to you of their own accord" (*Analects* 2:3, quoted in Jeffrey Riegel, "Confucius," in *Stanford Encyclopedia of Philosophy*, http://plato.stanford.edu/entries/confucius).

[4]Kwang-Kuo Hwang, *Foundations of Chinese Psychology: Confucian Social Relations* (New York: Springer, 2012), 254.

[5]Hwang, *Foundations*, 162-74.

Romans 14:1-6

As for the one who is weak in faith, welcome him, but not to quarrel over opinions. [2] One person believes he may eat anything, while the weak person eats only vegetables. [3] Let not the one who eats despise the one who abstains, and let not the one who abstains pass judgment on the one who eats, for God has welcomed him. [4] Who are you to pass judgment on the servant of another? It is before his own master that he stands or falls. And he will be upheld, for the Lord is able to make him stand. [5] One person esteems one day as better than another, while another esteems all days alike. Each one should be fully convinced in his own mind. [6] The one who observes the day, observes it in honor of the Lord. The one who eats, eats in honor of the Lord, since he gives thanks to God, while the one who abstains, abstains in honor of the Lord and gives thanks to God.

Whom does Paul address? We might say those who think eating meat is allowed and those who prohibit eating meat. However, Paul's comments are more nuanced. He divides people into two types:

1. those who are mistaken about not eating meat but who don't sin

2. those who understand correctly that believers are free to eat meat but make their brothers stumble when they eat

What clues suggest this distinction? First, Paul is not neutral about the issue. In Romans 14:1-2, the one who eats only vegetables is called "weak." Paul in Romans 14:14 adds, "nothing is unclean in itself" (compare Romans 14:20; 1 Corinthians 8:8-13). Paul's distinguishing "weak" and "strong" indicates that he takes sides, *theologically speaking*. Christ allows followers to eat vegetables *and* meat. The "weak" are mistaken about what believers can(not) eat.

Nevertheless, Paul's response is surprising. Instead of condemning the weak, he essentially commends them: "The one who observes the day, observes it in honor of the Lord. The one who eats, eats in honor of the Lord, since he gives thanks to God, while the one who abstains, abstains in honor of the Lord and gives thanks to God" (Romans 14:6). Although they have a mistaken perspective, they can still glorify God in practice. Being wrong about theological issues is not necessarily sin. Sadly, many churches divide because they forget this point.

How do we understand Paul's response? Two points provide clarification. First, he points out that when the weak eat only vegetables, they do it "in honor of the Lord."[6]

---

[6]Although the Greek lacks the word "honor" and only uses *kyriō* ("to the Lord"), the ESV translation captures the sense of the sentence. The one who eats "gives thanks to God" (14:6), in contrast to the unrighteous person in Romans 1:21 who neither glorifies nor thanks God. Also, Romans 14:7-9 makes clear that *kyriō* conveys allegiance, that something is done *for the sake of* the Lord.

This is the goal of all Christian living.[7] Sometimes the most important thing about people's behavior is not *what* they do but *how* they do it. In Romans 14, what the weak do, they do for the Lord's sake. Their actions seek to honor Christ above all.

Second, the controversy doesn't concern explicit commands but rather *potential implications* of Christ's work. We must not miss the seriousness of the debate, as though it simply concerned ancient cultural mores. First Corinthians 8 shows the gravity of this kind of dispute. The weak equate eating meat with honoring idols and perhaps denying the supremacy of the Creator God.

The two sides disagree about what logical inference is correct. The strong infer that eating meat offered to idols is allowed since "an idol has no real existence" and "there is no God but one" (1 Corinthians 8:4). For the weak, eating meat rejects a fundamental Christian truth. The weak understand "there may be so-called gods in heaven or on earth" (1 Corinthians 8:5). Both groups begin with true statements but draw different conclusions. This explains Paul's patience with the mistaken view of the weak, even urging the strong to restrict their own freedom (Romans 15:13-23; 1 Corinthians 8:9-13; 10:23-31).

In these situations, believers honor Christ and one another by distinguishing *what is the Lord's unambiguous will* from *what is simply a possible implication of biblical truth*. Such discernment requires humility, exegetical skill, theological knowledge, and the conviction that church unity is a gospel issue.

HONORING CHRIST AS LORD OF ALL

For Paul, the controversy concerns far more than theological correctness or cultural preference. He cares most about whether believers honor Christ as supreme Lord. The passage repeatedly emphasizes the expansive scope of Christ's reign. Christ is sovereign over life and death. He has authority over every person. Paul's comments are explicitly based on his view of God's kingdom (Romans 14:17).

Romans 14:7-19

For none of us lives to himself, and none of us dies to himself.[8] For if we live, we live to the Lord, and if we die, we die to the Lord. So then, whether we live or whether we die, we are the Lord's.[9] For to this end Christ died and lived again, that he might be Lord both of the dead and of the living.

[10] Why do you pass judgment on your brother? Or you, why do you despise your brother? For we will all stand before the judgment seat of God;[11] for it is written, "As I live, says the Lord, every knee shall bow to me, and every tongue shall confess to God."[12] So then each of us will give an account of himself to God.

---

[7]Compare 1 Corinthians 10:31, which concludes a passage similar to Romans 14. See also Romans 14:23; Colossians 3:17.

> [13] Therefore let us not pass judgment on one another any longer, but rather decide never to put a stumbling block or hindrance in the way of a brother. [14] I know and am persuaded in the Lord Jesus that nothing is unclean in itself, but it is unclean for anyone who thinks it unclean. [15] For if your brother is grieved by what you eat, you are no longer walking in love. By what you eat, do not destroy the one for whom Christ died. [16] So do not let what you regard as good be spoken of as evil. [17] For the kingdom of God is not a matter of eating and drinking but of righteousness and peace and joy in the Holy Spirit. [18] Whoever thus serves Christ is acceptable to God and approved by men. [19] So then let us pursue what makes for peace and for mutual upbuilding.

In Romans 14:11, Paul quotes Isaiah 45:23 to affirm Christ's universal lordship. The context of Isaiah is significant for Paul's argument. Isaiah 45 underscores that the Lord is the Creator. Just before the verse quoted by Paul, Isaiah writes, "And there is no other god besides me, a righteous God and a Savior; there is none besides me. Turn to me and be saved, all the ends of the earth! For I am God, and there is no other" (Isaiah 45:21-22; compare 45:5, 15). Isaiah repeatedly connects "one God" with God's kingship (for example, Isaiah 43:15; 44:6). He uses these themes to oppose idolatry. By worshiping idols, Israel rejects God as King. Those who make idols are put to shame and disgraced (Isaiah 45:16).

Both Romans 14 and 1 Corinthians 8 concern whether people can eat certain foods. Both connect "one God" and authority. Paul in 1 Corinthians 8 speaks directing about "one God" and indirectly addresses authority. In Romans 14, Paul directly mentions authority and indirectly discusses "one God." The chart below illustrates the link between the two chapters.

Table 5. Link between Romans 14 and 1 Corinthians 8

Common Themes	Eating food, church unity (stumbling, weak and strong)	
	Romans 14	**1 Corinthians 8–9**
Direct	Authority	"One God"/Idolatry
Indirect	"One God"/Idolatry	Authority

Church unity is another shared theme. In each text, the "strong" show humility by seeking to please the "weak." Believers should not cause brothers and sisters to "stumble." Therefore, Christians forsake certain rights as a way to love others.

THE ETHICS OF HONOR AND SHAME

Paul states in Romans 14:14, "I know and am persuaded in the Lord Jesus that nothing is unclean in itself, but it is unclean for anyone who thinks it unclean." Because God is Creator, creation is good. Objectively, food and drink are good in themselves. However, Paul's restriction in the second half of the verse is inherently *subjective*. His assessments of good/bad and right/wrong are based on specific situations and individuals.

Does this mean Paul suggests a relativistic view of Christian ethics? No.

A few elements ground Paul's thinking: God is Creator-King. Mutual love is essential and produces the church's unity, which must be prioritized. These values are unchanging absolutes. Yet the church flexibly applies these ethical principles. Judgments about right and wrong depend on one's worldview, identity, and community. What we regard as worthy of honor or shame frames our *moral lens*.

Honor and shame need not lead to relativism. Christ's followers understand honor and shame in view of God's self-revelation in history culminating in Christ's life, death, and resurrection. They discern true honor and shame because they know the Creator who alone manifests everlasting glory. His kingdom consists of all nations. He is worthy of supreme honor. This perspective is a firm framework that helps believers make moral decisions in ever-changing cultures. Christians affirm the existence of absolute moral standards precisely because honor and shame are defined relative to God.

HOW PAUL APPLIES THE GOSPEL

Romans 14 demonstrates how Paul applies the gospel laid out earlier in the letter and so how honor and shame shape Christian practice. The gospel declares Christ as the promised Davidic king (Romans 1:1-4). Those who dishonor God become shameful and lack his glory (Romans 1:18–3:23). Those whom he approves are justified, counted among his people (Romans 2–4). Whatever one's culture, collective identity is ultimately redefined in relation to Christ (Romans 4–6). Many of these related themes reappear and are applied to the Roman church in Romans 14.

Is what we eat or drink a gospel issue? What about clothing, music, or schooling? Most people would say no, yet each of these things *could* become gospel issues. Eating and drinking among Roman Christians effectively function as "works of law" do in Romans 2–4. Rival camps emerged because of different opinions about certain cultural practices and symbols. This implicitly reoriented their basis for unity and worth. Both Romans 2–4 and 14 address the same essential problem—the Roman Christians' group identity and unity were not in Christ. The contentious people of Romans 14 potentially denied in practice what Paul said earlier.

What made this a gospel issue? The Jew-Gentile division undermined the proclamation that Christ reigns over all nations. Similarly, the split over meat could imply Christ is Lord of only one group (Romans 14:7-12).

When eating and drinking are boundary markers, they become a "stumbling block" (Romans 14:13, 20-21). In Romans 9:32-33, Christ is also regarded as "a stumbling stone." Comparing the two passages, we see that a stone causing "stumbling" functionally determines one's group identity. In Romans 9 and 14, Jesus and food respectively serve as boundary markers defining insiders and outsiders. Those who reject the "stumbling stone" are reckoned as outsiders, and thus are lower in status.[8]

Romans 15:8-9 is also significant. Paul's statement there both supports the prior argument and encapsulates the entire letter's theological emphases. This observation has two implications. First, 14:1–15:7 is one of the main applications of Romans. It is not a mere implication or one side exhortation among others in Romans 12–16. Second, 14:1–15:7 clarifies Romans' earlier theological message (especially Romans 2–4). Put simply, eating and drinking *functionally* serve as boundary markers in the same way works and faith did in Paul's previous discussion.

In Romans 14, Paul again presents faith as the solution to church disunity. In Romans 14:23, faith determines right and wrong. He writes, "But whoever has doubts is condemned if he eats, because the eating is not from faith. For whatever does not proceed from faith is sin." Who is strong in faith like Abraham (Romans 4:20)? John Barclay says, "The strength in their faith is the degree to which they have been able to dissociate their faith in Christ from every norm or value that is not derived from the good news itself."[9]

In summary, Romans 14 shows us how Paul *applies* the gospel to the church. The gospel radically changes one's honor-shame perspective. Because the Romans serve a new king, they must redefine "insiders" and "outsiders" relative to Christ, who alone measures worth. Since there is one God, Christ's church consists of all nations, transcending cultural distinctions.

Unity is a gospel issue, but unity for unity's sake is not the goal. Paul seeks genuine unity based on Christ, *not* economics, nationality, denomination, hometown, language, education, gender, or any other measure. This perspective spurs Paul's questions: "Why do you pass judgment on your brother? Or you, why do you despise your brother? For we will all stand before the judgment seat of God" (Romans 14:10).

---

[8]Other details suggest that Romans 14 applies the theology from earlier chapters. In Romans 14:17, Paul mentions "kingdom" and "righteousness"; both were important themes from Romans 1, 5, 6. As we've seen, an underlying problem in Romans 14 concerns loyalty to Jesus as king.

[9]John Barclay, "Faith and Self-Detachment from Cultural Norms: A Study of Romans 14–15," *Zeitschrift für die neutestamentliche Wissenschaft* 194 (2013): 104.

THE GOD OF PEACE

Collectivistic societies that prioritize relationships emphasize the importance of peace. How much more those who proclaim the "God of peace" (Romans 15:33; 16:20)? The latter chapters of Romans give concentrated attention to the subject of peace, which is mentioned in Romans more than in Paul's other letters.[10] Paul characterizes peace in two ways. First, peace comes from God (Romans 1:7; 2:10; 15:13). Second, this peace primarily concerns community relationships (Romans 3:17; 8:6; 12:18; 14:17, 19; compare 16:17).

Later references to peace in Romans might shed light on Romans 5:1. The wording of Romans 5:1 is exceptional because of its explicit mention of having peace "with God." The precise meaning is ambiguous.[11] However, the stress on pursuing peace in Romans 12–15 strengthens the possibility that Paul urges believers in 5:1 to be at peace with God by seeking peace with one another. Both Romans 8:6 and 14:17 suggest believers have peace because of the Holy Spirit. The logic of these verses is comparable to that of Romans 5:1, 5.

Members of Christ's church should live at peace with one another. This thread undergirds Romans 12–15, with Paul's comments in Romans 14 linking back to Romans 12. In Romans 14:18, he says, "Whoever thus serves Christ [by living at peace with fellow believers] is acceptable to God and approved by men." The only other time Paul uses "acceptable" (*euarestos*) is Romans 12:1-2, where he urges believers "to present your bodies as a living sacrifice, holy and *acceptable* to God, which is your spiritual worship," wanting them to "discern what is the will of God, what is good and *acceptable* and perfect."

The peace that marks God's kingdom pursues mutual upbuilding (Romans 14:17, 19).[12] Paul clarifies the meaning of "mutual upbuilding" a few verses later:

> We who are strong have an obligation to bear with the failings of the weak, and not to please ourselves. Let each of us please his neighbor for his good, *to build him up*. For Christ did not please himself, but as it is written, "The reproaches of those who reproached you fell on me." (Romans 15:1-3)

Pursuing peace entails seeking the good of others, even at personal cost. This explains the need for endurance and encouragement (Romans 15:4-5). Just as Christ bore sin to bring about reconciliation among all nations, so his followers bear the failings and reproach of others.

---

[10]See Romans 1:7; 2:10; 3:17; 5:1; 8:6; 14:17, 19; 15:13, 33; 16:20. As a verb, see 12:18.

[11]Scholars debate whether 5:1 indicates what is already true (that is, "we have peace with God") or whether Paul exhorts readers to respond to their justification (that is, "[you] have peace with God"). External manuscript evidence favors the latter. See Stanley Porter, "The Argument of Romans 5: Can a Rhetorical Question Make a Difference?" *Journal of Biblical Literature* 110, no. 4 (1991): 662-65.

[12]Robert Jewett and Roy D. Kotansky, *Romans: A Commentary*, ed. Eldon J. Epp (Minneapolis: Fortress, 2007), 865-66.

Paul concludes the letter by summarizing how God secures peace among his people:

> I appeal to you, brothers, to watch out for *those who cause divisions* and create obstacles contrary to the doctrine that you have been taught; avoid them. For such persons do not serve our Lord Christ, but their own appetites, and by smooth talk and flattery they deceive the hearts of the naive. For your obedience is known to all, so that I rejoice over you, but I want you to be wise as to what is good and innocent as to what is evil. The *God of peace* will soon crush Satan under your feet. The grace of our Lord Jesus Christ be with you. (Romans 16:17-20; compare 1:7)

The combative imagery of crushing Satan highlights how God achieves peace. From an honor-shame perspective, this is significant. In relationship-sensitive contexts, people are especially prone to avoid and ignore conflict. One can lose face just by acknowledging conflict or disagreement. Peace requires managing public perception. It is maintained by giving others "face"—or minimally, not causing others to "lose face."

However, Paul indicates that conflict is inherent to securing peace in two ways. First, God in Christ will crush Satan under his feet (echoing Genesis 3:15). Paul refers to a future victory. Given 1 Corinthians 15:25-27, he seems to have in mind the final resurrection (compare Ephesians 1:22).

Second, for the sake of peace, the church anticipates another area of conflict. Divisive people will sneak into their midst (Romans 16:17). When this happens, believers must not turn a blind eye, which does not produce genuine peace. Rather, they "watch out" and "avoid" divisive people, not denying the problem. Properly responding to such contrarians brings conflict, either when confronting error or in breaking relationship (that is, avoiding them).

How do people divide the church? Paul says that "by smooth talk and *flattery* they deceive the hearts of the naive" (Romans 16:18). This echoes Galatians 4:17-18, where the church's enemies "make much of" them but for no good purpose. Accordingly, believers must understand how "face" works for the sake of the church's gospel witness. Believers are told to honor one another, yet some use "face" to manipulate and deceive. Flattery is a potent force. To prevent this, Christ's followers should be trained in sound doctrine. This provides discernment and conviction and makes it harder to be led astray (Romans 16:17-18).

DEVELOPING GUANXI FOR THE GLORY OF GOD

An American couple slowly became suspicious as a Korean woman they knew showered them with gifts and treated them to luxurious restaurants. They finally discovered why. After spending months attempting to establish *guanxi* ("relationship"), she hoped to obligate them to teach her son English. Reciprocity is a natural part of relationships. The mother tried to exploit this principle by putting these Westerners in her debt. East Asians routinely develop *guanxi* with various people *just in case* they someday need a favor. For many people, relationships are mere tools. Before long in this context, one can grow cynical and calculating rather than grateful and generous.

Romans 15:1-9a

We who are strong have an obligation to bear with the failings of the weak, and not to please ourselves. [2] Let each of us please his neighbor for his good, to build him up.

[3] For Christ did not please himself, but as it is written, "The reproaches of those who reproached you fell on me." [4] For whatever was written in former days was written for our instruction, that through endurance and through the encouragement of the Scriptures we might have hope. [5] May the God of endurance and encouragement grant you to live in such harmony with one another, in accord with Christ Jesus, [6] that together you may with one voice glorify the God and Father of our Lord Jesus Christ. [7] Therefore welcome one another as Christ has welcomed you, for the glory of God.

[8] For I tell you that Christ became a servant to the circumcised to show God's truthfulness, in order to confirm the promises given to the patriarchs, [9] and in order that the Gentiles might glorify God for his mercy.

When we arrive at Romans 15, readers ought not think Paul changes topics with a turn of the page. The verbal links in Romans 15:1-7 with the prior passage remind us that chapter divisions are not original to Paul. One could argue that Romans 15:7-33 is a unit of thought. This is made evident both by the ongoing focus on Jews and Gentiles and the concluding mention of "God of *peace*" (Romans 15:33; compare 14:17, 19; 15:13). Furthermore, the "for" in Romans 15:8 binds the entire chapter together, showing the following section (15:10-33) belongs with the previous discussion.[13]

Paul offers a hopeful view of Christian community. His exhortations in Romans 15–16 directly stem from the gospel. Romans 15:8-9a summarizes the theological core of Romans: "For I tell you that Christ became a servant to the circumcised to show God's truthfulness, in order to confirm the promises given to the patriarchs, and in order that the Gentiles might glorify God for his mercy."[14]

Verses 8-9a supports Romans 15:1-7, particularly Paul's claim, "We who are strong have an obligation ["are indebted"; *opheilō*] to bear with the failings of the weak, and

---

[13]In effect, the "therefore" and "for" in Romans 15:7-8 create the logical overlap that unites the chapter.

[14]Its importance is underscored by the numerous Old Testament citations that follow, including 2 Samuel 22:50; Psalm 18:49; Deuteronomy 32:43; Psalm 117:1; Isaiah 11:1, 10.

not to please ourselves" (Romans 15:1). Why do they have this debt? Paul has an Eastern view of relationships. He understands they entail mutual obligation. Having God as Father (Romans 15:6), Christians are "debtors" (Romans 8:12).[15] In Romans 13:8, their debt is to love one another. This debt is enduring, rooted in a permanent familial relationship.

In Romans 15:3, Paul applies Psalm 69:9 to Christ, demonstrating a practical implication of Christian relationships. By worldly expectations, relationships are means for gaining personal benefit and honor. However, the psalmist endures "dishonor" (Psalm 69:7, 19) because of his relationship to God. The speaker's words are effectively put on the lips of Christ, who suffers reproach for his Father's sake.

What motivates such endurance? Compare Romans with Psalm 69, which Paul says was written so that "through *endurance* and through the encouragement of the Scriptures we might have *hope*" (Romans 15:4). The psalmist says, "Let not those who *hope* in you be put to shame through me" (Psalm 69:6; compare Romans 5:3-5; 8:25). Scott Hafemann summarizes,

> The experience of the psalmist, now replayed in Christ's own experience, is a pathway to hope. So Paul's point in 15:3b is not simply, "act like Christ," as often argued. . . . The Scriptures and the experience of the Christ teach us that God's final redemptive triumph at the end-point of history, not following the moral example of Christ per se, is the *ultimate* foundation and motivating force of what the Romans would have heard to be Paul's social ethic of "obligation."[16]

Paul spurs his readers to persevere by directing their hope to "the God of endurance and encouragement" (Romans 15:5). Christ and his people are honored through shame. But as recipients of grace, believers know God will vindicate them. Paul reorients cultural expectations of reciprocity. Their fundamental obligation is to God. If controversy divides the church, God's name is dishonored. Just as Christ's sacrifice saves God's "face," so the strong uphold God's honor by bearing with the weak.

Paul's ethic is both Eastern and ancient. East Asians feel a stronger sense of indebtedness in daily relationships than do most Westerners.[17] Western notions of grace lead us to misunderstand and devalue relational debt language. Benjamin Shin and Sheryl Takagi Silzer "used to think that Asian culture was completely devoid of grace. But now [we] realize that it was just a different type of grace,

---

[15]Significantly, Romans 8:12 is followed by a flurry of verses highlighting the readers' identity as God's children. Compare Romans 1:7, 14.

[16]Scott Hafemann, "Eschatology and Ethics: The Future of Israel and the Nations in Romans 15:1-13," *Tyndale Bulletin* 51, no. 2 (2000): 167. Emphasis original.

[17]For one study among many, see Hidefumi Hitokoto, "Indebtedness in Cultural Context: The Role of Culture in the Felt Obligation to Reciprocate," *Asian Journal of Social Psychology* 19 (2015): 16-25.

not the Western kind that [we were] used to knowing as an evangelical, Western Christian."[18]

Obligation is an inherent aspect of relationships. Generally, Westerners separate grace and reciprocity such that grace is "non-circular," that is, it expects nothing in return from the recipient. But John Barclay points out, "This is not a common conception of perfect gifts in antiquity . . . it was rare to find the gift perfected as a 'one-way, unilateral donation'"[19] As a result of this misunderstanding, some Western scholars even argue (mistakenly) that Paul emphasizes "grace rather than obligation."[20]

An Eastern emphasis on reciprocity in relationships helps recover a more ancient view of grace and therefore the ability to bear with others. Barclay explains,

> What distinguishes the sphere of gift [from payment] is not that it is "unilateral," but that it expresses a social bond, a mutual recognition of the value of the *person*. It is filled with sentiment because it invites a personal, enduring, and reciprocal relationship—an ethos very often signaled by the use of the term *charis*. [By contrast,] the one-way gift establishes no relation, creates a permanent and potentially humiliating dependency, and frees the recipient of all responsibility.[21]

For Paul, relationships create "debts" that bond people together based on identity. It is no mere transactional cost simply tolerated for personal benefit. Accordingly, even Paul is a "debtor" who is "eager" to preach the gospel in Rome (Romans 1:14-15). Romans 15:27 applies this logic to Gentiles, who "owe" Jews "material blessings." In short, Paul's argument for church unity and call to gospel ministry are easily misunderstood without a proper emphasis on reciprocity—that is, relational debt.

THE SHARED BLESSING OF MINISTRY

Paul depicts himself as a Jewish priest who crosses cultures to bring Gentiles to God as an offering. Such work "fulfills" the gospel of Christ (Romans 15:16, 19).[22] For Paul, gospel ministry concerns far more than individual salvation. Two collective

---

[18]Shin and Silzer, *Tapestry of Grace: Untangling the Cultural Complexities in Asian American Life and Ministry* (Eugene, OR: Wipf & Stock, 2016), 59.

[19]Barclay, *Paul and the Gift* (Grand Rapids: Eerdmans, 2015), 74. On pages 79-188, Barclay traces how the Western church has veered away from ancient understandings of grace.

[20]J. R. Harrison, *Paul's Language of Grace in Its Graeco-Roman Context* (Tübingen: Mohr Siebeck, 2003), 331. Cited by Barclay, *Paul and the Gift*, 181.

[21]Barclay, *Paul and the Gift*, 31, 75. For examples where "*charis* is present as a reciprocal obligation, additional to the cash payment," see Paul Millett, *Lending and Borrowing in Ancient Athens* (Cambridge: Cambridge University Press, 2002), 123-26.

[22]The ESV gives a gloss, "I have fulfilled the ministry of the gospel of Christ." Significantly, the Greek (*peplērōkenai to euangelion tou Christou*) lacks "the ministry of."

identities—Jews and Gentiles—are basic to his understanding of the gospel. By the way, this could explain why Paul in Galatians 3:8 says the Abrahamic covenant *is* the gospel.

Harmony across racial, national, and cultural divides is no mere side effect to gospel ministry. In fact, rather than go straight to Spain, Paul first heads to Jerusalem. On behalf of Gentile churches, he delivers their financial gift to poor Jewish believers. Paul justifies their desire to help in this way: "If the Gentiles have come to share in their [Jews'] spiritual blessings, they ought also to be of service to them in material blessings" (Romans 15:27). Paul labors for church unity because unity across ethnic and social boundaries is a fundamental fruit of the gospel.

The poor Gentiles in Macedonia and Achaia poignantly illustrate in practice what Paul labors to convey throughout the letter. Delaying his trip to Spain for the sake of the Jerusalem saints only heightens the importance of the Gentiles' ministry. Their example of generosity achieves two goals. First, it humbles Roman Gentiles who might be "arrogant" toward Jews (Romans 11:18). Second, it gives greater impetus for the Roman church to support Paul's Spanish mission. Apathy and prejudice based on common social divisions are antithetical to the gospel.

In Romans 16, Paul exemplifies what it means to "welcome one another" (Romans 15:7).[23] Paul's honoring of women is extraordinary. He greets ten women. Paul regards them as significant contributors to gospel ministry. In addition to being his benefactor, Phoebe delivers and likely read the letter.[24] Prisca is a "fellow worker" listed before her husband Aquila (16:3). Mary and Persis have "worked hard" for Christ. Junia is a "fellow prisoner" well-known among the apostles. Tryphaena and Tryphosa are "workers in the Lord." He greets people across the economic and social spectrum—men/women, slave/free, Jew/Gentile. They form a new people "in Christ."[25]

Paul's reasons for honoring them are noteworthy. "Achieved honor" is given to "Prisca and Aquila . . . who risked their necks for my life" (Romans 16:3-4) and "Andronicus and Junia . . . my fellow prisoners" who "are well known to the apostles" (Romans 16:7).[26] Mary and Persis "worked hard" for the Romans and the Lord (Romans 16:6, 12). Phoebe is approved "for she has been a patron [benefactor] of

---

[23]Jewett and Kotansky, *Romans*, 952.
[24]The translation "patron" could be misleading as though Paul were Phoebe's "client." Therefore, I use "bene-factor" following the suggestion of Erland D. MacGillivray, "Romans 16:2, προστάτις/προστάτης, and the Application of Reciprocal Relationships to New Testament Texts." *Novum Testamentum* 53 (2011): 199.
[25]Romans 16 is distinct in its density of "in Christ" and "in the Lord" language, as in Romans 16:2, 3, 5, 7, 8, 9, 10, 11, 12, 13, 22.
[26]Ancient and linguistic evidence for "Junia" rather than "Junias" is overwhelming. Most recently, see Michael Burer, "ΕΠΙΣΗΜΟΙ ἘΝ ΤΟΙΣ ἈΠΟΣΤΟΛΟΙΣ in Romans 16:7 as 'Well Known to the Apostles': Further Defense and New Evidence," *Journal of the Evangelical Theological Society* 58, no. 4 (2015): 731-55.

many and of myself as well" (Romans 16:2). Since Christ is just called a "servant" (*diakonos*) in Romans 15:8, her commendation as a *diakonos* is especially honorific. Being "in Christ" doesn't nullify achieved honor; it simply changes one's standard of honor.

All Paul has said thus far impresses upon his readers *their* obligation to support his Spanish mission.[27] In Romans 15:26-27, Gentiles *owe* material support to the Jerusalem saints (most of whom they likely had never met). At a glance, Paul seems to solicit support from people who have neither met him nor owe him (Romans 15:24); yet this impression is only half true.[28]

One could easily miss a subtle detail underlying Romans 16. Paul has spent years investing in numerous relationships that extend deep into the Roman community. His many second-person greetings further suggest that Romans is more than a mere introductory letter to strangers.[29] Those he greets are more than coworkers; they are personal friends whom he sees as family.[30] He expresses close affection, calling some "beloved" (Romans 16:5, 8, 9, 12), "kinsmen" (Romans 16:7, 11, 21), "sister" (Romans 16:1), "brothers" (Romans 16:14, 17; compare 15:14, 30; 16:23), and even "mother" (Romans 16:13). They have ministered and suffered together (Romans 16:3, 7, 9).

Because Paul does not personally know various Romans, he "borrows face" from their network of shared relationships.[31] These serve as Paul's résumé, so to speak.[32] He seeks the same credibility given to these mutual friends whom he honors. This is a less superficial form of "name dropping," important when people are sensitive to ascribed honor.

PUTTING PEACE INTO PRACTICE

Romans 14 equips the church to *apply* the gospel from an honor-shame perspective. First, Paul helps us discern what counts as a "gospel issue." This discernment equips the church to avoid disputes about secondary issues. A "gospel issue" includes instances where people use a standard other than faith in Christ to distinguish insiders

---

[27] Key verses emphasizing a believer's debt include Romans 1:14; 8:12; 13:7-8; 15:1, 27. The frequency intensifies as Paul nears the letter's conclusion.

[28] Paul's reference to "Timothy, my fellow worker" (Romans 16:21), whom Eastern churches would have known, suggests Paul's need to introduce himself to many of his Roman readers. See Peter Lampe, "The Roman Christians in Romans 16," in *The Romans Debate*, rev. ed., ed. Karl Donfried (Grand Rapids: Baker Academic, 1991), 218.

[29] See Terence Mullins, "Greeting as a New Testament Form," *Journal of Biblical Literature* 87, no. 4 (1968): 425-26.

[30] Of the twenty-six people Paul greets, Jewett and Kotansky identify at least fifteen with whom Paul already has a close relationship. He seems not to know personally eleven people. See Jewett and Kotansky, *Romans*, 952-53.

[31] On "borrowing face," see Hwang, *Foundations*, 335-36.

[32] Compare Richard Longenecker, *The Epistle to the Romans* (Grand Rapids: Eerdmans, 2016), 1066.

from outsiders. Such problems not only concern how people gain salvation; they include threats against church unity. Cultural distinctions, debatable issues, ethnicity, economics, and even one's diet are just a few potential areas that could constitute a "gospel issue." In the Gospels, the Sabbath is treated like a fundamental issue, not merely a single moral infraction among others. In Romans, Galatians, and Acts 15, circumcision is a gospel issue. The Sabbath, circumcision, and regulations around food and drink *in themselves* are not bad. Nevertheless, how we treat these topics can become a gospel issue.

What about today? Below I list various issues that potentially could become gospel issues. This short list represents concerns from different cultures. In some cases, the entire matter depends on how one defines the activity. For instance, does "veneration" mean "worship" or simply "respect"?

Table 6. Potential gospel issues

Eating blood	Belonging to a political party
Drinking alcohol	Buying stocks and bonds
Ancestor veneration	Certain sexual practices
Practicing yoga	View on end times (eschatology)
Various issues surrounding	Practicing *feng shui*
baptism	Attending a meeting at a mosque
Use of tongues	Wearing certain clothing
Choice of Bible translation	Movies and music
Interpretation of Genesis 1–2	Head coverings during church
Evolution	Divorce and remarriage

Second, Paul equips the church to maintain a unity that gives honor to God. God's people don't seek unity for unity's sake. Paul does not endorse the mere toleration that is in vogue among modern, individualistic countries. Such toleration is little more than individuals coexisting with one another. Paul wants more from Christ's followers— we ought to love and welcome one another, being of one mind. This is a positive, proactive peace, not the apparent absence of conflict.

Christian unity is rooted in an essential gospel truth: Christ is Lord over all. What unites God's people is that they give allegiance to the same king and so belong to his kingdom. The gospel makes clear *who* Jesus is such that it becomes clear *who* his followers are in relationship to others.

For many, the gospel primarily concerns *how* individuals get saved.[33] When individual salvation is made central, people increasingly debate which doctrines must be accepted for salvation. Certainly, allegiance to Christ assumes basic theological beliefs like Christ's resurrection, monotheism, and so on. However, this more individualistic emphasis is prone to cultivate the contentious environment found in Romans 14.

Church unity is not based on convictions of conscience whose truth depends on *possible* inferences drawn from clearer truths. Many people are uncomfortable with theological "gray areas." Romans 14 is a warning to churches to humbly admit we can't always discern right and wrong with certainty. The existence of truth and our ability to discern truth are quite different things. Without humility in our limited perspectives, church unity is impossible.

On this point, Chinese culture offers wisdom. Chinese often seek a middle way between two extremes. While the middle way is not always correct, God's people would be wise to explore the possibility that others have truthful insights. Chinese pursue a middle way because they value harmony.[34] This tendency can certainly lead to compromise, yet this danger does not negate the wisdom of approach. After all, it attempts to prioritize sound relationships, not simply correct information.

Unity does not require having the same convictions. It is possible for people with opposite convictions to glorify God. As we've seen, someone might be *wrong* yet still honor God. People confuse the Bible with their conscience when they don't realize that what is sin for them might not be sin for others.

Third, Paul warns against confusing uniformity with unity. This danger is probably most pronounced in strong collectivist cultures. Traditions, ceremonies and rules bring about outward conformity and the impression of unity. Communities shame those who do not comply. Passages like Romans 12:3-8 and 14:1-9 underscore the importance of diversity for Christian unity.

People naturally gather with others like themselves and then use their group to measure harmony. Such a limited perspective inhibits our ability to assess and achieve true unity. Within a typical congregation, twenty people might hold one view and perhaps thirty people have another opinion. However, just because one's own group

---

[33]Scot McKnight, *The King Jesus Gospel: The Original Good News Revisited* (Grand Rapids: Zondervan, 2011). The "King Jesus gospel" and the message of salvation are inseparable. Nevertheless, priority is consistently given to *how one is saved*. I explained how one leads to the other earlier in this book. For more discussion, see Jackson W., *One Gospel for All Nations: A Chinese Contextualization of Salvation through Honor and Shame* (Pasadena: WCL, 2015).

[34]For Filipinos, this is *pakikisama*. For Japanese, *wa*.

agrees does not mean the church is unified. We fool ourselves by using a less-than-biblical measure of unity.

Cultural distinctions are no foundation for Christian unity. Ethnicity, hobbies, or life background cannot sustain lasting unity. In fact, these things typically divide people. One's nationality, skin color, education, and gender determine identity based on differences rather than a common commitment to Christ. Wherever conformity begins to trump true unity, people will likely forge "unity" based on cultural similarities. Churches do well to ask, "Is the basis of our unity more cultural or Christian?"

Fourth, Paul serves as a model for Christian leaders to combat division and controversy. True Christian unity is fragile when leaders use highly authoritarian approaches, which are common in honor-shame cultures. Such leaders often intensify divisions of hierarchy. They exert authority by issuing demands and raising expectations. We need to remember that rules are important, but they don't change hearts.

Fifth, authoritarian use of the Bible threatens church unity by subtly undermining biblical authority. Consider what happens when people do not distinguish the Bible's original meaning from their personal interpretation. Practically speaking, the leader's authority replaces biblical authority. In those settings, teachers too often appeal to "biblical inerrancy" to defend interpretations that deserve legitimate debate. Biblical truth loses out to theological opinion.

To avoid division, Christian leaders need extraordinary humility. They should allow, *even encourage*, contrary opinions. Since all believers have the Holy Spirit, leaders should expect others will have important insights and corrections for them. Humble leaders relentlessly seek to know and overcome their own shortcomings. They are teachable.

This chapter has shown how the gospel transforms Christians' honor-shame perspective. This change has several implications. Constant comparison and competition yield to humility and unity. An honor-shame perspective reshapes our view of the church. The gospel creates a new people bound to one another by Christ, not social distinctions. Church unity is a gospel issue. Because the gospel changes collective identity, Christian ethical decisions must be considered within the context of Christ's church.

REDEEMING RELATIONSHIPS

Paul redeems *guanxi*. In Christ, relationships are neither tools for selfish gain nor burdens to be tolerated. If we find ourselves struggling with Paul's debt language, we should reconsider our assumptions about reciprocity and obligation. In Christ, our "ought to" is also a "want to." Relationships are a means of blessing others. In large part, this is an undercurrent throughout Paul's letter. God, not Abraham, takes initiative to establish relationship, blessing Abraham's family and all nations. Being in covenant relationship with God is not enslaving but freeing.

When we see our sense of identity as distinct from others and habitually insist on our rights and prerogatives above others with whom we have relationship, we become isolated individualists. When people insist on satisfying "their own appetites," they use "smooth talk and flattery" to manipulate others. Consequently, they "cause divisions and create obstacles" contrary to the gospel. We must be clear that valuing distinctions (Romans 12) does not spawn divisions (Romans 14). Recovering a collectivist perspective equips the church to honor other members of Christ's body.

Relationships "in Christ" make *practical* demands on our lives. Paul doesn't settle for mere theological or theoretical unity. Reading Romans through an Eastern lens thus restores a more Pauline perspective by bringing together the false Western dichotomy between "spiritual" and "secular." We need not accept the false dilemma between evangelism and social ministry. Hence Paul intertwines spiritual blessing and material obligation in Romans 15:27 (compare 1 Corinthians 9:11).

Paul's admonitions remind us afresh that faith, like honor, is inherently public:

> American Christians will often say that true character is what you do when no one is watching. . . . In stark contrast to this perspective, Paul was very concerned about how his followers' behavior was perceived by others. The reason for this, to be frank, is because the reputation of some of Paul's churches was in the sewer.[35]

Shame prefers to remain hidden. It creeps into our lives when faith remains private. The seeds of hypocrisy take root where our private life is divided from our public life. The church is the unique context where Christian views of honor and shame make sense and produce "the obedience of faith."

---

[35]Brandon O'Brien and E. Randolph Richards, *Paul Behaving Badly: Was the Apostle a Racist, Chauvinist Jerk?* (Downers Grove, IL: InterVarsity Press, 2016), 46.

DISCUSSION GUIDE

CHAPTER 1: HOW TO READ WITH EASTERN EYES

1. What are some common characteristics between ancient Near Eastern cultures and traditional East Asian cultures?

2. In your community, what are the typical things that give people "face"?

3. Why do honor-shame cultures tend to be collectivistic (that is, group oriented)?

4. What are some common social groups in your culture? What values and perspectives tend to characterize them?

5. Who are the formal or informal authorities in your community? How do people practically show respect?

6. How have honor and shame influenced your life?

CHAPTER 2: PAUL'S MISSION FRAMES HIS MESSAGE (ROMANS 1, 15)

1. How does Paul use indirect speech in Romans? Why does he use this approach?

2. What are Paul's purposes for writing Romans?

3. How does Paul's mission influence his theological message in Romans?

4. How does our sense of identity reflect our honor-shame perspective?

CHAPTER 3: DISHONORING GOD AND OURSELVES (ROMANS 1–3)

1. In Romans, how does Paul describe sin? List verses to support your answer.

2. How do you and those you know typically talk about sin? Do you tend to list examples, use certain metaphors, or cite certain verses?

3. In your context, what are common ways you and others tend to seek "face," honor, fame, or a reputation? Be specific.

4. Typically, from what people do you most seek approval? Why? How?

5. How might you need to repent? How can you change your perspective and actions so that they honor God, even if it means "losing face" in front of other people?

CHAPTER 4: DISTINGUISHING "US" AND "THEM" (ROMANS 2–3)

1. In Romans, how do people categorize themselves and others? What distinctions and values are these labels based on?

2. How do you distinguish "insiders" and "outsiders"? How does that tend to influence your attitudes and behaviors?

3. List a few symbols or traditions that potentially divide the church.

4. Typically, with whom do you most identify? The church? Coworkers? Classmates? Family? Another group? What evidence might other people see to confirm this?

5. How might a collectivistic (or group-oriented) perspective help you
   . . . better communicate the gospel?
   . . . identify practical ways to strengthen the local church?

CHAPTER 5: CHRIST SAVES GOD'S FACE (ROMANS 3)

1. Why is God declared righteous in Romans 3:4?

2. How does Christ save God's "face"?

3. What's the relationship between God's righteousness and our justification?

4. How should Paul's perspective on God's righteousness and glory influence how you read the Bible and live in your community?

5. How should concern for God's reputation reorient your desire to seek "face" and honor?

CHAPTER 6: WHO IS WORTHY OF HONOR? (ROMANS 4)

1. How does Romans 3:27-31 prepare readers to interpret Romans 4?

2. What key question does Paul answer in Romans 4? Which verses most helpfully show the relationship between the "who" and "what" questions of justification?

3. How do we distinguish whether Paul primarily emphasizes faith as the condition or as the proof of justification in Romans 4?

4. List a few ways your church or ministry might compromise unity in Christ by appealing to other standards or symbols besides Christ.

5. How does faith glorify God and justify people in a way that keeping the Mosaic law cannot?

6. How might you vary the way you present the gospel to others?

7. How does Paul's argument link the gospel and the church?

CHAPTER 7: FAITH IN THE FILIAL CHRIST (ROMANS 5–6)

1. How does filial piety tie together faithfulness and sonship?

2. How does Christ's faithfulness glorify God and restore honor to his family?

3. How does Paul use "in Christ" language to discuss collective identity?

4. How does Christ's achieved honor lead to the church's ascribed honor?

CHAPTER 8: THE HOPE OF GLORY THROUGH SHAME (ROMANS 5–8)

1. Why is Christ's resurrection the basis for Paul's hope of glory?

2. How does boasting express loyalty and group identity?

3. How does one practically boast in the Lord?

4. Both Paul and his Jewish opponents "boast in God." What's the difference? In practice, what type of glory do you seek?

5. What is the "glory of God," the "hope that does not put us to shame"?

6. Why does Christian suffering not lead to shame?

7. Salvation includes what "subjective" blessing? How does this lead to a life of honor, not shame?

CHAPTER 9: SHAMED FROM BIRTH? (ROMANS 7)

1. How might traditional individualistic readings of Romans foster shame in the church?

2. What clues suggest Paul has a collectivistic perspective in Romans 7?

3. Who seems to be the "I" in Romans 7?

4. How does Paul present an optimistic perspective of sinners?

5. What implications might Romans 7 have for our view of culture?

CHAPTER 10: THEY WILL NOT BE PUT TO SHAME (ROMANS 9–11)

1. Paul frequently appeals to Old Testament passages that speak about being (or not being) "put to shame." In the Old Testament, what does it mean to be "put to shame"?

2. Why do Old Testament passages about idols often mention people being put to shame?

3. What is the relationship between "hope" and "boasting"?

4. In Isaiah, what does the prophet use "put to shame" language to highlight?

5. In view of Old Testament background, how does the potter-clay analogy honor God and humble people in Romans 9?

6. How can the potter-clay analogy in Romans 9 motivate perseverance in readers?

CHAPTER 11: HONOR ONE ANOTHER (ROMANS 12–13)

1. Why is honor an essential aspect of love?

2. How does our sense of group identity influence how and to whom we show honor?

3. How is it possible to honor authorities without completely obeying them?

4. In what way is Romans 13:1-7 a Trojan-horse argument?

5. How might Romans 13 reframe debates about tradition, ancestor veneration, and other similar issues?

6. How can you and your church bring benefit to your broader social community?

CHAPTER 12: THE CHURCH AS "HARMONIOUS SOCIETY" (ROMANS 14-16)

1. How does Romans 14 relate to Paul's teaching in Romans 1–11?

2. What constitutes a "gospel problem"? In Romans 14, why are activities like eating or drinking gospel problems?

3. What potential issues threaten to become gospel issues in your community?

4. Practically speaking, how much do you and your church prioritize and strive for unity in Christ?

5. In your church or organization, around what might people seek unity other than Christ? In other words, how might people settle for sub-Christian unity?

6. What are some ways you have and have not contributed to church unity?

BIBLIOGRAPHY

Achtemeier, Elizabeth. "Righteousness." In *Interpreter's Dictionary of the Bible*. 4 vols., edited by George A. Buttrick, 4:80-99. Nashville: Abingdon, 1962.

Adams, Edward. "Abraham's Faith and Gentile Disobedience: Textual Links Between Romans 1 and 4." *Journal for the Study of the New Testament* 65 (1997): 47-66.

———. "Paul's Story of God and Creation: The Story of How God Fulfills His Purposes in Creation." In *Narrative Dynamics in Paul: A Critical Assessment*, edited by Bruce W. Longenecker, 19-43. Louisville: Westminster John Knox, 2002.

Adams, Richard. "The Israel of God: The Narrative Rhetoric of Paul's Letter to the Galatians." PhD diss., Emory University, 2012.

Aktaş, Mert. "Cultural Values and Learning Styles: A Theoretical Framework and Implications for Management Development." *Procedia–Social and Behavioral Sciences* 41 (2012): 357-62.

Anderson, Bernard. "Exodus Typology in Second Isaiah." In *Israel's Prophetic Heritage: Essays in Honor of James Muilenburg*, edited by Bernard Anderson and Walter Harrelson, 177-95. New York: Harper, 1962.

Anderson, Garwood. *Paul's New Perspective: Charting a Soteriological Journey*. Downers Grove, IL: IVP Academic, 2016.

Anderson, Gary A. *Sin: A History*. New Haven, CT: Yale, 2009.

Anderson, Leith, and Ed Stetzer. "Defining Evangelicals in an Election Year." *Christianity Today*, March 2, 2016. www.christianitytoday.com/ct/2016/april/defining-evangelicals-in-election-year.html.

Arndt, William, Frederick W. Danker, Walter Bauer, and F. Wilbur Gingrich. "ἀποδίδωμι." *A Greek-English Lexicon of the New Testament and Other Early Christian Literature*, 109-10. Chicago: University of Chicago Press, 2000.

———. "ἀπόστολος." *A Greek-English Lexicon of the New Testament and Other Early Christian Literature*, 122. Chicago: University of Chicago Press, 2000.

———. "ὅπως" *A Greek-English Lexicon of the New Testament and Other Early Christian Literature*, 718. Chicago: University of Chicago Press, 2000.

———. "καύχημα." *A Greek-English Lexicon of the New Testament and Other Early Christian Literature*, 536–37. Chicago: University of Chicago Press, 2000.

————. "πίστις." *A Greek-English Lexicon of the New Testament and Other Early Christian Literature*, 818. Chicago: University of Chicago Press, 2000.

————. "προηγέομαι." *A Greek-English Lexicon of the New Testament and Other Early Christian Literature*, 869. Chicago: University of Chicago Press, 2000.

————. "στοιχεῖον." *A Greek-English Lexicon of the New Testament and Other Early Christian Literature*, 946. Chicago: University of Chicago Press, 2000.

————. "ταλαίπωρος." *A Greek-English Lexicon of the New Testament and Other Early Christian Literature*, 988. Chicago: University of Chicago Press, 2000.

————. "ταπεινός." *A Greek-English Lexicon of the New Testament and Other Early Christian Literature*, 989. Chicago: University of Chicago Press, 2000.

Barclay, John. "Faith and Self-Detachment from Cultural Norms: A Study of Romans 14–15." *Zeitschrift für die neutestamentliche Wissenschaft* 194 (2013): 192-208.

————. *Paul and the Gift*. Grand Rapids: Eerdmans, 2015.

————. "Pure Grace? Paul's Distinctive Jewish Theology of Gift." *Studia Theologica* 68, no. 1 (2014): 4-20.

Barnett, Adam. "David Cameron Christmas Message: PM Calls Britain a 'Christian Country.'" *Independent*, December 24, 2015. www.independent.co.uk/news/uk/politics/david-cameron-christmas-message-pm-to-hail-britains-christian-values-a6785021.html.

Barnett, P. W. "Apostle." In *Dictionary of Paul and His Letters*, edited by Gerald F. Hawthorne, Ralph P. Martin, and Daniel G. Reid, 45-51. Downers Grove, IL: InterVarsity Press, 1993.

Barrett, Nathaniel. "A Confucian Theory of Shame." *Sophia* 54 (2015): 143-63.

Bateman, Steve. *Brothers, Stand Firm: Seven Things Every Man Should Know, Practice, and Invest in the Next Generation*. Eugene, OR: Wipf & Stock, 2014.

Bauckham, Richard. *Gospel Women: Studies of Named Women in the Gospels*. Grand Rapids: Eerdmans, 2002.

Bechtel, Lyn M. "Shame as a Sanction of Social Control in Biblical Israel: Judicial, Political, and Social Shaming." *Journal for the Study of the Old Testament* 49 (1991): 47-76.

Bell, Duncan. "Mythscapes: Memory, Mythology, and National Identity." *British Journal of Sociology* 54, no. 1 (April 2003): 63-81.

Berring, Robert C., Jr. "Rule of Law: The Chinese Perspective." *Journal of Social Philosophy* 35, no. 4 (Winter 2004): 453-55.

Berry, Donald. *Glory in Romans and the Unified Purpose of God in Redemptive History*. Eugene, OR: Pickwick, 2016.

Bird, Michael. "'Raised for our Justification': A Fresh Look at Romans 4:25." *Colloquium* 35 (2003): 39-44.

————. *Romans*. The Story of God Bible Commentary. Grand Rapids: Zondervan, 2016.

————. *The Saving Righteousness of God: Studies on Paul, Justification, and the New Perspective*. Waynesboro, GA: Paternoster, 2007.

Bird, Michael, and Preston Sprinkle, eds. *The Faith of Jesus Christ.* Peabody, MA: Hendrickson, 2009.

Blackwell, Benjamin C. "Immortal Glory and the Problem of Death in Romans 3.23." *Journal for the Study of the New Testament* 32, no. 3 (2010): 285-308.

Bo, Zhu. "Chinese Cultural Values and Chinese Language Pedagogy." Master's thesis, Ohio State University, 2008.

Boren, Cindy. "Colin Kaepernick Protest Has 49ers Fans Burning Their Jerseys." *Washington Post,* August 28, 2016. www.washingtonpost.com/news/early-lead/wp/2016/08/28/colin -kaepernick-protest-has-49ers-fans-burning-their-jerseys.

Brooks, David. "The Uses of Patriotism." *New York Times,* September 16, 2016. www .nytimes.com/2016/09/16/opinion/the-uses-of-patriotism.html.

Brown, Michael. "Have Evangelicals Lost Their Credibility by Voting for Trump?" *Christian Post,* November 20, 2016. www.christianpost.com/news/have-evangelicals -lost-their-credibility-by-voting-for-trump-171566.

Brown, Ryan. *Honor Bound: How a Cultural Ideal Has Shaped the American Psyche.* New York: Oxford University Press, 2016.

Burer, Michael. "ΕΠΙΣΗΜΟΙ ΈΝ ΤΟΙΣ ἈΠΟΣΤΟΛΟΙΣ in Romans 16:7 as 'Well Known to the Apostles': Further Defense and New Evidence." *Journal of the Evangelical Theological Society* 58, no. 4 (2015): 731-55.

Burrowes, Brett David. "From Letter to Spirit: The Transformation of Torah in Paul's Symbolic World as Reflected in His Letter to the Romans." PhD diss., Durham University, 2004.

Byrne, Brendan. *Romans.* Collegeville, MN: Liturgical Press, 1996.

———. *Romans.* 2nd ed. Collegeville, MN: Liturgical Press, 2007.

Callahan, William C. "History, Identity, and Security: Producing and Consuming Nationalism in China." *Critical Asian Studies* 38, no. 2 (June 2006): 179-208.

———. "National Insecurities: Humiliation, Salvation, and Chinese Nationalism." *Alternatives: Global, Local, Political* 29, no. 2 (March–May 2004): 199-218.

Calvin, John. *Institutes of the Christian Religion.* Edited by Anthony Uyi. Translated by Henry Beveridge. Woodstock, Ontario: Devoted Publishing, 2016.

Campbell, Constantine R. *Paul and Union with Christ: An Exegetical and Theological Study.* Grand Rapids: Zondervan, 2012.

Cao, Nanlai. *Constructing China's Jerusalem.* Stanford, CA: Stanford University Press, 2001.

Carson, Biz. "Arizona Is Publicly Shaming Deadbeat Dads on Twitter." *Business Insider,* February 12, 2016. www.businessinsider.com/arizona-shames-deadbeat-dads-2016-1.

Carter, Joe. "No, the Majority of American Evangelicals Did Not Vote for Trump." The Gospel Coalition, November 15, 2016. www.thegospelcoalition.org/article/no-the -majority-of-american-evangelicals-did-not-vote-for-trump.

Ceresko, Anthony R. "The Rhetorical Strategy of the Fourth Servant Song (Isaiah 52:13–53:12): Poetry and the Exodus–New Exodus." *Catholic Biblical Quarterly* 56, no. 1 (1994): 42-55.

Chan, Che-po, and Brian Bridges. "China, Japan, and the Clash of Nationalisms." *Asian Perspective* 30, no. 1 (2006): 127-56.

Chan, Simon. *Grassroots Asian Theology*. Downers Grove, IL: IVP Academic, 2014.

Chang, Hui Ching, and G. Richard Holt. "A Chinese Perspective on Face as Inter- Relational Concern." In *The Challenge of Facework: Cross-Cultural and Interpersonal Issues*, edited by Stella Ting-Toomey, 95-132. Albany: State University of New York Press, 1994.

Chen, Wenhong, and Kye-Hyoung Lee. "Sharing, Liking, Commenting, and Distressed? The Pathway Between Facebook Interaction and Psychological Distress." *Cyberpsychology, Behavior, and Social Networking* 16, no. 10 (2013): 728-34.

Cheng, Chung-Ying. "The Concept of Face and Its Confucian Roots." *Journal of Chinese Philosophy* 13 (1986): 329-48.

Chesterton, G. K. *Orthodoxy*. Walnut, CA: MSAC Philosophy Group, 2008.

Cicero, Marcus Tullius, *XVIII Philosophical Treatises: Tusculanae Disputationes, Tusculan Disputations,* J. E. King (trans.), Loeb Classical Library (Cambridge, MA: Harvard University, 1927).

Cirafesi, Wally V. "'To Fall Short' or 'To Lack?' Reconsidering the Meaning and Translation of 'ΥΣΤΕΡΕΩ' in Romans 3:23." *Expository Times* 123, no. 9 (2012): 429-34.

Clark, David K. *To Know and Love God: Method for Theology*. Wheaton, IL: Crossway, 2003.

Cohen, Dov, and Richard Nisbett. "Self-Protection and the Culture of Honor: Explaining Southern Violence." *Personality and Social Psychology Bulletin* 20 (1994): 551-67.

Condon, John. *With Respect to the Japanese: A Guide for Americans*. Yarmouth, ME: Intercultural Press, 1984.

Covell, Ralph. *Confucius, the Buddha, and Christ: A History of the Gospel in Chinese*. Maryknoll, NY: Orbis, 1986.

Cranfield, C. E. B. *A Critical and Exegetical Commentary on the Epistle of Romans*, vol. 1. International Critical Commentary. Edinburgh: T&T Clark, 1975.

Crook, Zeba. "Honor, Shame, and Social Status Revisited." *Journal of Biblical Literature* 128, no. 3 (2009): 591-611.

Crouch, Andy. "The Return of Shame." *Christianity Today*, March 2015. www.christianity today.com/ct/2015/march/andy-crouch-gospel-in-age-of-public-shame.html.

Crowley, J. D. *Commentary on Romans for Cambodia and Asia*. Phnom Penh: Fount of Wisdom, 2013.

Daniel, Jerry. "Anti-Semitism in the Hellenistic-Roman Period." *Journal of Biblical Literature* 98 (1979): 45-65.

Davis, Mark. "Kaepernick Anthem Snub Is Not a Free Speech Issue." *Townhall.com*, August 29, 2016. http://townhall.com/columnists/markdavis/2016/08/29/kaepernick-anthem -snub-is-not-a-free-speech-issue-n2211297.

De Boer, Martinus. *Galatians: A Commentary*. New Testament Library. Louisville: Westminster John Knox, 2011.

Delling, G. "στοιχέω, συστοιχέω, στοιχεῖον." In *Theological Dictionary of the New Testament*, edited by Gerhard Kittel, Geoffrey W. Bromiley, and Gerhard Friedrich, 7:670-87. Grand Rapids: Eerdmans, 1964–.

Demarest, Bruce. *The Cross and Salvation: The Doctrine of God*. Wheaton, IL: Crossway, 2006.

Deng, Fucun. "The Basis for the Reconstruction of Chinese Theological Thinking." In *Christianity and Chinese Culture*, edited by Miikka Ruokanen and Paulos Huang, 297-308. Grand Rapids: Eerdmans, 2010.

deSilva, David. *Despising Shame: Honor Discourse and Community Maintenance in the Epistle to the Hebrews*. Revised ed. Atlanta: SBL, 2008.

———. *Honor, Patronage, Kinship and Purity*. Downers Grove, IL: IVP Academic, 2000.

———. *The Hope of Glory: Honor Discourse and New Testament Interpretation*. Collegeville, MN: Liturgical Press, 1999.

DeYoung, Rebecca Konyndyk. *Vainglory: The Forgotten Vice*. Grand Rapids: Eerdmans, 2014.

Dickson, John. *Humilitas: A Lost Key to Life, Love, and Leadership*. Grand Rapids: Zondervan, 2011.

Dio Chrysostom. *Discourses, 31-6*. Translated by J. W. Cohoon and H. L. Crosby. Cambridge, MA: The Loeb Classical Library, 1939.

Duncan, John. "The Hope of Creation: The Significance of ἐφ᾽ ἐλπίδι (Rom 8.20c) in Context." *New Testament Studies* 61 (2015): 411–427.

Dunn, James D. G. *The New Perspective on Paul*. Grand Rapids: Eerdmans, 2008.

———. *Romans 1–8*. Word Biblical Commentary. Dallas: Word, 1988.

———. *Romans 9–16*. Word Biblical Commentary. Dallas: Word, 1998.

Easter, Matthew. "The *Pistis Christou* Debate: Main Arguments and Responses in Summary." *Currents in Biblical Research* 9, no. 1 (2010): 33-47.

Enderlein, Steven E. "To Fall Short or Lack the Glory of God? The Translation and Implications of Romans 3:23." *Journal for the Study of Paul and His Letters* 1, no. 2 (2011): 213-24.

Endicott, Leilani, Tonia Bock, and Darcia Narvaez. "Moral Reasoning, Intercultural Development, and Multicultural Experiences: Relations and Cognitive Underpinnings." *International Journal of Intercultural Relations* 27 (2003): 403-19.

Engberg-Pedersen, Troels. "Gift-Giving and Friendship: Seneca and Paul in Romans 1-8 on the Logic of God's χαρις and Its Human Response." *The Harvard Theological Review* 101, no. 1 (2008): 15-44.

Esler, Philip F. *Conflict and Identity in Romans: The Social Setting of Paul's Letter*. Minneapolis: Fortress, 2003.

"Evangelicals and Catholics Together: The Christian Mission in the Third Millennium." *First Things*, May 1994. www.firstthings.com/article/1994/05/evangelicals-catholics -together-the-christian-mission-in-the-third-millennium.

"Experiences of Human Trafficking and Related Exploitation: Victim/Survivors' Stories." *Research and Public Policy Series* (April 2015): 121-40. https://aic.gov.au/publications /rpp/rpp124/experiences-human-trafficking-and-related-exploitation-victimsurvivors -stories.

Fang, Berlin. "Parents Must Let Kids Leave the Nest." *China Daily*, June 27, 2012. www .chinadaily.com.cn/opinion/2012-06/27/content_15524988.htm.

Farh, Jiing-Lih, and Bo-Shiuan Cheng. "A Cultural Analysis of Paternalistic Leadership in Chinese Organizations." In *Management and Organization in the Chinese Context*, edited by J. Li, A. Tsui, and E. Weldon. New York: St. Martin's Press, 2000.

Fernos, Rodrigo. *Medicine and International Relations in the Caribbean: Some Historical Variants*. New York: iUniverse, 2006.

Fisher, Max. "Yes, It Really Was a Crime in France to Insult the President until This Week. Here's Why." *Washington Post*, July 26, 2013. www.washingtonpost.com/blogs /worldviews/wp/2013/07/26/yes-it-really-was-a-crime-in-france-to-insult-the -president-until-this-week-heres-why.

Fitzmyer, Joseph A. *Romans*. Anchor Yale Bible. New York: Doubleday, 1993.

Flanders, Christopher. "Face." In *Global Dictionary of Theology*, edited by William A. Dyrness and Veli-Matti Kärkkäinen, 308-9. Downers Grove, IL: IVP Academic, 2008.

Forbes, Christopher. "Comparison, Self-Praise and Irony: Paul's Boasting and the Conventions of Hellenistic Rhetoric." *New Testament Studies* 32 (1986): 1-30.

Fraser, Suzan. "Turkish Teen Release: His Crime? Insulting the President." *Christian Science Monitor*, December 26, 2014. www.csmonitor.com/World/Latest-News -Wires/2014/1226/Turkish-teen-release-His-crime-Insulting-the-president.

Fuller, Thomas. "Thai Court Gives 10-Year Sentence for Insult to King." *New York Times*, January 23, 2013. www.nytimes.com/2013/01/24/world/asia/thai-court-gives-10-year -sentence-for-insult-to-king.html.

Garcia, Mark A. "Imputation as Attribution: Union with Christ, Reification and Justification as Declarative Word." *International Journal of Systematic Theology* 11, no. 4 (2009): 415-27.

Gathercole, Simon. "Justified by Faith, Justified by his Blood: The Evidence of Rom 3:21– 4:25." In *Justification and Variegated Nomism, Vol. 2: The Paradoxes of Paul*, edited by D. A. Carson, P. T. O'Brien, and M. A. Seifrid, 147-84. Tübingen: Mohr, 2004.

Geertz, Clifford. *The Interpretation of Cultures*. New York. Basic Books, 1973.

Goleman, Daniel. "The Focused Leader." *Harvard Business Review* 91, no. 12 (Dec 2013). http://hbr.org/2013/12/the-focused-leader.

Golgowski, Nina. "Washington Teen Jumps to Death after Being Shamed in Online Video Taken by Dad." *New York Daily News*, June 5, 2015. www.nydailynews.com/news/national /teen-kills-public-shaming-allegedly-dad-article-1.2247168.

Goodrich, John K. "Sold Under Sin: Echoes of Exile in Romans 7:14-25." *New Testament Studies* 59, no. 4 (2013): 476-95.

———. "From Slaves of Sin to Slaves of God: Reconsidering the Origin of Paul's Slavery Metaphor in Romans 6." *Bulletin for Biblical Research* 23, no. 4 (2013): 509-30.

Green, Matthew. "A Grim and Gruesome History of Public Shaming in London: Part 1." *Londonist*, January 26, 2016. https://londonist.com/2015/12/publicshaming1.

Greenwood, Dara N. "Fame, Facebook, and Twitter: How Attitudes About Fame Predict Frequency and Nature of Social Media Use." *Psychology of Popular Media Culture* 2, no. 4 (2013): 222-36.

Greig, Geordie. "Why My Children Will Not Be Inheriting my £180 Million Fortune: Sting Wants His Sons and Daughters to Earn Their Way (and Says He's Spending All His Money Anyway)." *Daily Mail*, June 21, 2014. www.dailymail.co.uk/home/event /article-2662557/Sting-I-earned-money-hard-work-You-try-singing-two-hours -getting-plane-day.html.

Grindheim, Sigurd. "A Theology of Glory: Paul's Use of Δόξα Terminology in Romans." *Journal of Biblical Literature* 136, no. 2 (2017): 451-65.

Gruen, Erich. *Heritage and Hellenism: The Reinvention of Jewish Tradition*. Berkeley: University of California Press, 2002.

Hafemann, Scott. "Eschatology and Ethics: The Future of Israel and the Nations in Romans 15:1-13." *Tyndale Bulletin* 51, no. 2 (2000): 167.

Hagedorn, Anselm C. "Guarding the Parents' Honour—Deuteronomy 21.18-21." *Journal for the Study of the Old Testament* 88 (2000): 101-21.

Haritatos, Jana, and Veronica Benet-Martinez. "Bicultural Identities: The Interface of Cultural, Personality, and Socio-cognitive Processes." *Journal of Research in Personality* 36 (2002): 598-606.

Harrison, J. R. *Paul's Language of Grace in its Graeco-Roman Context*. Tübingen: Mohr Siebeck, 2003.

———. "The Erasure of Distinction Paul and the Politics of Dishonour." *Tyndale Bulletin* 67, no. 1 (2016): 63-86.

Hart, John. "Paul as Weak in Faith in Romans 7:7-25." *Bibliotheca Sacra* 170 (July–Sept 2013): 315-43.

Hays, Richard B. *The Conversion of the Imagination: Paul as Interpreter of Israel's Scripture*. Grand Rapids: Eerdmans, 2004.

———. "'Have We Found Abraham to Be Our Forefather According to the Flesh?' A Reconsideration of Rom 4:1." *Novum Testamentum* 27, no. 1 (Jan 1985): 76-98.

Headlam, A. C., and W. Sanday. *Romans*. New York. Scribner's Sons, 1904.

Heiser, Michael. *The Unseen Realm: Recovering the Supernatural Worldview of the Bible*. Bellingham, WA: Lexham Press, 2015.

Hellerman, Joseph. *Embracing Shared Ministry: Power and Status in the Early Church and Why It Matters Today*. Grand Rapids: Kregel, 2013.

Hitokoto, Hidefumi. "Indebtedness in Cultural Context: The Role of Culture in the Felt Obligation to Reciprocate." *Asian Journal of Social Psychology* 19 (2015): 16-25.

Hobbs, T. R. "Critical Notes: Reflections on Honor, Shame, and Covenantal Relations." *Journal of Biblical Literature* 116, no. 3 (1997): 501-3.

Holland, Tom. *Contours of Pauline Theology: A Radical New Survey of the Influences on Paul's Biblical Writings*. Fearn: Mentor, 2004.

———. *Romans: The Divine Marriage*. Eugene, OR: Pickwick, 2011.

Holmes, Christopher. "Utterly Incapacitated: The Neglected Meaning of ΠΑΡΕΣΙΣ in Romans 3:25." *Novum Testamentum* 55 (2013): 349-66.

Hong, Ying-Yi. "The Dynamics of Multicultural Identities." In *Social Categories in Everyday Experience*, edited by Shaun Wiley, Tracey Revenson, and Gina Philogène, 1-41. Singapore: American Psychological Association Press, 2011.

Hood, Steven. "The Myth of Asian-Style Democracy." *Asian Survey* 38, no. 9 (1998): 853-66.

Hooker, Morna D. "Adam in Romans 1." *New Testament Studies* 6 (1960): 297-306.

Hu, Wenzhong, and Cornelius Lee Grove. *Encountering the Chinese: A Guide for Americans*. Yarmouth, ME: Intercultural Press, 1991.

Hultgren, Arland J. *Paul's Letter to the Romans: A Commentary*. Grand Rapids: Eerdmans, 2011.

Hurst, Charles, Heather Fitz Gibbon, and Anne Nurse. *Social Inequality: Forms, Causes, and Consequences*. New York: Routledge, 2016.

Hwang, Kwang-Kuo. *Foundations of Chinese Psychology: Confucian Social Relations*. New York: Springer, 2012.

Ingram, Jason, and Ruben Morgan. "Forever Reign." Hillsong. Sony/ATV Music Publishing.

Jackson, W. Daniel. "The Logic of Divine Presence in Romans 3:23." *The Catholic Biblical Quarterly* 80 (2018): 293-305.

Jacob, Haley Goranson. *Conformed to the Image of His Son: Reconsidering Paul's Theology of Glory in Romans*. Downers Grove, IL: IVP Academic, 2018.

Jacquet, Jennifer. *Is Shame Necessary? New Uses for an Old Tool*. New York: Vintage, 2016.

Jessup, Meredith. "Weiner Responds to Voter: 'Sure, I Dishonored My Wife . . . but I Didn't Do Anything to You!'" *The Blaze*, August 1, 2013. www.theblaze.com/news/2013/08/01/weiner-responds-to-voter-sure-i-dishonored-my-wife-but-i-didnt-do-anything-to-you/.

Jewett, Robert. "Honor and Shame in the Argument of Romans." In *Putting Body and Soul Together: Essays in Honor of Robin Scroggs*, edited by Virginia Wiles, Alexandra R. Brown, and Graydon F. Snyder, 258-76. Valley Forge, PA: Trinity Press International, 1997.

Jewett, Robert, and Roy D. Kotansky. *Romans: A Commentary.* Edited by Eldon J. Epp. Hermeneia. Minneapolis: Fortress, 2007.

Jie, Zhong, Aimin Wang, Mingyi Qian, Lili Zhang, Jun Gao, Jianxiang Yang, Bo Li, and Ping Chen. "Shame, Personality, and Social Anxiety Symptoms in Chinese and American Nonclinical Samples: A Cross-Cultural Study." *Depression and Anxiety* 25, no. 5 (2008): 449-60.

Johnson, Lee. "Social Stratification." *Biblical Theology Bulletin* 43, no. 3 (2013): 155-68.

Johnson, Phil. "Stand Fast in Your Liberty." In *Law and Liberty: A Biblical Look at Legalism*, edited by Don Kistler, 94-104. Orlando: Northampton Press, 2013.

Johnston, Sarah Iles. *Religions of the Ancient World: A Guide.* Cambridge, MA: Harvard University Press, 2004.

Jones, Robert P. "Donald Trump and the Transformation of White Evangelicals." *Time*, November 19, 2016. http://time.com/4577752/donald-trump-transformation-white -evangelicals/.

—————. *The End of White Christian America.* New York: Simon and Schuster, 2016.

Jordon, Winthrop. *White Over Black: American Attitudes toward the Negro, 1550–1812.* 2nd ed. Chapel Hill: University of North Carolina Press, 2012.

Junghyun, Kim, LaRose Robert, and Peng Wie. "Loneliness as the Cause and the Effect of Problematic Internet Use: The Relationship between Internet Use and Psychological Well-Being." *Cyberpsychology & Behavior* 12, no. 4 (2009): 451-55.

Kalton, Michael. "Extending the Neo-Confucian Tradition: Questions and Reconceptual- ization for the Twenty-First Century." In *Confucianism and Ecology*, edited by Mary Evelyn Tucker and John Berthrong, 77-101. Cambridge: Harvard University Center for the Study of World Religions, 1998.

Kampert, Patrick. "After Trump, I Can't Relate to My Evangelical Faith." *Chicago Tribune*, November 15, 2016. www.chicagotribune.com/news/opinion/commentary/ct-trump -evangelical-christians-faith-challenged-perspec-1116-md-20161115-story.html.

Keener, Craig S. *Romans: A New Covenant Commentary.* Eugene, OR: Cascade, 2009.

Keesmat, Sylvia. *Paul and His Story: (Re)Interpreting the Exodus Tradition.* Sheffield: Shef- field University Press, 1999.

Kelly, J. M. *Studies in the Civil Judicature of the Roman Republic.* Oxford: Clarendon, 1976.

Kim, Donghoon, Yigang Pan, and Heung Soo Park. "High-versus Low-Context Culture: A Comparison of Chinese, Korean, and American Cultures." *Psychology & Marketing* 15, no. 6 (1998): 507-21.

Kim, Kun-Ok. "What Is Behind 'Face-Saving' in Cross-Cultural Communication?" *Inter-cultural Communication Studies* 3, no. 1 (1993): 39-47.

Kim, Yung-myung. "Understanding East Asian Political Systems: Origins, Characteristics, and Changes." *Sungkyun Journal of East Asian Studies* 3, no. 1 (2003): 45-78.

Kipnis, Andrew. *Producing Guanxi: Sentiment, Self, and Subculture in a North China Village*. Durham: Duke University Press, 1997.

Kittel, Gerhard. "δοκέω, δόξα, δοξάζω, συνδοξάζω, ἔνδοξος, ἐνδοξάζω, παράδοξος." In *Theological Dictionary of the New Testament*, edited by Gerhard Kittel, Geoffrey W. Bro-miley, and Gerhard Friedrich, 2:232-55. Grand Rapids: Eerdmans, 1964–.

Ko, N. H. "Familism in Confucianism." Paper presented at the International Conference of Women's Global Connection (San Antonio, 2004). www.yumpu.com/en/document /view/10003369/familism-in-confucianism-womens-global-connection.

Kruse, Colin. *Paul's Letter to the Romans*. Pillar New Testament Commentary. Grand Rapids: Eerdmans, 2012.

Lai, Pan-chiu. "Sino-Christian Theology, Bible, and Christian Tradition." In *Sino-Christian Theology*, edited by Jason Lam and Pan-chiu Lai, 161-77. New York: Peter Lang, 2010.

Lakoff, George, and Mark Johnson. *The Metaphors We Live By*. Chicago: University of Chicago Press, 2003.

Lam, Andrew. "Asian-Americans' Rising Suicide Rates: Three Students Take Their Lives." *New America Media*, August 13, 2009.

Lampe, Peter. "The Roman Christians in Romans 16." In *The Romans Debate*, revised edition, edited by Karl Donfried, 216-30. Grand Rapids: Baker Academic, 1991.

Lebra, Takie Sugiyama. "Shame and Guilt: A Psychocultural View of the Japanese Self." *Ethos* 11, no. 3 (1983): 192-209.

Lebra, Takie Sugiyama. "Compensative Justice and Moral Investment among Japanese, Chinese, and Koreans." In *Japanese Culture and Behavior: Selected Readings*, 2nd edition, edited by Takie Sugiyama Lebra and William P. Lebra, 43-60. Hawaii: University of Hawaii Press, 1986.

Lee, Zuk-Nae. "Korean Culture and Sense of Shame." *Transcultural Psychiatry* 36, no. 2 (1999): 181-94.

Lei, Duo. "Guanxi and Its Influence on Chinese Business Practices." *Harvard China Review* (Spring 2005): 81-84.

Leithart, Peter. *Delivered from the Elements of the World: Atonement, Justification, Mission*. Downers Grove, IL: IVP Academic, 2016.

———. "Justification as Verdict and Deliverance: A Biblical Perspective." *Pro Ecclesia* 16, no. 1 (2007): 56-72.

Lendon, J. E. *Empire of Honour: The Art of Government in the Roman World*. Oxford: Clarendon, 2002.

Li, Jin, Lianqin Wang, and Kurt W. Fischer. "The Organisation of Chinese Shame Concepts." *Cognition and Emotion* 18, no. 6 (2004): 767-97.

Li, Mia. "Faithful Rush to Protect Church with a Cross Deemed Too Tall." *New York Times*, April 4, 2014. http://sinosphere.blogs.nytimes.com/2014/04/04/faithful-rush-to -protect-church-with-a-cross-deemed-too-tall.

Li, Pingye. "The Characteristics of Chinese Religion and the Development of Christianity in China." In *Sino-Christian Studies in China*, edited by Yang Huilin and Daniel H. N. Yeung, 325-32. Newcastle, UK: Cambridge Scholars, 2006.

———. "How Do Social and Psychological Needs Impact the Existence and Growth of Christianity in Modern China?" In *Christianity and Chinese Culture*, edited by Mikka Ruokanen and Paulos Huang, 211-27. Grand Rapids: Eerdmans, 2010.

Lightfoot, J. B. *Saint Paul's Epistle to the Philippians*. Whitefish, MT: Kessinger, 2010.

Liu, Dilin. *Metaphor, Culture and Worldview*. Lanham, MD: University Press of America, 2002.

Liu, James, Mei-chih Li, and Xiao Dong Yue. "Chinese Social Identity and Inter-Group Relations: The Influence of Benevolent Authority." In *Oxford Handbook of Chinese Psychology*, edited by Michael Harris Bond, 579-98. Oxford: Oxford University Press, 2010.

Liu, Li. "Filial Piety, Guanxi, Loyalty, and Money: Trust in China." In *Trust and Distrust: Sociocultural Perspectives*, edited by Ivana Marková and Alex Gillespie, 51-73. Charlotte: Information Age Publishing, 2008.

Lloyd, G. E. R. *Demystifying Mentalities*. New York: Cambridge, 1990.

Locker, Melissa. "Chinese Publicly Shames Its Own Worst Tourists." *Travel and Leisure*, December 27, 2015. www.travelandleisure.com/articles/china-tourism-blacklist.

Longenecker, Richard. *Introducing Romans: Critical Issues in Paul's Most Famous Letter*. Grand Rapids: Eerdmans, 2011.

———. *The Epistle to the Romans*. New International Greek Testament Commentary. Grand Rapids: Eerdmans, 2016.

Louie, Sam. *Asian Honor: Overcoming the Culture of Silence*. Bloomington, IN: Westbow, 2012.

Luo, Ruiyao. "Shanghai Says People Who Fail to Visit Parents Will Have Credit Scores Lowered." *Caixin*, April 11, 2016. www.caixinglobal.com/2016-04-11/101011746.html.

Luraghi, Silvia. *On the Meaning of Prepositions and Cases: The Expression of Semantic Roles in Ancient Greek*. Philadelphia: John Benjamins Publishing, 2003.

Lust, Johan, Karin Hauspie, and Erik Eynikel. "ὅπως." *A Greek-English Lexicon of the Septuagint*, revised edition. Stuttgart: Deutsche Bibelgesellschaft, 2003.

Luther, Martin. *Luther's Works, Vol. 21: The Sermon on the Mount and the Magnificat*. Edited by J. Pelikan and H. Lehmann. Philadelphia: Fortress, 1955.

MacArthur, John. *The MacArthur Daily Bible: Read the Bible in One Year, with Notes from John MacArthur*. Nashville: Thomas Nelson, 2003.

MacGillivray, Erland D. "Romans 16:2, προστάτις/προστάτης, and the Application of Reciprocal Relationships to New Testament Texts." *Novum Testamentum* 53 (2011): 183-199.

Macaskill, Grant. *Union with Christ in the New Testament.* Oxford: Oxford University Press,
2014.

Madison, Jennifer. "World's Meanest Parents? The Mother Who Tricked Her Son into
Thinking He Got an Xbox for Christmas Sparks Fury as Video Goes Viral." *Daily Mail,*
June 25, 2011. www.dailymail.co.uk/news/article-2008095/World-s-meanest-parents
-The-mother-tricked-son-thinking-got-Xbox-Christmas-sparks-fury-video-goes-viral
.html.

Malina, Bruce J., and John J. Pilch. *Social-Science Commentary on the Letters of Paul.* Minneapolis: Fortress, 2006.

Martyn, J. Louis. *Theological Issues in the Letters of Paul.* Nashville: Abingdon, 1997.

Maston, Jason. "Sirach and Romans 7:1-25: The Human, the Law, and Sin." In *Reading
Romans in Context: Paul and Second Temple Judaism,* edited by Ben Blackwell, John
Goodrich, and Jason Maston, 93-99. Grand Rapids: Zondervan, 2015.

McKaughan, Daniel J. "On the Value of Faith and Faithfulness." *International Journal for
Philosophy of Religion* 81 (2017): 7-29.

McKnight, Scot. *The King Jesus Gospel: The Original Good News Revisited.* Grand Rapids:
Zondervan, 2011.

Mencius. *Mengzi with Selections from Traditional Commentaries.* Translated by Bryan W.
Van Norden. Indianapolis, IN: Hackett Publishing Co, Inc. 2008.

Merkin, Rebecca S. "Cross-Cultural Communication Patterns—Korean and American
Communication." *Journal of Intercultural Communication* 20 (May 2009): 5-15.

Michaud, Derek, and James Wu. "C. S. Song." In *Boston Collaborative Encyclopedia of
Western Theology* (1994–). people.bu.edu/wwildman/bce/song.htm.

Michel, Otto. *Der Brief an die Römer.* Göttingen: Vandenhoeck & Ruprecht, 1978.

Millett, Paul. *Lending and Borrowing in Ancient Athens.* Cambridge. Cambridge University
Press, 2002.

Mischke, Werner. *The Global Gospel: Achieving Missional Impact in Our Multicultural
World.* Scottsdale, AZ: Mission One, 2015.

Mock, Dennis. *New Testament Survey.* Atlanta: Bible Training Centre for Pastors, 1998.

Moo, Douglas J. *The Epistle to the Romans.* New International Commentary on the New
Testament. Grand Rapids: Eerdmans, 1996.

Moon, Ruth. "Segregated Surveys: How Politics Keeps Evangelicals White." *Christianity
Today,* November 13, 2014. www.christianitytoday.com/ct/2014/november/segregated
-surveys-how-politics-keeps-evangelicals-white.html.

Morley, Jefferson. *Snow-Storm in August: The Struggle for American Freedom and Washington's Race Riot of 1835.* New York: Anchor, 2013.

Morris, Leon. *The Epistle to the Romans*. Pillar New Testament Commentary. Grand Rapids: Eerdmans, 1988.

Motyer, J. A. *The Prophecy of Isaiah: An Introduction & Commentary*. Downers Grove, IL: InterVarsity Press, 1996.

Mounce, Robert. *Romans*. New American Commentary Nashville: B&H, 1995.

Moxnes, Halvor. "Honour and Righteousness in Romans." *Journal for the Study of the New Testament* 10, no. 32 (1988): 61-78.

Mullins, Terence. "Greeting as a New Testament Form." *Journal of Biblical Literature* 87, no. 4 (1968): 425-26.

Murray, Andrew. *Humility: The Beauty of Holiness*. Brisbane: Ichthus Publications, 2014.

Murray, John. *Redemption: Accomplished and Applied*. Grand Rapids: Eerdmans, 1980.

———. *The Epistle to the Romans*. Grand Rapids: Eerdmans, 1997.

Musolff, Andreas. "The Metaphor of the 'Body Politic' Across Language and Cultures." In *Cognitive Explorations into Metaphor and Metonymy*, edited by Polzenhagen, Frank, Zoltán Kövecses, Stefanie Vogelbacher, and Sonja Kleinke, 85-99. New York: Peter Lang, 2014.

National Association of Evangelicals. "What Is an Evangelical?" http://nae.net/what-is-an -evangelical. Accessed November 22, 2016.

Neuliep, James, Michelle Chaudior and James McCoskey. "A Cross-Cultural Comparison of Ethnocentrism Among Japanese and United States College Students." *Communication Research Reports* 18, no. 2 (2001): 137-46.

Newman, Cary C. *Paul's Glory-Christology: Tradition and Rhetoric*. Novum Testamentum Supplements, vol. 69. Leiden: Brill, 1992.

Neyrey, Jerome. *Honor and Shame in the Gospel of Matthew*. Louisville: Westminster John Knox, 1998.

Ni, Huiliang. "Sinicizing Jesus in the First Half of the Twentieth Century: How Chinese Christians Understood Jesus." PhD diss., Claremont Graduate University, 2008.

Nisbett, Richard. *The Geography of Thought: How Asians and Westerners Think Differently . . . and Why*. New York: Simon & Schuster, 2003.

Nisbett, Richard, and Dov Cohen. *Culture of Honor: The Psychology of Violence in the South*. Boulder, CO: Westview, 1996.

O'Dea, Gregory. "Framing the Frame: Embedded Narratives, Enabling Texts, and *Frankenstein*." *Romanticism on the Net* 31 (2003): n.p. www.erudit.org/revue/ron/2003/v /n31/008697ar.html.

Olson, Robert. *The Gospel as the Revelation of God's Righteousness: Paul's Use of Isaiah in Romans 1:1-3:26*. Tübingen: Mohr Siebeck, 2016.

Olyan. Saul M. "Honor, Shame, and Covenant Relations in Ancient Israel and Its Environment." *Journal of Biblical Literature* 115, no. 2 (1996): 201-18.

Osnos, Evan. *Age of Ambition: Chasing Fortune, Truth, and Faith in the New China*. New York: Farrar, Straus and Giroux, 2015.

Osnos, Evan, and Nancy Updike. "Poetry of Propaganda." *This American Life*, December 18, 2015. www.thisamericanlife.org/radio-archives/episode/575/transcript.

Oswalt, John. *The Book of Isaiah, Chapters 40–66*. New International Commentary on the Old Testament. Grand Rapids: Eerdmans, 1998.

Ott, Craig. "The Power of Biblical Metaphors for the Contextualized Communication of the Gospel." *Missiology* 42, no. 4 (2014): 357-74.

Pappin, Gladdin J. "A Virtue Betrayed, A Review of *Loyalty: The Vexing Virtue* by Eric Felten." *First Principles Journal* 47, no. 1 (2012): n.p. www.firstprinciplesjournal.com /articles.aspx?article=1818.

Park, Jerry, Joshua Tom, and Brita Andercheck. "CCF Civil Rights Symposium." Council on Contemporary Families, February 4, 2014. contemporaryfamilies.org/50-years-of -religious-change.

Paulson, Christina Bratt. "'Biculturalism': Some Reflections and Speculations." In *Intercultural Discourse and Communication: The Essential Readings*, edited by Scott F. Kiesling and Christina Bratt Paulston, 277-87. Malden, MA: Wiley-Blackwell, 2004.

Penman, R. "Facework in Communication: Conceptual and Moral Challenges." In *The Challenge of Facework: Cross-Cultural and Interpersonal Issues*, edited by Stella Ting-Toomey, 15-45. Albany: State University of New York Press, 1994.

Peterman, Gerald. "Social Reciprocity and Gentile Debt to Jews in Romans 15:26-27." *Journal of the Evangelical Theological Society* 50, no. 4 (2007): 746.

Pew Research Center. "Racial and Ethnic Composition." Religious Landscape Study. www .pewforum.org/religious-landscape-study/racial-and-ethnic-composition.

Philonenko, Marc. "Sur l'expression "vendu au péché" dans l' 'Epître aux Romains.'" *Revue de l'histoire des religions* 103 (1986): 41-52.

Pinter, Dean. "Josephus and Romans 13:1-14: Providence and Imperial Power." In *Reading Romans in Context*, edited by Ben Blackwell, John Goodrich, and Jason Maston, 143-50. Grand Rapids: Zondervan, 2015.

Piper, John. *The Future of Justification: A Response to N. T. Wright*. Wheaton, IL: Crossway, 2008.

———. "How Is God's Passion for His Own Glory Not Selfishness?" *Desiring God*, November 24, 2007. www.desiringgod.org/articles/how-is-gods-passion-for-his-own-glory-not -selfishness.

———. "Is Jesus an Egomaniac?" Sermon delivered at the Passion Conference, January 4, 2010. www.desiringgod.org/messages/is-jesus-an-egomaniac.

Pizzuto-Pomaco, Julia. *From Shame to Honor: Mediterranean Women in Romans 16*. Lexington, KY: Emeth Press, 2017.

Platt, David. "Free as Sons." *Radical.net*, December 21, 2008. www.radical.net/sermon /free-as-sons.

Plunkett, Suzanne. "Bahrain Toughens Penalties for Insulting King." *Reuters*, February 5, 2014. www.reuters.com/article/2014/02/05/us-bahrain-law-idUSBREA140KX20140205.

Porter, Stanley. "The Argument of Romans 5: Can a Rhetorical Question Make a Difference?" *Journal of Biblical Literature* 110, no. 4 (1991): 655-77.

Pratt, Zane. "Here's What We Mean by Unreached Peoples and Places." November 22, 2016. https://www.imb.org/2016/11/22/what-do-we-mean-by-unreached-peoples-and -places.

Prudchenko, Kate. "What Are the Effects of a Frame Narrative?" Accessed August 25, 2018. https://penandthepad.com/effects-frame-narrative-1733.html.

Quintilian, *Institutio oratoria*, Book 9.Translated by H. E. Butler, Loeb Classical Library. Cambridge, MA: Harvard University Press, 1920.

Reumann, John. "Righteousness." In *The Anchor Yale Bible Dictionary*, edited by David Noel Freedman, 5:724-73. New York: Doubleday, 1992.

Richards, E. Randolph, and Brandon J. O'Brien. *Misreading Scripture with Western Eyes: Removing Cultural Blinders to Better Understand the Bible*. Downers Grove, IL: Inter-Varsity Press, 2012.

———. *Paul Behaving Badly: Was the Apostle a Racist, Chauvinist Jerk?* Downers Grove, IL: InterVarsity Press, 2016.

Riegel, Jeffrey. "Confucius." In *Stanford Encyclopedia of Philosophy*, revised March 23, 2013. http://plato.stanford.edu/entries/confucius.

Robertson, O. Palmer. "Genesis 15:6: New Covenant Exposition of an Old Testament Text." *Westminster Theological Journal* 42, no. 2 (1980): 285-86.

Ronson, Jon. *So You've Been Publicly Shamed*. New York: Riverhead Books, 2015.

Roth, Dieter. "What ἐν τῷ κόσμῳ are the στοιχεῖα τοῦ κόσμου?" *HTS Theological Studies* 70, no. 1 (2014). https://hts.org.za/index.php/hts/article/view/2676.

Rulmu, Callia. "The Use of Psalm 69:9 in Romans 15:3: Shame as Sacrifice." *Biblical Theology Bulletin* 40, no. 4 (2010): 227-33.

S. C. S. "Why Adoptions Are So Rare in South Korea." *The Economist*, May 27, 2015. www .economist.com/blogs/economist-explains/2015/05/economist-explains-32.

Saad, Carmel S., Rodica Ioana Damian, Verónica Benet-Martínez, Wesley G. Moons, and Richard W. Robins. "Multiculturalism and Creativity: Effects of Cultural Context, Bicultural Identity, and Ideational Fluency." *Social Psychological and Personality Science* 4, no. 3 (2013): 369-75.

Sanchez, Mark. "Colin Kaepernick's Birth Mom Ironically Shames Him on Twitter." *New York Post*, August 30, 2016. http://nypost.com/2016/08/30/colin-kaepernicks-birth -mom-ironically-shames-him-on-twitter.

Schreiner, Thomas. "'Works of Law' in Paul." *Novum Testamentum* 33, no. 3 (1991): 217-44.

———. *Romans*. Baker Exegetical Commentary on the New Testament. Grand Rapids: Baker Academic, 1998.

Scott, James M. "Exile and the Self-Understanding of Diaspora Jews in the Greco-Roman Period." In *Exile: Old Testament, Jewish, and Christian Conceptions*, edited by James M. Scott, 173-218. Supplements to the Journal for the Study of Judaism 56. Leiden: Brill, 1997.

Searle, John R. *Expression and Meaning: Studies in the Theory of Speech Acts*. Cambridge: Cambridge University Press, 1979.

See, Lisa. *On Gold Mountain: The One-Hundred-Year Odyssey of My Chinese-American Family*. New York: Vintage, 1996.

Seifrid, Mark. *Christ, Our Righteousness: Paul's Theology of Justification*. New Studies in Biblical Theology. Downers Grove, IL: IVP Academic, 2000.

———. "Righteousness, Justice, and Justification." In *New Dictionary of Biblical Theology*, edited by T. Desmond Alexander and Brian S. Rosner, 740-45. Downers Grove, IL: InterVarsity Press, 2000.

———. "Romans." In *Commentary on the New Testament Use of the Old Testament*, edited by G. K. Beale and D. A. Carson, 607-94. Grand Rapids: Baker, 2007.

Selz, Genhard J. "The Divine Prototypes." In *Religion and Power: Divine Kingship in the Ancient World*, edited by Nicole Brisch, 13-32. Chicago: University of Chicago Press, 2008.

Sheldon, Kennon M., Neetu Abad, and Christian Hinsch. "A Two-Process View of Facebook Use and Relatedness Need-Satisfaction: Disconnection Drives Use, and Connection Rewards It." *Journal of Personality and Social Psychology* 100, no. 4 (2011): 766-75.

Shin, Benjamin, and Sheryl Takagi Silzer. *Tapestry of Grace: Untangling the Cultural Complexities in Asian American Life and Ministry*. Eugene, OR: Wipf & Stock, 2016.

Shive, Glenn. "Conclusion: The Future of Chinese Religious Life." In *Chinese Religious Life*, edited by David A. Palmer, Glenn Shive, and Philip L. Wickeri, 241-54. New York: Oxford University Press, 2011.

ShuFang Dien, Dora. *The Chinese Worldview Regarding Justice and the Supernatural: The Cultural and Historical Roots of Rule by Law*. New York: Nova Science Publishers, 2007.

Shum, Shiu-Lun. *Paul's Use of Isaiah in Romans: A Comparative Study of Paul's Letter to the Romans and the Sibylline and Qumran Sectarian Texts* (WUNT 2/156; Tübingen: Mohr Siebeck, 2002).

Sivonen, Mikko. "The *Doxa* Motif in Paul." PhD diss., University of Helsinki, 2018.

Smith, James K. A. "Revolution*ism* and Our Secular Age." *Comment*, Fall 2016. www .cardus.ca/comment/article/4927/revolutionism-and-our-secular-age.

Sprinkle, Preston. "The Afterlife in Romans: Understanding Paul's Glory Motif in Light of the Apocalypse of Moses and 2 Baruch." in *Lebendige Hoffnung–ewiger Tod?!:*

Jenseitsvorstellungen im Hellenismus, Judentum und Christentum, edited by Manfred Lang and Michael Labhan, 201-33. Leipzig: Evangelische Verlagsanstalt: 2007.

Stanley, Christopher. "'Neither Jew Nor Greek': Ethnic Conflict in Graeco-Roman Society." *Journal for the Study of the New Testament* 64 (1996): 101-24.

Stark, Rodney. "Early Christianity: Opiate of the Privileged?" *Faith & Economics* 54 (Fall 2009): 1-18.

Stephens, Mark B. and Georgiane Deal. "The God Who Gives Generously: Honour, Praise and the Agony of Celebrity." *Scottish Journal of Theology* 71, no 1 (2018): 52-66.

Stendahl, Krister. "Paul and the Introspective Conscience of the West." *Harvard Theological Review* 56, no. 3 (1963): 199-215.

Steward, Tom. *True Mind: How Truth Can Change What You Believe and How You Live.* Bloomington, IN: Westbow, 2001.

Stowers, Stanley K. *A Rereading of Romans: Justice, Jews, and Gentiles.* New Haven, CT: Yale University Press, 1994.

Strand, Mark. "Explaining Sin in a Chinese Context." *Missiology* 28, no. 4 (2000): 427-41.

Sun, Catherine Tien-Lun. *Themes in Chinese Psychology.* Singapore: Cengage Learning, 2008.

Sun, Wendel. *A New People in Christ: Adam, Israel, and Union with Christ in Romans.* Eugene, OR: Pickwick, 2018.

———. "Seeking (Exchanged) Glory: The Gentiles of Romans 2." *Journal of Asian Evangelical Theology* 20, no. 2 (2016): 45-64.

Tacitus, Cornelius. *The Histories and the Annals.* Translated by Clifford Moore and John Jackson. 4 vols. Loeb Classical Library. Cambridge: Harvard University Press, 1925–37.

Tadmor, Carmit T., Adam Galinsky, and William Maddux. "Getting the Most Out of Living Abroad: Biculturalism and Integrative Complexity as Key Drivers of Creative and Professional Success." *Journal of Personality and Social Psychology* 103, no. 3 (Sept 2012): 520-42.

Tak, Sing Cheung, Man Chan Hoi, Man Chan Kin, Ambrose Y. C. King, Yue Chiu Chi, and Fang Yang Cheng. "How Confucian Are Contemporary Chinese? Construction of an Ideal Type and Its Application to Three Chinese Communities." *European Journal of East Asian Studies* 5, no. 2 (2006): 157-80.

Tan, Andrew Kim Seng. "The Rhetoric of Abraham's Faith." PhD diss., University of Cape Town, 2016.

Tan, Hann-Tzuu (Joey). *The Chinese Way: Contextualizing the Gospel for the Chinese.* Self-published, 2012.

Tangney, June Price, and Jessica L. Tracy. "Self-Conscious Emotions." In *Handbook of Self and Identity*, edited by Mark R. Leary and June Price Tangney, 446-80. New York: Guilford Press, 2011.

Tennent, Timothy. *Theology in the Context of World Christianity.* Grand Rapids: Zondervan, 2007.

Thielman, Frank. *Paul and the Law: A Contextual Approach.* Downers Grove, IL: IVP Academic. 1994.

———. "The Story of Israel and the Theology of Romans 5–8." In *Pauline Theology Volume IV: Looking Back, Pressing On,* edited by E. Elizabeth Johnson and David M. Hay, 169-95. Atlanta: Scholars Press, 1997.

Thompson, Curt. *Soul of Shame: Retelling the Stories We Believe About Ourselves.* Downers Grove, IL: InterVarsity Press, 2015.

Thompson, Michael B. *The New Perspective on Paul.* Cambridge: Grove, 2011.

Ting, K. H. *God Is Love: Collected Writings of Bishop K. H. Ting.* Colorado Springs: David C. Cook, 2004.

Towner, Philip H. "Can Slaves Be Their Masters' Benefactors? 1 Timothy 6:1-2a in Literary, Cultural and Theological Context." *Current Trends in Scripture Translation* 182/183 (1997): 39-52.

———. "Romans 13:1-7 and Paul's Missiological Perspective: A Call to Political Quietism or Transformation?" In *Romans and the People of God: Essays in Honor of Gordon D. Fee on the Occasion of His 65th Birthday,* edited by Sven K. Soderlund and N. T. Wright, 149-69. Grand Rapids: Eerdmans, 1999.

Tracy, Kate. "China Lifts High the Cross (Right Off Dozens of Churches)." *Christianity Today,* May 30, 2014. www.christianitytoday.com/gleanings/2014/may/china-lifts -high-cross-right-off-dozens-churches-zhejiang.html.

Trebilco, Paul R. *Outsider Designations and Boundary Construction in the New Testament: Christian Communities and the Formation of Group Identity.* Cambridge: Cambridge University Press, 2017,

Tweed, Roger G., and Darrin R. Lehman. "Learning Considered within a Cultural Context: Confucian and Socratic Approaches." *American Psychologist* 57, no. 2 (2002): 89-99.

Van Wolde, Ellen. "Who Guides Whom? Embeddedness and Perspective in Biblical Hebrew and in 1 Kings 3:16-28." *Journal of Biblical Literature* 14, no. 4 (1995): 623-42.

Vandello, Joseph A., and Dov Cohen. "Patterns of Individualism and Collectivism Across the United States." *Journal of Personality and Social Psychology* 77, no. 2 (1999): 279-92.

Vanhoozer, Kevin. "Wrighting the Wrongs of the Reformation? The State of the Union with Christ in St. Paul and Protestant Soteriology." In *Jesus, Paul and the People of God: A Theological Dialogue with N. T. Wright,* edited by Nicholas Perrin and Richard B. Hays, 235-59. Downers Grove, IL: IVP Academic, 2012.

Venter, Dirk J. "The Implicit Obligations of Brothers, Debtors and Sons (Romans 8:12-17)." *Neotestamentica* 48, no. 2 (2014): 283-302.

von Harnack, A. *The Expansion of Christianity in the First Three Centuries*, vol. 2. New York: G. P. Putnam's Sons, 1905.

W., Jackson. "Authority in a Collectivistic Church: Identifying Crucial Concerns for a Chinese Ecclesiology." *Global Missiology* 1, no. 9 (Oct 2011): n.p. http://ojs.globalmissio logy.org/index.php/english/article/view/679/1689.

———. "Have Theologians No Sense of Shame? How the Bible Reconciles Objective and Subjective Shame." *Themelios* 43, no. 2 (2018): 205-19.

———. *One Gospel for All Nations: A Chinese Contextualization of Salvation through Honor and Shame*. Pasadena, CA: William Carey Library, 2015.

———. "Paul Writes to the Greek First and also the Jew." *Journal of the Evangelical Theological Society* 65, no. 4 (2013): 765-79.

———. *Saving God's Face: A Chinese Contextualization of Salvation Through Honor and Shame*. Pasadena, CA: William Carey International University Press, 2013.

———. "We Compromise the Gospel When We Settle for Truth: How 'Right' Interpretations Lead to 'Wrong' Contextualization." *Global Missiology* 2, no. 10 (2013): n.p. http://ojs .globalmissiology.org/index.php/english/article/view/1130/2614

———. "Why Is God Justified in Romans? Vindicating Paul's Use of Psalm 51 in Romans 3:4." *Neotestamentica* 51, no. 2 (2017): 291-314.

Wagner, Ross. *Heralds of the Good News: Isaiah and Paul in Concert in the Letter to the Romans*. Boston: Brill, 2003.

Walker, D. D. "Benefactor." In *Dictionary of New Testament Background*, edited by Craig A. Evans and Stanley E. Porter, 157–59. Downers Grove, IL: InterVarsity Press, 2000.

Wallace, Daniel B. *Greek Grammar Beyond the Basics*. Grand Rapids: Zondervan, 1996.

Wan, Enoch. "Practical Contextualization: A Case Study of Evangelizing Contemporary Chinese." *Global Missiology* 1, no. 1 (2003): n.p. http://ojs.globalmissiology.org/index .php/english/issue/view/27.

Wang, Zheng. "National Humiliation, History Education, and the Politics of Historical Memory: Patriotic Education Campaign in China." *International Studies Quarterly* 52 (2008): 783-806.

Waters, Guy Prentiss. *Justification and the New Perspective on Paul: A Review and Response*. Phillipsburg, NJ: P&R, 2004.

Watts, Jack, and Robert S. McGee. *Recovering from Religious Abuse: 11 Steps to Spiritual Freedom*. New York: Simon and Schuster, 2012.

Watts, Rikki E. "Consolation or Confrontation? Isaiah 40–55 and the Delay of the New Exodus." *Tyndale Bulletin* 41, no. 1 (1990): 31-59.

———. "Echoes from the Past: Israel's Ancient Traditions and the Destiny of the Nations in Isaiah 40–55." *Journal for the Study of the Old Testament* 28, no. 4 (2004): 481-508.

Wedderburn, A. J. M. "Some Observations on Paul's Use of the Phrases 'in Christ' and 'with Christ.'" *Journal for the Study of the New Testament* 25 (1985): 88-91.

West, Diana. *The Death of the Grown-Up: How America's Arrested Development Is Bringing Down Western Civilization.* New York: St. Martin's Press, 2007.

Westerholm, Stephen. *Perspectives Old and New on Paul: The "Lutheran" Paul and His Critics.* Grand Rapids: Eerdmans, 2004.

White, Joel. "N. T. Wright's Narrative Approach." In *God and the Faithfulness of Paul: A Critical Examination of the Pauline Theology of N. T. Wright,* edited by Christoph Heilig, J. Thomas Hewitt, and Michael Bird, 181-204. Tübingen: Mohr Siebeck, 2016.

Wilckens, Ulrich. *Der Brief an die Römer,* I. Evangelisch-katholischer Kommentar zum. Neukirchen-Vluyn: Neukirchener, 1980.

Williams, Arthur. "Brother on Christmas. . . ." *YouTube,* December 31, 2007. https://youtu .be/VhO-OE931D4.

Williams, Sam K. "The 'Righteousness of God' in Romans." *Journal of Biblical Literature* 99, no. 2 (1980): 241-90.

Wilmore, Gayraud S. *African American Religious Studies: An Interdisciplinary Anthology.* Durham, NC: Duke University Press, 1989.

Winter, Bruce. "The Public Honoring of Christian Benefactors." *Journal for the Study of the New Testament* 34 (1988): 87-103.

——. *Seek the Welfare of the City: Christians as Benefactors and Citizens.* Grand Rapids: Eerdmans, 1994.

——. *Divine Honours for the Caesars: The First Christian Responses.* Grand Rapids, MI: Eerdmans, 2015.

Witherington, Ben, III, and Darlene Hyatt. *Paul's Letter to the Romans: A Socio-Rhetorical Commentary.* Grand Rapids: Eerdmans, 2004.

Wolseley, Garnet. *Narrative of the War with China in 1860.* London: Longman, Green, Longman, and Roberts, 1862.

Wright, Christopher J. H. "The Israelite Household and the Decalogue: The Social Background and Significance of Some Commandments." *Tyndale Bulletin* 30 (1979): 101-24.

Wright, N. T. *The Climax of the Covenant: Christ and the Law in Pauline Theology.* Minneapolis: Fortress, 1992.

——. *Justification: God's Plan and Paul's Vision.* Downers Grove, IL: IVP Academic, 2009.

——. "The Letter to the Romans." In *The New Interpreter's Bible,* 12 vols., edited by Leander E. Keck, 10:396-770. Nashville: Abingdon, 1994–2004.

——. "New Exodus, New Inheritance: The Narrative Substructure of Romans 3–8." In *Romans and the People of God: Essays in Honor of Gordon D. Fee on the Occasion of His 65th Birthday,* edited by Sven K. Soderlund and N. T. Wright, 26-35. Grand Rapids: Eerdmans, 1999.

———. "The New Inheritance According to Paul." *Bible Review* 14, no. 3 (1998): 16, 47.

———. *Paul and the Faithfulness of God*, vol. 1. Minneapolis: Fortress, 2013.

———. "Response to Kevin Vanhoozer." In *Jesus, Paul and the People of God: A Theological Dialogue with N. T. Wright*, edited by Nicholas Perrin and Richard B. Hays, 259-61. Downers Grove, IL: IVP Academic, 2012.

———. "Righteousness." In *New Dictionary of Theology*, edited by Sinclair B. Ferguson and J. I. Packer, 590-92. Downers Grove, IL: InterVarsity Press, 2000.

———. "Romans and the Theology of Paul." In *Pauline Perspectives: Essays on Paul, 1978–2013*, 93-125. Minneapolis: Fortress, 2013.

Wu, Daniel. "Honor, Shame, and Guilt: Social Scientific Approaches to the Book of Ezekiel." PhD diss., University of Sydney, 2013.

Xinhua News Service. "CPC Promotes 'Core Value System' to Lay Moral Foundation for Social Harmony," October 18, 2006. www.gov.cn/english/2006-10/18/content_417140.htm.

Yau Fai Ho, David, and Rainbow Tin Hung Ho. "Knowledge Is a Dangerous Thing: Authority Relations, Ideological Conservatism, and Creativity in Confucian-Heritage Cultures." *Journal for the Theory of Social Behavior* 38, no. 1 (2008): 67-86.

Yen, Hung-Chung. "Human Nature and Learning in Ancient China." In *Education as Cultivation in Chinese Culture*, edited by Shikkuan Hsu and Yuh-Yin Wu, 19-43. Singapore: Springer, 2015.

Yinger, Kent L. *The New Perspective on Paul: An Introduction*. Eugene, OR: Cascade, 2011.

Young, Gweon You. "Shame and Guilt Mechanisms in East Asian Culture." *The Journal of Pastoral Care and Counseling* 51, no. 1 (Spring 1997): 57-64.

Yu, Zhang. "Concern Rises in Wenzhou as Christianity Booms in Capitalist Fashion." *Global Times*, April 17, 2014. www.globaltimes.cn/content/855208.shtml.

Zeleny, Jeff. "Obama's Lapels." *New York Times*, October 4, 2007. http://thecaucus.blogs.nytimes.com/2007/10/04/obamas-lapels.

Zhang, Haihua, and Geoffrey Baker. *Think Like Chinese*. Annandale, NSW: Federation Press, 2008.

Zhang, Xian. "Christianity, Marxism, and 'The End of History': An Analysis of History Strung Together with the Examples of Liberation Theology." In *Sino-Christian Studies in China*, edited by Huilin Yang and Daniel H. N. Yeung, 204-21. Newcastle: Cambridge Scholars, 2006.

Zylstra, Sarah. "Are Evangelicals Bad for Marriage?" *Christianity Today*, February 14, 2014. www.christianitytoday.com/ct/2014/february-web-only/are-evangelicals-bad-for-marriage.html.

AUTHOR INDEX

SUBJECT INDEX

SCRIPTURE INDEX

45:16, *120, 146, 152, 153,*
  154, 179
45:17, *155*
45:18, *153*
45:19, *152, 154, 155*
45:21, *151, 155, 179*
45:22, *106, 110*
45:23, *106, 110, 154, 155,*
  156, 179
45:24, *106, 146, 152, 155*
45:25, *110, 154, 155, 156,*
  159
46:13, *106, 156*
49, *147*
49–51, *149*
49:3, *106, 149*
49:5, *149*
49:22, *147, 148, 149*
49:23, *148*
49:24–50:2, *133*
49:25, *148*
50, *142, 147, 148*
50:1, *133*
50:6, *147*
50:7, *148*
50:8, *106, 121, 147, 148,*
  149
51:1, *149*
51:3, *149*
51:5, *106, 149, 154*
51:7, *149*
52–53, *106*
52:2, *149*
52:3, *133*
52:5, *46*
52:15, *31*
53, *110*
53:11, *121, 151*
54:10, *92*

54:22, *106*
58:8, *121*
60:19, *121*
60:21, *151*
61:11, *154*
62:2, *121*
62:10, *148*
62:12–63:16, *106*
64:8, *151, 158*
66:18, *161*

Jeremiah
2:5, *43*
2:11, *42, 43, 158*
2:14, *44*
2:26, *52*
2:36, *52*
9:19, *52*
9:23, *154*
10:14, *156*
13:11, *109*
14:4, *52*
14:21, *79*
15:9, *52*
16:14, *121*
18:2, *151*
20:11, *52*
31:9, *103, 121*
31:31, *118*
31:33, *61*
31:34, *61*
32:40, *118*
51:9, *92*
51:10, *146, 154*
51:17, *120*
51:51, *52*

Lamentations
4:2, *151*

Ezekiel
16:27, *52*
20:33, *121*
28:22, *106*
34:23, *103*
36:16, *118*
36:26, *61*
38:23, *106*
39:29, *117*

Daniel
12:1, *146*

Hosea
2:14, *121, 139*
3:5, *103*
4:7, *156*
4:12, *156*
10:6, *52, 120*
11:1, *103, 121*
13:14, *105*

Joel
1:1–2:11, *146*
1:11, *52*
2, *142, 146*
2:17, *146, 148*
2:19, *146*
2:23, *145, 146*
2:26, *145*
2:28, *117*
2:32, *145*

Micah
7:9, *146*

Habakkuk
2:14, *121*

Finding the Textbook You Need

The IVP Academic Textbook Selector
is an online tool for instantly finding the IVP books
suitable for over 250 courses across 24 disciplines.

ivpacademic.com